# Spring Wildflowers of Utah's Red Rock Desert

by

## Peter Lesica
and
## Walter Fertig

TRILLIUM
P·R·E·S·S

ISBN 978-0-87842-685-0

DISCLAIMER: Consuming or using plants for medicinal purposes is dangerous and may result in death or serious injury. The authors, publishers and distributors of this book do not recommend experimentation with edible and medicinal plants by readers.

# Acknowledgements

Matt Betenson of Grand Staircase-Escalante National Monument provided the base map of national parks and monuments in Utah. Funding to W.F. for floristic research in national parks and monuments was provided by the National Park Service. David Rockwell and Jeannie Nuckolls helped with design and layout. Kathy Lloyd and Laura Fertig graced us with their editorial skills. Rosella Mosteller helped edit photos. Laura Fertig introduced W.F. to the Colorado Plateau. Ann DeBolt introduced P.L. to the Red Rock Desert and taught him to avoid stepping on the soil crust.

**Errata:** P. 216. The text accurately describes winterfat (*Krascheninnikovia lanata*); however, the photograph depicts the related green molly (*Neokochia americana*)

# Table of Contents

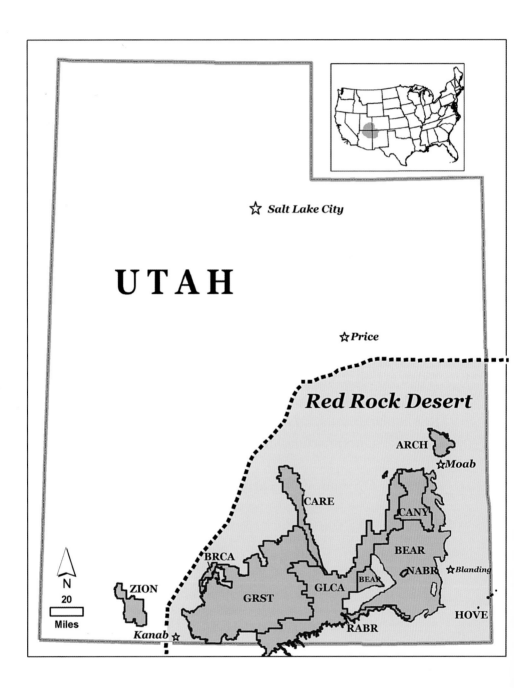

☆ Salt Lake City

# UTAH

☆ Price

## Red Rock Desert

ARCH
☆ Moab

CARE

CANY

BEAR

BRCA

BEAR
NABR
☆ Blanding

ZION

GRST
GLCA

HOVE

N
20
Miles

Kanab ☆

RABR

# Introduction

Relatively few people live in Utah's Red Rock Desert, but many visit in order to hike, climb, mountain bike, boat, explore or just take in the fabulous scenery. The most popular time to visit the region is surely in the spring when the weather is benign, especially compared to areas farther north. This is also the best time of year to see wildflowers and one of the best places in the West to see wildflowers at this time of year. Knowing and understanding the plants of the region enhances appreciation of the scenery and canyon country's natural history. This book was designed to provide an easy-to-use yet thorough introduction to the springtime flowering plants of this spectacular part of western North America. It is not intended for use in the montane or alpine zones of the La Sal or Abajo ranges. Plants of the ponderosa pine and higher vegetation zones are not included.

## Utah's Red Rock Desert: Where is it?

This book focuses on southeast Utah, in particular the area designated as Plateau Country but not including the Uinta Basin. There are nine national parks and monuments in the area. These include Arches (ARCH), Bryce Canyon (BRCA), Canyonlands (CANY) and Capitol Reef (CARE) national parks and Bears Ears (BEAR), Grand Staircase-Escalante (GRST), Hovenweep (HOVE), Natural Bridges (NABR) and Rainbow Bridge (RABR) national monuments as well as Glen Canyon National Recreation Area (GLCA). Zion National Park (ZION) is just outside the area. Boundaries shown on the map are current as of 2017. This book is also useful throughout the Colorado Plateau which includes portions of southwest Colorado, northwest New Mexico and northeast Arizona; i.e., the Four Corners region (see map inset on page iv).

## Climate

Climate of southeast Utah is semi-arid and continental. Average annual precipitation at Moab, one of the lowest recording stations at 4,000 ft in elevation, is nine inches. Average precipitation at Boulder, at the upper edge of the pinyon-juniper zone with an elevation of 6,700 ft, is nearly 11 inches. The southern monsoon brings somewhat more precipitation between July and October compared to the rest of the year. Summers are hot and winters are cold. Average maximum July temperature is over 98°F and 85°F at Moab and Boulder respectively, while mean January minimum temperatures are 18°F and 17°F respectively.

## Geology

The Colorado Plateau of southeast Utah is composed of mostly horizontal layers of sedimentary rocks: sandstone, shale and occasionally limestone. Age of the numerous sedimentary formations varies from 325 million years (Pennsylvanian) to 65 million years (Cretaceous). Cliffs and canyons provide most of the region's topographic relief and spectacular scenery. Uplifts were the result of vertical movement along faults caused by tectonic activity. This uplifting resulted in impressive escarpments such as the Book Cliffs, the Vermillion Cliffs and the White Cliffs; the different colors contributed by the different geologic formations. Canyons were formed through downcutting by the Colorado River and its tributaries, including the San Juan, Green, Price, San Rafael, Fremont, and Escalante. In many cases the relatively level portions of the Colorado Plateau between major rivers have been recognized as distinct plateaus, such as the Kaiparowits, Paunsaugunt and Tavaputs and the San Rafael Swell. The La Sal, Abajo and Henry mountains are three small ranges that rise above the level of the plateaus, providing climate and habitats otherwise unknown in Utah's canyon country.

## Soils

Vegetation and plant distributions in southeast Utah are strongly influenced by soils. Texture is the single most important soil attribute controlling plant distributions. Well-drained sands and sandy soils are most common on the Colorado Plateau, reflecting the predominance of sandstone geology. Wind deposition of sand can form dunes such as those east of the San Rafael Swell. Otherwise sandy soil occurs in association with sandstone, especially on broad stream terraces and alluvial plains. Gravelly soils are also well-drained and occur on slopes or more exposed sites where erosion by wind or water has slowed soil development and kept bedrock close to the surface. Both sandy and gravelly soils usually have relatively low concentrations of salts.

Fine-textured silts and clays are derived from shale, formed in marine environments where salts are at high concentrations. Clay soils are poorly drained because particles are densely packed, slowing the downward move-ment of water. Thus precipitation remains close to the surface rather than percolating down. Much of the water falling as rain runs off of sloping surfaces. Warm temperatures and low humidity cause much of the precipi-tation that penetrates the soil to be drawn back to the surface, bringing salts with it and concentrating them near the surface in the rooting zone. The dense matrix of particles and high salt concentration make clay soils a very different environment for plants than sandy or gravelly soils.

## Vegetation

Low-elevation vegetation of Utah's Painted Desert can be divided into nine plant communities described below.

**Riparian** plant communities occur most often on level terraces along perennial or near-perennial streams, but also around seeps and in other areas with near-surface water tables. Cottonwood trees (*Populus deltoides*) and willows (*Salix* spp.) are usually the dominant woody plants. Sedges (*Carex* spp.) and rushes (*Juncus* spp.), most of which bloom in the summer, comprise much of the herbaceous vegetation.

**Hanging gardens** are also a wet habitat, but one that occurs on the steep faces of cliffs and canyon walls where water springs from between two impervious layers of rock. Maidenhair fern (*Adiantum capillus-veneris*) as well as species of thistle (*Cirsium* spp.) and columbine (*Aquilegia* spp.) are common plants in these communities.

**Salt desert** shrub communities occur on broad, relatively level terraces and alluvial plains in valleys where soils are often derived, at least in part, from marine shales. Dominant shrubs include shadscale (*Atriplex confertifolia*), Gardner saltbush (*A. gardneri*), fourwing saltbush (*A. canescens*) and greasewood (*Sarcobatus vermiculatus*). Broom snakeweed (*Gutierrezia sarothrae*) and several grasses (e.g., *Sitanion, Agropyron*) may be common between shrubs where soils are somewhat silty. Very dense clays may support little or no perennial vegetation but can be ablaze with tolerant annuals in wet years.

Communities dominated by **Blackbrush** (*Coleogyne ramosissima*) occur on gentle terrain with shallow, stony and often somewhat sandy soil. Shallow bedrock below the surface restricts water infiltration in these areas. Other shrubs, such as rabbitbrush (*Chrysothamnus*) and sand sagebrush (*Artemisia filifolia*) may also occur with blackbrush, but never approach dominance, and there are few herbaceous plants present.

**Sand sagebrush** (*Artemisia filifolia*) can dominate plant communities in valley bottoms with deep, sandy soil. Mormon tea (*Ephedra* spp.) and yucca (*Yucca* spp.) are other common woody plants in these habitats. Indian ricegrass (*Oryzopsis hymenoides*), needle-and-thread (*Stipa comata*) and scurf pea (*Psoralidium* spp.) are common herbaceous plants.

**Big sagebrush** (*Artemisia tridentata*) plant communities are most often found on top of the plateaus in silty or somewhat clayey soils. Other common shrubs include winterfat (*Krascheninnikovia lanata*) and rabbitbrush. The herbaceous layer is dominated by perennial grasses, including galleta (*Hilaria jamesii*), Indian ricegrass and needle-and-thread.

**Mixed desert shrub** communities often support what appear to be combinations of two or more of the above shrub-dominated communities. Shadscale, four-wing saltbush, rabbitbrush, sagebrush and blackbrush may be common as well as a myriad of grasses and wildflowers. Mixed desert shrub communities are often found in stony soil on or at the base of gentle slopes.

**Shale barrens** occur on slopes and alluvial plains where dense, shale-derived clay is at the surface. There is little or no organic matter in the soil, and water runs off rather than percolating downward. These soils are also prone to shrinking and swelling and forming polygonal cracks which make it

difficult for many seedlings to become established. There is little or no vegetation in most years, but spectacular blooms of annuals, such as brittle phacelia (*Phacelia demissa*) or Colorado Plateau stinkweed (*Cleomella palmeriana*, pictured above), may occur following a wet winter.

**Pinyon-juniper woodlands** are the only common tree-dominated plant communities outside of riparian areas on the Colorado Plateau. These woodlands occur wherever there is fractured bedrock close to the surface. At lower elevations and warmer slopes, Utah juniper (*Juniperus osteosperma*) is the most common or only tree. Pinyon pine (*Pinus edulis*) becomes more common with increased moisture or cooler temperatures. Big sagebrush, rabbitbrush, snakeweed, bitterbrush (*Purshia tridentata*) and serviceberry (*Amelanchier utahensis*) are common shrubs in the understory. Many of the herbaceous species common in big sagebrush and mixed desert shrub communities occur here as well. Scattered individuals of Utah juniper can often be seen in shrub-dominated habitats with stony soils.

## Cryptobiotic soil crusts

Cryptobiotic or biological soil crusts are a thin, dark veneer on the soil surface composed of tiny lichens, mosses, algae and most importantly, nitrogen-fixing bacteria. They usually appear as blackish, rough patches. The bacteria produce a gelatinous film that covers the bare soil particles and binds them together, stabilizing the surface and helping to reduce wind and water erosion. The bacteria and some lichens fix atmospheric nitrogen, thus enriching the soil and enhancing plant growth. Soil crusts have also been shown to facilitate seedling establishment by providing "safe sites" with enhanced moisture and nutrient environments. Cryptobiotic crusts are most common on erosion-prone, fine, sandy soils. Trampling by livestock or humans can easily destroy these crusts. It is best to avoid stepping on soil crust when exploring the desert.

## Flora of the Red Rock Desert

About 2700 species of vascular plants are known from Utah's Red Rock Desert. Nearly one-quarter of these are restricted to this region and adjacent portions of the Colorado Plateau in Colorado, New Mexico, and Arizona. The degree of endemism in the flora of the Colorado Plateau is one of the highest in North America. Many of the plateau endemics are among the rarest species in the flora, while others are common in the Four Corners area but not found beyond. Often the plateau endemics are restricted to specific geologic formations, such as the Carmel limestone, Mancos shale, Chinle volcanic ash, and Navajo sandstone. The Colorado River has also acted as an important barrier promoting isolation of plant populations and new speciation, with several "species pairs" found on opposite banks.

The flora of the Red Rock Desert has also been enriched by species that are more typical of the Great Basin, Mojave Desert, Great Plains, and Rocky Mountains. Just over 100 species in the flora are introduced from other parts of the world, especially southwest Asia and Central America. Sagebrush and pinyon-juniper habitats have the highest number of plant species. More than 1000 are adapted to these sites, while about 700 species prefer wetland environments.

## How to use this book

With few exceptions, this book includes only those species with peak flowering on or before mid-June. The majority of these are broad-leaved wildflowers. Most of the common trees indigenous to the region, but only the most common grasses are also included. This book describes and illustrates with photographs approximately 300 of the most common species. Half again that many species are mentioned and sometimes illustrated. Looking at all of those pictures to find the right one can be a daunting task. The organization of this book will help to make the task easier. Plants are first divided into three groups: trees, grasses and wildflowers (including shrubs). There are relatively few trees and grasses described in this book; most descriptions are of wildflowers which are organized primarily by flower color (white, yellow, red/orange, blue/purple, and green). Users of this book can more easily identify a wildflower by taking into account the flower color and a few characteristics that describe the flower. The questions you should ask yourself are:

Is the plant a tree (go to P. 14) or a grass (go to P. 22)
If the plant is an herb or a shrub, what color are the flowers: white (P. 28), yellow (P. 89), blue/purple/pink (P. 142), red/orange (P. 198), green or inconspicuous (P. 209)?

Each color group is subsequently divided into four subgroups: (1) flowers with 4 or 5 separate petals, (2) flowers with 4 or 5 petals united at the base into a short or long tube, (3) flowers clustered together into an aster-like or sunflower-like head, often with strap-shaped ray flowers around the edge, or (4) flowers with 3 or 6 petals that are separate or united. These groups and subgroups are indicated at the top of each page. Shrubs follow herbaceous forbs within each subgroup.

## Taxonomy

There are several recent treatments of the flora of southeast Utah. These include *A Utah Flora* (Welsh et al. 2003), *Intermountain Flora* (Cronquist et al. 1972-2012) and *Flora of the Four Corners Region* (Heil et al. 2013). These publications do not always agree on taxonomy. We have chosen to follow the taxonomic nomenclature of the *Intermountain Flora*. Synonyms for the scientific names we employ can be found in Appendix A.

## Selected References

Belnap, J. and O.L. Lange (eds.). 2002. Biological soil crusts: structure, function and management. Springer-Verlag, Berlin.

Cronquist, A., A.H. Holmgren, N.H. Holmgren, J.L. Reveal, P.K. Holmgren and R.C. Barneby. 1972-2012. Intermountain Flora, volumes 1-6. New York Botanical Garden Press, New York.

Dunmire, W.W. and G.D. Tierney. 1997. Wild plants and native peoples of the Four Corners. Museum of New Mexico Press, Santa Fe.

Fertig, W. and M. Hill. 2005-2009. Annotated checklists for the floras of Arches, Bryce Canyon, Canyonlands, Capitol Reef, Hovenweep, Natural Bridges, and Zion, as well as other national parks and monuments in Utah's Red Rock country are available for free download as PDFs at https://science.nature.nps.gov/im/units/ncpn/Index.cfm

Fagan, D. 1998. Canyon country wildflowers. Falcon Press, Helena, Montana.

Flora of North America Editorial Committee. 1993-2016. Flora of North America north of Mexico. Vols. 2-9, 19-26. Oxford University Press, New York, NY.

Heil, K.D., S.L. O'Kane, L.M. Reeves and A. Clifford. 2013. Flora of the Four Corners region. Missouri Botanical Garden Press, St. Louis.

Moerman, D.E. 1998. Native American ethnobotany. Timber Press, Portland, Oregon.

Welsh, S.L., N.D. Atwood, S. Goodrich and L.C. Higgins. 2003. A Utah flora, 3rd Edition. Brigham Young University Press, Provo, Utah.

# Glossary

**Alternate**. Single at each node around the stem.

**Annual**. Germinating, growing, flowering and dying in one year or less time.

**Auricle**. Linear or ear-shaped appendage at the top of a grass leaf sheath.

**Awn**. Slender, bristle-like appendage.

**Axil**. Angle or space between leaf and stem or between other organs of the plant.

**Basal**. Positioned at the base.

**Biennial**. Growing vegetatively for one or more years followed by a single episode of blooming and then death.

**Blade**. Expanded, often flat portion of a leaf or petal.

**Bract**. Leaf- or scale-like structure at the base of a flower or inflorescence.

**Calyx**. Outermost or lowermost whorl of flower parts, generally green and enclosing inner flower parts.

**Capsule**. A dry, globose to tubular fruit opening to release the seeds.

**Catkin**. Spike-like, usually pendent inflorescence of unisexual flowers.

**Cone**. A dense cluster of sterile bracts with seed or pollen in between the bracts (e.g., pine cone).

**Coniferous**. Cone-bearing, often referring to trees in the Pine Family.

**Deciduous**. Pertaining to plants with leaves that all fall following the growing season.

**Disk flower**. A symmetric flower in the Sunflower Family, often in the center of the flower head surrounded by ray flowers.

**Endemic**. Restricted to a specified (usually small) area.

**Evergreen**. Having green leaves through the winter.

**Fruit**. A plant's seed-bearing structure.

**Genus**. (plural = genera). A circumscribed group of closely related species.

**Glabrous**. Smooth; devoid of hairs or other surface structures.

**Gland**. Small bodies on the plant surface or at the tip of a hair that exude a generally sticky substance.

**Head**. A dense cluster of flowers surrounded by bracts in the Sunflower Family, and resembling a single flower.

**Hood**. A hollow, arch-shaped flower part, usually with a turned-down margin.

**Inflorescence**. An arrangement of flowers with associated stalks and bracts.

**Involucral bract**. Small leaf- or scale-like structure at the base of the flower head in the Sunflower Family.

**Lanceolate**. Lance-shaped, widened near the base and tapering to the tip; longer than wide.

**Leaflet**. A distinct, leaf-like segment of a compound leaf.

**Lemma**. The lowermost bract enclosing the grass flower.

**Ligule**. A hairy or membranous projection at the top of a grass leaf sheath.

**Lobe**. A rounded or pointed projection, separated from adjacent lobes by a fissure or sinus.

**Midrib**. The central vein of a leaf or leaflet.

**Needle**. A slender, needle-like leaf of a tree in the Pine Family.

**Node**. Point on the stem where leaves or branches are attached.

**Opposite**. Two leaves or other structures per node, on opposite sides of the stem.

**Ovary**. Basal flower part that contains immature seeds.

**Ovate**. Egg-shaped in outline, widest axis below middle.

**Perennial**. Living more than two years and flowering more than once.

**Petals**. A usually colored segment of a flower.

**Petiolate**. Having a leaf stalk.

**Petiole**. Leaf stalk.

**Pinnate**. With leaflets arranged in one plane along either side of the axis.

**Pod**. A bean- or balloon-like fruit that dries out when mature.

**Pollination**. Transfer of pollen to fertilize an ovary.

**Ray flower.** A strap-shaped flower in the Sunflower Family, often around the periphery of a flower head.

**Sepal**. Outermost flower part, forming the calyx that encloses the inner flower parts.

**Sessile**. Lacking a stalk.

**Shrub**. A woody plant with numerous stems arising from the base.

**Spikelet**. An elongate cluster of unstalked grass flowers, usually subtended by two sterile bracts.

**Spur**. A pointed projection.

**Stalk**. A slender stem suppoting a leaf, flower or inflorescence.

**Stamen**. The male flower part containing the pollen.

**Stipule**. A small, leaf-like appendage at the junction of leaf and stem.

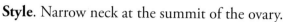

**Style**. Narrow neck at the summit of the ovary.

**Taproot**. The primary, vertical, usually stout part of the root system.

**Trunk**. The main stem of a tree below the branches.

**Tufted**. Having a dense cluster of basal leaves.

# Utah juniper  (*Juniperus osteosperma*)
## Cypress Family  (Cupressaceae)

**DIAGNOSTIC CHARACTERS:** Coniferous tree or large shrub to 16 ft (5 m) tall, often with several trunks. **Bark** gray, stringy and furrowed. **Leaves** are triangular, hardened, scale-like, about ⅛ in (2-3 mm) long, overlapping and surrounding the twigs. **Male cones** are less than ¼ in (3-5 mm) long on branch tips. **Female cones** globose, mostly ¼-½ in (6-12 mm) across, maturing after 2 years into a blue, berry-like fruit with 1 or 2 seeds.

**HABITAT AND RANGE:** Abundant, especially in well-drained soil, rock outcrops or slickrock. Idaho and Montana south to California and New Mexico. Found in ARCH, BEAR, BRCA, CANY, CARE, GLCA, GRST, HOVE, NABR, RABR, and ZION.

**NOTES:** This is the most common tree on the Colorado Plateau. Plants over 1,000 years old have been documented. The abundance of Utah juniper was once held in check by wildfires, but has increased as a result of fire suppression and the loss of grassy fuel resulting from cattle grazing. Native Americans in the area used decoctions of the berries or leaves to treat several ailments including headaches, menstrual cramps, colds and rheumatism. Utah juniper was the "cedar" used by pioneer settlers for fence posts and fuel and is the namesake of Cedar Breaks National Monument.

14

# Two-needle pinyon pine (*Pinus edulis*)
## Pine Family (Pinaceae)

**DESCRIPTION:** Coniferous evergreen tree up to 50 ft (15 m) tall, but usually shorter. **Bark** gray, furrowed, polygonal plates. **Needles** are pointed, ½-2 in (2-4 cm) long and grouped in pairs towards the branch tips. **Male cones** are globose, yellow and ¼ in (6 mm) long with many clustered on branch tips. **Female cones** are brown, resinous, ovoid, 1-2 in (3-6 cm mm) long, composed of numerous overlapping, oblong scales that are thickened at the tip and eventually spread apart to release the large, wingless, nut-like seeds.

**HABITAT AND RANGE:** Shallow or stony soil in the pinyon-juniper zone. Nevada and Wyoming south to Mexico. Known from ARCH, BEAR, BRCA, CANY, CARE, GLCA, GRST, NABR, RABR, and ZION.

**NOTES:** Pinyon pine nuts (seeds) are eaten by birds and mammals, including Native Americans and Europeans. Pinyon pine does not extend into as many dry habitats as Utah juniper, but becomes more common in places with higher precipitation. Two-needle pinyon is replaced by one-needle pinyon (*P. monophylla*) in the Great Basin, including the lower, western portion of Zion National Park. It can be recognized by its single needle per bundle. The two species intergrade in northern and central Arizona, suggesting they may be varieties of the same species.

15

# Douglas fir
## (*Pseudotsuga menziesii*)
## Pine Family (Pinaceae)

**DESCRIPTION:** Coniferous evergreen tree up to 95 ft (30 m) tall, but shorter in our area. **Bark** gray, with brown, longitudinal furrows. **Needles** occur singly and are rounded at the tip, ½-2 in (1-4 cm) long, densely and evenly spread along the twigs. **Male cones** are narrowly ovoid, reddish-brown, ¼ in (5-8 mm) long and arising from terminal leaf axils. **Female cones** are green, becoming brown, about 2 in (4-6 cm) long and composed of numerous overlapping fan-shaped scales, each with a narrow 3-lobed appendage extending beyond it.

**HABITAT AND RANGE:** Occasional on lower slopes of steep canyons and in higher pinyon-juniper woodlands. Throughout most of temperate western North America. Occurs in BEAR, BRCA, CANY, CARE, GLCA, GRST, NABR, and ZION.

**NOTES:** Douglas fir usually occurs at higher elevations than those of the Colorado Plateau; however, it sometimes can be found in shady canyons or the base of north-facing cliffs.

# Russian olive
## (*Elaeagnus angustifolia*)
## Oleaster Family (Elaeagnaceae)

**DESCRIPTION:** Small tree up to 32 ft (10 m) tall. **Twigs** thorny, scurfy-white when young, purplish with age. **Leaves** are alternate, stalked; the blades lanceolate, scurfy white-hairy and 1-3 in (2-9 cm) long. **Flowers are** borne in leaf axils and are fragrant and have four spreading, yellow, petal-like sepals about ⅛ in (3 mm) long. **Fruit** is a hard, globose, yellowish-green olive-like berry about ½ in (1 cm) across with a white-scaly surface.

**HABITAT AND RANGE:** Lower terraces along rivers and streams. Introduced from Europe throughout temperate North America, but most common in the west. Occurs in ARCH, BRCA, CANY, CARE, GLCA, GRST, and ZION.

**NOTES:** Mammals, such as raccoons, as well as birds eat the fruit. Russian olive has a symbiotic relationship with nitrogen-fixing bacteria which allows the plant to grow quickly but still have very hard wood. Beavers, who prefer native willows and cottonwood, rarely attack Russian olive.

# Box elder  (*Acer negundo*)
## Maple Family  (Aceraceae)

**DESCRIPTION:** Deciduous tree up to 40 ft (12 m) tall with separate sexes. **Twigs** velvety-hairy when young. **Leaves** are opposite and stalked, each having 3 stalked, ovate leaflets 1-4 in (2-10 cm) long with toothed margins. **Inflorescence:** male flowers are clustered at leaf nodes; numerous stalked female flowers are borne on pendent branches. **Flowers** have 4 to 5 small, green sepals with either a 2-parted ovary or 4 or 5 conspicuous, long stamens. **Fruit** is a pair of spreading, winged, seeds ½-1 in (2-4 cm) long, united at the seed end.

**HABITAT AND RANGE:** Stream banks and large washes and canyons. Throughout most of temperate North America. Found in ARCH, BEAR, CANY, CARE, GLCA, GRST, NABR, and ZION.

**NOTES:** Box elder is a maple with typical maple-like whirligig seeds, and sap that can be boiled to make syrup. Box elder will sprout from the base if the trunk is damaged.

# Gambel oak
## (*Quercus gambelii*)
## Fagaceae  (Oak Family)

**DESCRIPTION:** Deciduous clonal shrub or small tree up to 32 ft (10 m) tall. **Twigs** appressed-hairy when young. **Leaves** are alternate, stalked; the blades elliptic in outline 1-7 in (3-17 cm) long with 5-9 deep rounded lobes. **Female flowers** have tiny, hairy sepals; few are clustered at leaf nodes. **Male flowers** usually have 6 stamens and are borne on pendent branches (catkins), 1-2 in (3-5 cm) long. **Fruit** is an ellipsoid acorn, ½-1 in (1-3 cm) long with a scaly cap at the base.

**HABITAT AND RANGE:** Stream terraces and around springs or sandy to alluvial plains in the sagebrush or pinyon-juniper zones. Nevada to Colorado south to Mexico. Occurs in ARCH, BEAR, BRCA, CANY, CARE, GLCA, GRST, HOVE, NABR, RABR, and ZION.

**NOTES:** Gambel oak is a member of the white oaks, species with rounded leaf lobes and acorns that mature in one year rather than two. Leaves contain tannins that are mildly poisonous. The acorns are eaten by deer, squirrels and turkeys. Gambel oak readily crosses with scrub oak (*Q. turbinella*) to form the hybrid species *Quercus x pauciloba*.

# Singleleaf ash *(Fraxinus anomala)*
## Olive Family (Oleaceae)

**DESCRIPTION:** Small tree up to 20 ft (6 m) tall with gray bark. **Twigs** 4-angled, light brown and short-hairy. **Leaves** are opposite, stalked; the blades ovate with wavy margins or with 3 short-stalked, ovate leaflets ½-2 in (2-5 cm) long. **Inflorescence** from leaf nodes, branched with many flowers. **Male flowers** reduced to 2 stamens and a sterile ovary. **Female flowers** only a single ovary and style. **Fruit** is an oar-shaped, winged seed ½-1 in (1-3 cm) long.

**HABITAT AND RANGE:** Washes, woodlands and rocky, lower slopes, mainly in the pinyon-juniper zone. Wyoming and Nevada south to California through New Mexico and Mexico. Found in ARCH, BEAR, CANY, CARE, GLCA, GRST, HOVE, NABR, RABR, and ZION.

**NOTES:** Velvet ash (*F. velutina*) has leaves with 3 to 7 leaflets and is confined to stream banks. Box-elder (*Acer negundo*, P. 17) has toothed leaflets and paired winged fruits.

18

# Fremont cottonwood (*Populus deltoides*)
## Willow Family (Salicaceae)

**DESCRIPTION:** Large tree to 80 ft (25 m) high with furrowed bark. **Twigs** brittle, tan to gray with resinous buds. **Leaves** alternate, long-stalked; the blades are triangular and 1-5 in (3-12 cm) long with wavy-toothed margins. **Inflorescence** many-flowered, cylindrical catkins; male and female on different trees. **Male catkins** purplish with numerous stamens, expanding to 2-4 in (4-10 cm) long. **Female catkins** many-flowered, green, expanding to 2-5 in (6-12 cm) long. **Fruits** are numerous, resinous, ellipsoid capsules about ½ in (10 mm) long containing minute cottony seeds.

**HABITAT AND RANGE:** Margins of rivers and larger streams and canyons. Plains cottonwood (*P. deltoides*) occurs throughout temperate North America; Fremont cottonwood (var. *fremontii*) is found in Nevada to Colorado south to Arizona and New Mexico. Found in ARCH, BEAR, BRCA, CANY, CARE, GLCA, GRST, HOVE, NABR, RABR, and ZION.

**NOTES:** Hybridization is common in this group of cottonwoods, so treating our plants as forms of plains cottonwood is reasonable. Plants establish following floods but may be washed away in subsequent flood events. Named for John Fremont who led exploratory expeditions in the mid-1800's. The brittle, punky branches of Fremont cottonwood leave holes in tree trunks when they break off, creating hollows for nesting birds.

19

# Hoptree (*Ptelea trifoliata*)
## Rutaceae (Citrus Family)

**DESCRIPTION:** Shrub or small tree to 6 ft (2 m) high with yellow to brown twigs. **Leaves** are alternate and have 3 lanceolate to ovate, glabrous or finely hairy, minutely-toothed leaflets, ½-3 in (1-7 cm) long with conspicuous pits. **Inflorescence** hemispheric, openly branched with stalked flowers. **Flowers** have 4 to 6 greenish petals ¼ in (5-7 mm) long. **Fruit** flattened, circular, ½-1 in (1-3 cm) wide including the broad veiny wings.

**HABITAT AND RANGE:** Stony soil of stream banks and canyons at low elevations. Eastern seaboard west to Utah and Arizona. Occurs in GLCA.

**NOTES:** Probably confined to the Colorado and Virgin rivers in our area. Havasupai treated arrowheads with crushed leaves to make them poisonous. Hoptree flowers and foliage have a strong citrus odor like the fleshy fruits of many other members of the citrus family.

# Netleaf hackberry
## (*Celtis reticulata*)
## Elm Family (Ulmaceae)

**DESCRIPTION:** Deciduous clonal shrub or small tree up to 16 ft (5 m) tall with corky bark. **Twigs** gray, hairy when young. **Leaves** are alternate, stalked; the blades ovate with toothed margins, 1-3 in (2-8 cm) long. **Flowers** are borne in leaf axils and are bisexual or unisexual; each has 5 sepals less than ⅛ in (2-3 mm) long, but no petals. **Fruit** is a hard, globose, green berry ¼ in (5-8 mm) across.

**HABITAT AND RANGE:** Sandy or stony soils in canyons and on stream banks in the desert shrub to sagebrush zones. Eastern Washington to California and Mexico east to Kansas and Louisiana. Found in ARCH, BEAR, CANY, CARE, GLCA, GRST, HOVE, NABR, RABR, and ZION.

**NOTES:** Netleaf hackberry is slow-growing, long-lived and usually resprouts after fire. The fruits are eaten by Native Americans and small mammals. Navajo used the leaves to make a red dye. Hackberry has been included in the Elm Family, but taxonomists now believe it may be more closely related to hops and marijuana in the Cannabaceae. Hackberry leaves are usually covered with ball-like insect galls caused by aphid-like psyllid flies.

# Tamarisk, saltcedar  (*Tamarix chinensis, T. ramosissima*)
## Tamarisk Family  (Tamaricaceae)

**DESCRIPTION:** Shrub or small tree up to 20 ft (6 m) tall with brown bark. **Leaves** are alternate, lanceolate, scale-like, less than ⅛ in (1-3 mm) long, overlapping and appressed to the twig. **Inflorescences** cylindrical, ½-3 in (2-7 cm) long on upper portions of side branches; each has numerous crowded, short-stalked flowers. **Flowers** have 5 pink petals ⅛ in (1-3 mm) long. **Fruit** is a conical capsule ⅛ in (3-4 mm) long containing numerous seeds with cottony filaments on top.

**HABITAT AND RANGE:** Banks of streams and washes. Introduced from Asia to most of temperate western North America. Occurs in ARCH, BEAR, BRCA, CANY, CARE, GLCA, GRST, HOVE, NABR, RABR, and ZION.

**NOTES:** Researchers have found that most tamarisk plants in our area are hybrids between two Eurasian species, *T. chinensis* and *T. ramosissima*. Like cottonwood and willow, tamarisk establishes on banks following floods. Unlike these native species however, it produces seed during most of the growing season instead of only in the spring and thus has an advantage over native riparian species, especially along regulated rivers. Small-flowered tamarisk (*T. parviflora*) has flowers with 4 petals and is uncommon.

# Purple three-awn
### (*Aristida purpurea*)
### Grass Family (Poaceae)

**DESCRIPTION:** Tufted perennial 4-28 in (10-70 cm) tall. **Leaf blades** less than ⅛ in (1-2 mm) wide with long and short hairs at the base. **Inflorescence** of short-stalked, often purplish spikelets. **Spikelets** 1-flowered. **Lemmas** are about ½ in (10-15 mm) long with 3 purple, stiff, thread-like awns, 1-3 in (2-8 cm) long at the tip.

**HABITAT AND RANGE:** Silty or gravelly soil of blackbrush, sagebrush or pinyon-juniper habitats. Throughout most of western and central temperate North America. Found in ARCH, BEAR, BRCA, CANY, CARE, GLCA, GRST, HOVE, NABR, RABR, and ZION.

**NOTES:** Plants are eaten by ungulates and livestock early in the year, but the stiff awns make it unpalatable later. This species often forms dense reddish bands along roadsides where growth is encouraged by the extra runoff.

# Cheatgrass
### (*Bromus tectorum*)
### Grass Family (Poaceae)

**DESCRIPTION:** Stiff-hairy annual with 1 to many stems 4-20 in (10-50 cm) high. **Leaf blades** are less than ¼ in (1-6 mm) wide with a jagged-edged membrane (ligule) at the base. **Inflorescence** of spreading-stalked, often purplish, sometimes nodding spikelets. **Spikelets** have 3 to 6 flowers. **Lemmas** are about ½ in (9-13 mm) long, each with a stiff awn about ½ in (10-17 mm) long, from the 2-lobed tip.

**HABITAT AND RANGE:** Sandy or silty, often sparsely-vegetated or disturbed soil in nearly all but saline habitats. Introduced from Europe throughout temperate North America. Known from ARCH, BEAR, BRCA, CANY, CARE, GLCA, GRST, HOVE, NABR, RABR, and ZION.

**NOTES:** Cheatgrass germinates in autumn and grows throughout the winter whenever conditions are adequate. It is believed to fuel more frequent range fires, thereby reducing the cover of sagebrush. Red brome (*B. rubens*) and Japanese brome (*B. japonicus*) are two other introduced annuals; the former is more common in arid areas; the latter is found in moist areas.

# Squirreltail (*Sitanion hystrix*)
## Grass Family  (Poaceae)

**DESCRIPTION:** Tufted, mostly glabrous perennial 4-26 in (10-65 cm) tall. **Leaf blades** less than ¼ in (1-4 mm) wide with a minute (0.5 mm) membrane (ligule) at the base surrounded by a pair of ear-like flaps (auricles). **Inflorescence** of crowded, sessile spikelets, narrow at first, becoming brush-like and shattering at maturity. **Spikelets** 1- to 6-flowered with numerous needle-like awns. **Lemmas** are ⅜ in (8-10 mm) long with 3 purple, stiff, erect and then spreading, thread-like awns, 1-3 in (2-7 cm) long at the tip.

**HABITAT AND RANGE:** Most habitats; most common in sagebrush and pinyon-juniper communities. Throughout temperate western North America. Occurs in ARCH, BEAR, BRCA, CANY, CARE, GLCA, GRST, HOVE, NABR, RABR, and ZION.

**NOTES:** Squirreltail barley (*Hordeum jubatum*) has a similar inflorescence but a slightly larger ligule and is usually found in vernally moist sites such as roadsides or pond margins. Squirreltail can hybridize with nearly every western species of wheatgrass (*Agropyron*) and the hybrids are often intermediate, but always have readily-shattering spikelets.

# Slender wheatgrass
## (*Agropyron trachycaulum*)
## Grass Family (Poaceae)

**DESCRIPTION:** Tufted, glabrous or short-hairy perennial up to more than 3 ft (100 cm) tall. **Leaf blades** are less than ¼ in (2-7 mm) wide with a minute membrane (ligule) at the base and small ear-like lobes (auricles) surrounding the stem. **Inflorescence** slender, composed of sessile, partly overlapping spikelets. **Spikelets** have 3 to 7 flowers with the wide side facing the stem. **Lemmas** are ⅜ in (5-12 mm) long, each sometimes with a short needle-like awn at the tip.

**HABITAT AND RANGE:** Stream banks, grasslands and woodlands of sagebrush and pinyon-juniper communities. Throughout temperate North America except the southeast. Found in ARCH, BEAR, BRCA, CANY, CARE, GLCA, GRST, HOVE, NABR, and ZION.

**NOTES:** Bluebunch wheatgrass (*A. spicatum*) is a bunchgrass with long, bent awns and more widely-spaced spikelets; western wheatgrass (*A. smithii*) has single stems from underground rhizomes and awnless spikelets.

# Annual wheatgrass
## (*Eremopyrum triticeum*)
## Grass Family (Poaceae)

**DESCRIPTION:** Tufted, short-hairy annual ½-2 in (1-4 cm) high. **Leaf blades** are less than ¼ in (1-4 mm) wide with a 0.5 mm membrane (ligule) at the base and minute ear-like lobes (auricles) surrounding the stem. **Inflorescence** ovoid in outline, composed of sessile, tightly overlapping spikelets. **Spikelets** have 3 to 6 flowers with the wide side facing the stem. **Lemmas** are about ¼ in (5-8 mm) long, each with a short, needle-like tip.

**HABITAT AND RANGE:** Disturbed silty or clay, often salty soil in salt desert shrub, sagebrush and pinyon-juniper habitats. Introduced from Eurasia to much of temperate western North America. Occurs in ARCH and CANY.

**NOTES:** Annual wheatgrass is especially common on soils derived from Mancos Shale in the area around Moab and Green River.

# Indian ricegrass (*Oryzopsis hymenoides*)
## Grass Family (Poaceae)

**DESCRIPTION:** Bunch-forming, mostly glabrous perennial 8-28 in (20-70 cm) tall. **Leaf blades** are usually tubular and less than ⅛ in (1 mm) wide with a membrane less than ¼ in (2-8 mm) high at the base. **Inflorescence** is highly branched and composed of long-stalked, widely-separated spikelets. **Spikelets** are 1-flowered, pear-shaped. **Lemmas** are densely long-hairy and ⅛ in (2-4 mm) long with a short awn.

**HABITAT AND RANGE:** Sandy or occasionally gravelly soil from desert shrub to pinyon-juniper communities. Throughout most of temperate, western North America. Occurs in ARCH, BEAR, BRCA, CANY, CARE, GLCA, GRST, HOVE, NABR, RABR, and ZION.

**NOTES:** Hopi, Navajo and numerous other Native American tribes ground the seeds of Indian ricegrass to make bread or other baked goods. Littleseed ricegrass (*O. micrantha*) is smaller than Indian ricegrass, but the lemmas have longer awns and are hairless.

## Galleta (*Hilaria jamesii*)
## Poaceae (Grass Family)

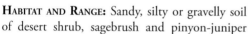

**DESCRIPTION:** Tufted, short-rhizomatous, short-hairy perennial 4-24 in (10-60 cm) tall. **Leaf blades** are ⅛ in (1-3 mm) wide with a fringed membrane ⅛ in (1-3 mm) high at the base. **Inflorescence** is slender and composed of sessile, barely overlapping clusters of 3 purplish spikelets that are long-hairy at the base. **Spikelets** are of 2 kinds: outside spikelets are 2-flowered and have only stamens; central spikelets have only 1 bisexual flower. **Lemmas** are ¼ in (5-8 mm) long; the central one with a short needle-like awn at the bilobed tip.

**HABITAT AND RANGE:** Sandy, silty or gravelly soil of desert shrub, sagebrush and pinyon-juniper habitats. Southwest deserts from southern Wyoming to Mexico. Found in ARCH, BEAR, BRCA, CANY, CARE, GLCA, GRST, HOVE, NABR, RABR, and ZION.

**NOTES:** Plants are more tolerant of grazing than many other native grasses, and thus tend to become dominant in rangelands. Hopi used galleta to make baskets.

## Six-weeks fescue
### (*Vulpia octoflora*)
### Grass Family (Poaceae)

**DESCRIPTION:** Tufted, usually short-hairy annual 6-12 in (15-30 cm) tall. **Leaf blades** usually rolled and less than ⅛ in (1 mm) wide with a short membrane at the base. **Inflorescence** is narrow with erect, short-stalked spikelets. **Spikelets** are somewhat flattened with 6 to 12 flowers. **Lemmas** are lanceolate and less than ¼ in (3-5 mm) long with an apical awn about ⅛ in (1-5 mm) long.

**HABITAT AND RANGE:** Sparsely-vegetated, sandy or silty soil, often along streams or in other disturbed sites throughout our area. Throughout most of temperate North America. Known from ARCH, BEAR, BRCA, CANY, CARE, GLCA, GRST, HOVE, NABR, RABR, and ZION.

**NOTES:** Unlike cheatgrass (P. 22), six-weeks fescue germinates in the spring and so usually does not attain the height or mass of the introduced annual bromes. Navajo used the seeds for food.

## Needle-and-thread (*Stipa comata*)
### Grass Family (Poaceae)

**Description:** Bunch-forming, mostly glabrous perennial 1-3 ft (30-90 cm) tall. **Leaf blades** are usually rolled and less than ⅛ in (1 mm) wide with a membrane less than ¼ in (2-6 mm) high at the base. **Inflorescence** is open with long-stalked, widely-spreading spikelets. **Spikelets** are 1-flowered and spindle-shaped with a sharp-pointed base. **Lemmas** are narrow, short-hairy and about ½ in (8-14 mm) long with a mostly glabrous, bent and twisted awn up 8 in (20 cm) long from the pointed tip.

**Habitat and Range:** Sandy or gravelly soil in all habitats except those with salty or heavy soil. Throughout temperate western North America. Found in ARCH, BEAR, BRCA, CANY, CARE, GLCA, GRST, HOVE, NABR, RABR, and ZION.

**Notes:** The long awns of needle-and-thread twist and untwist with diurnal changes in humidity, and can drill the seed into the ground in the process. Mormon needlegrass (*S. arida*) has a more compact inflorescence with smaller lemmas and shorter awns; awns of New Mexico feathergrass (*S. neomexicana*) have spreading hairs to the tip.

## White-cup spring-parsley (*Cymopterus bulbosus*)
### Parsley Family (Apiaceae)

DESCRIPTION: Perennial. **Stems** are leafless and 2-8 in (5-20 cm) long. **Leaves** are all basal, whitish-green and 1-4 in (2-10 cm) long with 3 to 9 ovate and deeply lobed leaflets. **Flowers** are white in a hemispheric inflorescence in clusters subtended by white bracts with a single purple vein. **Fruits** are 2-4 in (5-10 mm) long with several wavy-margined wings about ⅛ in (3 mm) wide.

HABITAT AND RANGE: Sandy to clayey, often well-drained, sometimes salty soil of salt and mixed desert shrub communities and juniper woodlands. Cold deserts from southern Wyoming to Arizona and New Mexico. Found in ARCH, CANY, CARE, and HOVE.

NOTES: Like several other species in its genus, white-cup spring-parsley has a thick, starchy taproot. Archaeological studies indicate that white-cup spring-parsley had a high enough caloric content to be an important root crop for the Ute and other tribes who ate the roots. Young shoots were also consumed as a potherb. Since many species in the Parsley Family are poisonous, great care should be taken in eating any plants that have not been positively identified. Two similar species, basin spring-parsley (*Cymopterus purpurascens*) and purple-nerved spring-parsley (*C. multinervatus*) also occur in The Red Rock Desert and differ in having more tightly packed fruiting heads or a purplish cup of bracts with green veins.

# Desert rockcress
### (*Boechera pulchra*)
## Mustard Family (Brassicaceae)

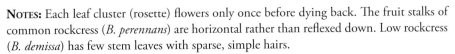

**DESCRIPTION:** Perennial with 1 to many basal leaf clusters. **Stems** unbranched, 6-24 in (15-60 cm) tall. **Leaves** are basal and alternate, narrow, short-hairy and ½-2 in (1-6 cm) long. **Flowers** are white to purplish and have 4 petals, up to 2/3 in (9-18 mm) long, that spread outward. **Fruits** are narrow pods, 1-2 in (3-6 cm) long, that become reflexed with age.

**HABITAT AND RANGE:** Sandy, silty or gravelly soil of desert shrub and pinyon-juniper communities. Western North American deserts from Oregon to Wyoming and south to Baja, Arizona and New Mexico. Occurs in ARCH, BEAR, CANY, CARE, GLCA, GRST, HOVE, NABR, RABR, and ZION.

**NOTES:** Each leaf cluster (rosette) flowers only once before dying back. The fruit stalks of common rockcress (*B. perennans*) are horizontal rather than reflexed down. Low rockcress (*B. demissa*) has few stem leaves with sparse, simple hairs.

## Spectacle pod (*Dimorphocarpa wislizenii*)
## Mustard Family (Brassicaceae)

**DESCRIPTION:** Gray-hairy annual or biennial. **Stems** often branched, 4-20 in (10-50 cm) tall. **Leaves** alternate; the basal lobed and often withered; stem leaves mostly unlobed and ½-4 in (1-10 cm) long. **Flowers** have 4 white petals up to ⅓ in (4-8 mm) long. **Fruits** on long, spreading stalks, flattened with 2 adjacent, 1-seeded lobes.

**HABITAT AND RANGE:** Sandy soil of blackbrush, sagebrush and pinyon-juniper communities. Colorado Plateau and warm deserts from Nevada to Texas and Mexico. Occurs in ARCH, BEAR, CANY, CARE, GLCA, GRST, HOVE, and ZION.

**NOTES:** Navajo and Hopi ground the plant to treat wounds, insect bites and hemorrhoids. The species epithet commemorates Friedrich Wislizenus, a German naturalist who travelled across northern Mexico in the 1840s and was arrested by the Mexican government for being a spy.

# Wedge-leaf whitlow-wort (*Draba cuneifolia*)
## Mustard Family (Brassicaceae)

**DESCRIPTION:** Annual to 8 in (3-20 cm) tall. **Stems** short with few narrow leaves. **Basal leaves** wedge-shaped, ¼-2 in (5-40 mm) long with branched hairs. **Flowers** have 4 white petals up to ¼ in (3-5 mm) long. **Fruits** on ascending stalks are flattened and narrowly elliptic with several seeds in 2 rows.

**HABITAT AND RANGE:** Sandy or silty soil of desert shrub to pinyon-juniper habitats. Across southern U.S. and Mexico but most common in the desert Southwest. Known from ARCH, BEAR, CANY, CARE, GLCA, GRST, HOVE, NABR, and ZION.

**NOTES:** Our plants are var. *cuneifolia.* Dwarf whitlow-wort (*D. reptans*) has similar fruits and growth form, but the hairs of the leaves and stems are mostly unbranched.

# Perennial pepperweed
## (*Lepidium latifolium*)
## Mustard Family
## (Brassicaceae)

**DESCRIPTION:** Rhizomatous, mostly glabrous perennial. **Stems** erect, branched and 20-60 in (50-150 cm) tall. **Leaves** basal and alternate; lower leaves stalked; the blades elliptic to lanceolate with toothed margins 2-5 in (4-13 cm) long. **Inflorescence** branched, spreading with numerous flowers. **Flowers** have 4 white petals 1-2 mm long. **Fruits** are sparsely hairy, ovoid and ⅛ in (2-3 mm) long.

**HABITAT AND RANGE:** Riparian areas and roadsides. Introduced from Eurasia to most of temperate western North America. Occurs in ARCH, CANY, and GLCA

**NOTES:** Perennial pepperweed is officially classified as a noxious weed by the state of Utah. Whitetop (*Cardaria draba*) is a closely-related, introduced weed found in similar habitats; it is smaller and has fruits that are broader than long and short-hairy foliage.

# Mountain pepperwort
## (*Lepidium montanum*)
## Mustard Family (Brassicaceae)

**DESCRIPTION:** Clump-forming, glabrous or short-hairy perennial. **Stems** branched, usually up to 20 in (3-50 cm) tall. **Leaves** basal and alternate; the basal are often stalked and lobed, 1-6 in (3-15 cm) long. **Flowers** have 4 white petals ⅛ in (2-5 mm) long. **Fruits** are glabrous, ovoid and up to ¼ in (2-5 mm) long on spreading stalks.

**HABITAT AND RANGE:** All types of soil in all habitats. Oregon to Montana south to California through west Texas. Found in ARCH, BEAR, BRCA, CANY, CARE, GLCA, GRST, HOVE, NABR, RABR, and ZION.

**NOTES:** This is a variable species. At least 3 forms occur in our area; var. *jonesii* with glabrous stems and lobed stem leaves, pictured here, is the most common form on the Colorado Plateau. Mountain pepperwort contains linolenic acid, which is a form of omega-3 acids important for dietary health. Densecress (*L. densiflorum*) and Virginia pepperwort (*L. virginicum*) are annuals with toothed leaves and elliptic fruits that are notched at the tip.

# Little twistflower
## (*Streptanthella longirostris*)
## Mustard Family (Brassicaceae)

**DESCRIPTION:** Waxy-smooth annual. **Stems** 4-20 in (10-50 cm) tall, usually branched. **Leaves** alternate, narrow, ½-4 in (1-10 cm) long. **Flowers** have 4 whitish petals, ¼ in (3-7 mm) long, enclosed by sepals that are white at the base with purple tips. **Fruits** are long-beaked, linear pods, 1-2 in (3-5 cm) long, that dangle from recurved stalks.

**HABITAT AND RANGE:** Usually sandy or silty, sparsely-vegetated soil of desert shrub, sagebrush and pinyon-juniper habitats. Southern Washington to Montana and south to Mexico. Occurs in ARCH, BEAR, BRCA, CANY, CARE, GLCA, GRST, HOVE, NABR, RABR, and ZION.

**NOTES:** This is the only member of the genus *Streptanthella*. The distinctive fruits and winged seeds of little twistflower have been recovered from ancient pack rat middens in Capitol Reef National Park.

# Fendler's sandwort
## (*Eremogone fendleri*)
## Pink Family (Caryophyllaceae)

**DESCRIPTION:** Perennial forming loose mats. **Stems** unbranched, sticky-hairy, up to 10 in (25 cm) tall. **Leaves** are mostly basal and opposite, linear, stiff, glabrous and up to 4 in (10 cm) long. **Inflorescence** of few stalked flowers on stem tips. **Flowers** have 5 white petals ¼ in (4-8 mm) long and 5 pointed sepals with white margins.

**HABITAT AND RANGE:** Silty or gravelly soil of blackbrush, sagebrush and pinyon-juniper habitats. Idaho and Wyoming south to Arizona and New Mexico. Occurs in ARCH, BEAR, CANY, CARE, GLCA, GRST, HOVE, NABR, and ZION.

**NOTES:** Most of our plants belong to var. *eastwoodiae* which has larger flowers, fewer stem leaves, and is less glandular than other varieties. Navajo inhaled powdered root to treat a congested nose. Shrubby sandwort (*E. macradenia*) is taller and woody at the base.

# Fendler's spurge (*Chamaesyce fendleri*)
## Spurge Family (Euphorbiaceae)

**DESCRIPTION:** Glabrous perennial with milky sap. **Stems** purple, prostrate to ascending, 2-8 in (5-20 cm) long. **Leaves** opposite, short-stalked; the blades ovate and up to ½ in (3-11 mm) long. **Inflorescence** composed of small, white and green flowers in leaf axils. **Fruits** are short-stalked, nodding, 3-ribbed, 3-seeded, globose capsules ⅛ in (2-3 mm) long.

**HABITAT AND RANGE:** Sparsely vegetated, sandy soil of desert shrub and pinyon-juniper habitats. Southern Great Plains and intermountain region from Wyoming south to California, Texas and Mexico. Found in ARCH, BEAR, BRCA, CANY, CARE, GLCA, GRST, HOVE, NABR and ZION.

**NOTES:** Several similar-appearing, prostrate, annual species of *Chamaesyce* occur in our area and are told apart by minute characters of the flowers and fruits. This group of spurges has the water-conserving C4 mode of photosynthesis.

# Two-grooved milkvetch (*Astragalus bisulcatus*)
## Pea Family (Fabaceae)

**DESCRIPTION:** Robust, sparsely-hairy perennial. **Stems** erect, leafy, 6-28 in (15-70 cm) tall. **Leaves** are alternate, pinnately compound, and 1-6 in (3-15 cm) long with 9 to 19 narrowly-elliptic leaflets. **Inflorescence** of erect stalks from leaf axils with 25 to 80 flowers. **Flowers** are pea-like, nodding, about ½ in (10-18 mm) long and white with purple tips. **Pods** droop and are narrowly ellipsoid, ½ in (12-20 mm) long with 2 longitudinal grooves on the bottom and a short stalk hidden by the calyx.

**HABITAT AND RANGE:** Silty or clay, usually selenium-bearing, shale-derived soils of sage-brush and pinyon-juniper habitats. Great Plains, Great Basin and Colorado Plateau from southern Canada south to Nevada and Arizona to Texas. Found in BEAR, BRCA, GRST, and ZION.

**NOTES:** Our plants are var. *major*; the less common var. *bisulcatus* occurs in similar habitats but has purplish flowers. Plants sequester selenium, making them ill-smelling and poisonous to livestock.

# Lesser rushy milkvetch *(Astragalus convallarius)*
## Pea Family (Fabaceae)

**DESCRIPTION:** Silvery perennial. **Stems** slender, erect, 6-24 in (15-60 cm) long. **Leaves** are alternate, pinnately compound, thread-like and 1-4 in (2-10 cm) long with few or no linear leaflets. **Inflorescence** ascending from leaf axils with 3 to 25 well-spaced flowers. **Flowers** are pea-like, whitish, less than ½ in (7-11 mm) long. **Pods** pendulous, linear, flattened and 1-2 in (2-5 cm) long.

**HABITAT AND RANGE:** Sagebrush, pinyon-juniper and less commonly desert shrub communities. Intermountain region from southwest Montana to Nevada, Utah and Colorado. Occurs in BRCA, CARE, GRST, and ZION.

**NOTES:** Bishop's milkvetch (*A. episcopus*) and great rushy milkvetch (*A. lonchocarpus*) are slender with linear leaflets and pendulous pods, but the former has pinkish flowers, and the latter has pods that are triangular in cross-section. The herbage of lesser rushy milkvetch is highly toxic to sheep.

# Small-flowered milkvetch *(Astragalus nuttallianus)*
## Pea Family (Fabaceae)

**DESCRIPTION:** Appressed-hairy annual. **Stems** prostrate to erect, usually unbranched, 1-14 in (2-36 cm) tall. **Leaves** are alternate, pinnately compound, and ½-3 in (1-8 cm) long with 7 to 15 well-spaced leaflets. **Inflorescence** ascending to erect with few flowers.

**Flowers** pea-like, purple to white, spreading, up to ⅜ in (4-8 mm) long. **Pods** are curved-linear, about ½ in (1 cm) long and 2-lobed in cross-section.

**HABITAT AND RANGE:** Sandy or gravelly soil of blackbrush, sagebrush and pinyon-juniper communities. Deserts and Great Plains from California and Nevada to Kansas, Texas and Mexico. Found in BEAR, CANY, CARE, GLCA, GRST, HOVE, RABR, and ZION.

**NOTES:** This variable species is composed of nine forms, but only var. *micranthiformis* occurs on the Colorado Plateau. It is inconspicuous except when in flower and abundance varies depending on winter rainfall. Most other milkvetch species in the Colorado Plateau are perennials.

# Stinking milkvetch (*Astragalus praelongus*)
## Pea Family (Fabaceae)

**Description:** Mostly glabrous perennial. **Stems** erect, branched, 8-36 in (20-90 cm) tall. **Leaves** are alternate, pinnately compound, and 2-7 in (4-18 cm) long with 9 to 33 leaflets. **Inflorescence** erect with 10 to 33 flowers. **Flowers** nod and are cream-colored and ½-1 in (15-24 mm) long. **Pods** spread horizontally and are green, ellipsoid and 1-2 in (2-4 cm) long.

**Habitat and Range:** Sandy, gravelly or clay soils of desert shrub, salt desert shrub and pinyon-juniper communities, often in wash bottoms. Nevada to Colorado and Texas. Known from ARCH, BEAR, BRCA, CANY, CARE, GLCA, GRST, and ZION.

**Notes:** True to its name, stinking milkvetch is foul-smelling due to the accumulation of toxic selenium. There are three forms in our area: var. *lonchopus* has stalked pods; var. *ellisiae* has pods less than ½ in (1 cm) thick, while those of var. *praelongus* are about ½ in (1 cm) thick. The dried pods of this species rattle when brushed against, tricking hikers into thinking a rattlesnake may be nearby.

# Canyonlands prairie-clover (*Dalea flavescens*)
## Pea Family (Fabaceae)

**DESCRIPTION:** Silvery-hairy or white-waxy perennial. **Stems** erect, 8-20 in (20-50 cm) tall. **Leaves** are alternate, pinnately compound, 1-2 in (2-5 cm) long with 3 to 7 leaflets. **Inflorescence** an erect spike ½-4 in (1-10 cm) long composed of numerous, densely packed, small flowers. **Flowers** are ⅜ in (6-11 mm) long with 5 unequal, white petals and a long-hairy, bumpy calyx. **Pods** are ovoid, 1-seeded, flattened, hairy, bumpy and ⅛ in (3-4) mm long.

**HABITAT AND RANGE:** Desert shrub, blackbrush and pinyon-juniper habitats. Endemic to the Colorado Plateau of Utah and Arizona. Occurs in ARCH, BEAR, CANY, CARE, GLCA, GRST, and NABR.

**NOTES:** There are two forms of Canyonlands prairie-clover; the flowering spikes of var. *epica* are greater than 2 in (5 cm) long, while those of var. *flavescens* are shorter. Var. *epica* was named to commemorate the epic migration of Mormon pioneers across the Colorado River south of Escalante. White prairie-cover (*D. candida*) has a similar inflorescence, but the foliage is green and glabrous.

# Wild licorice (*Glycyrrhiza lepidota*)
## Pea Family (Fabaceae)

**DESCRIPTION:** Rhizomatous, often sticky perennial. **Stems** erect, 1-4 ft (40-120 cm) tall. **Leaves** are alternate, pinnately compound, 3-8 in (8-19 cm) long with 13 to 19 leaflets that are gland-dotted and thinly-hairy beneath. **Inflorescence** erect, cylindrical, ½-2 in (1-5 cm) long with 20 to 50 ascending flowers. **Flowers** whitish, pea-like, about ½ in (9-13 mm) long. **Pods** are ellipsoid, ½-1 in (13-20 mm) long and beset with hooked prickles.

**HABITAT AND RANGE:** Deep, moist soil of streambanks, occasionally roadsides. Throughout all of temperate North America except the southeast. Known from ARCH, CANY, CARE, GLCA, GRST, and ZION.

**NOTES:** The roots of this plant have the aroma of licorice. It is closely related to the European licorice of commerce (*G. glabra*), which differs in having smooth pods.

# Large-flowered breadroot (*Pediomelum megalanthum*)
## Pea Family (Fabaceae)

**DESCRIPTION:** Spreading-hairy perennial up to 10 in (25 cm) tall. **Leaves** are palmately compound, all basal, and long-stalked with 5 to 8 leaflets up to 1½ in (4 cm) long. **Inflorescence** ascending to erect, hemispheric with 6 to 24 flowers. **Flowers** are pea-like, ½-1 in (12-21 mm) long; the lower petals purple; the upper white. **Pods** ellipsoid, less than ¼ in (4-5 mm) long, included in the calyx.

**HABITAT AND RANGE:** Clay, sandy or gravelly soil of desert shrub, blackbrush and pinyon-juniper habitats. Deserts of western Nevada to eastern Colorado and New Mexico. Found in ARCH, BEAR, CANY, and GLCA.

**Notes:** Plants have a slender below-ground stem attached to a large ellipsoid, tuberous root. Aromatic breadroot (*P. aromaticum*, right) has a similar growth form but smaller flowers.

37

## Spiny false milkvetch (*Peteria thompsoniae*)
### Pea Family (Fabaceae)

**Description:** Appressed-hairy perennial. **Stems** erect, 4-20 in (10-50 cm) long, branched below. **Leaves** are alternate, pinnately compound, 1½-7 in (4-18 cm) long with 9 to 27 leaflets and a pair of spines at the base of the petiole. **Inflorescence** a loose spike with 18 to 25 flowers. **Flowers** off-white to pinkish, up to 1 in (18-25 mm) long; the calyx with sticky hairs. **Pods** strap-shaped, about 2 in (5-6 cm) long.

**Habitat and Range:** Sandy or gravelly to clay soils of desert shrub or pinyon-juniper habitats. Southern Idaho south to California and northern Arizona. Found in CANY, CARE, GLCA, GRST, and ZION.

**Notes:** The spine-like stipules at the base of the leaf petiole distinguish this plant from true milkvetches (*Astragalus* spp.). Sereno Watson of Harvard University named the species after Ellen Powell Thompson, the sister of John Wesley Powell, who discovered it and several other species while exploring around Kanab, Utah, in the 1870s.

# Desert green gentian (*Frasera albomarginata*)
## Gentian Family (Gentianaceae)

**DESCRIPTION:** Nearly glabrous biennial. **Stems** erect, branched above, 8-24 in (20-60 cm) tall. **Leaves** are basal and in whorls of 3 or 4, linear-oblong, white-margined and ¾-4 in (2-10 cm) long. **Inflorescence** open, with many-flowered branches from upper leaves. **Flowers** are ½-1 in (14-24 mm) across and have 4 white petals with green markings and a depressed, hair-fringed gland. **Fruit** an ovoid capsule about ½ in (12-19 mm) long.

**HABITAT AND RANGE:** Gravelly soil of desert shrub, sagebrush and pinyon-juniper communities. Intermountain deserts, California east to Colorado and New Mexico. Found in BEAR, CARE, GLCA, GRST, and ZION.

**NOTES:** The plants may live for several years as clusters of basal leaves, but they only flower once before dying. A poultice of the plant was used by Navajo to treat gunshot wounds. Utah green gentian (*F. paniculata*) has opposite rather than whorled stem leaves and is found in sandy sites.

## Tufted evening-primrose (*Oenothera caespitosa*)
### Evening-primrose Family (Onagraceae)

DESCRIPTION: Hairy, stemless, clump-forming perennial. **Leaves** are 1-12 in (3-30 cm) long, narrowly lanceolate or oblanceolate with entire to wavy or lobed margins. **Flowers** arise from axils of leaves; each has a narrow tube 1-6 in (3-14 cm) long expanding to 4 white, bilobed petals 1-2 in (2-6 cm) long that turn pink or purple with age. **Fruit** a woody, ellipsoid, bumpy capsule 1-2 in (25-50 mm) long hidden among leaf bases.

HABITAT AND RANGE: Sparsely-vegetated sandy, gravelly or clay soils in most habitats. Throughout most of temperate, western North America. Found in ARCH, BEAR, BRCA, CANY, CARE, GLCA, GRST, HOVE, NABR, RABR, and ZION.

NOTES: Tufted evening-primrose is a highly variable species that inhabits numerous habitats; three forms are usually found on different soils in our area: var *crinita* occurs on gravelly or clay soils; var. *navajoensis* is found on sandy or clay soil; var. *marginata* usually occurs in gravelly or stony soils. Hopi used the plant to treat sore eyes. Tufted evening-primroses open in the evening and their large, fragrant, long-tubed white flowers are adapted for pollination by long-tongued hawk moths.

# White-stem evening-primrose
## (*Oenothera albicaulis*)
### Evening-primrose Family  (Onagraceae)

**DESCRIPTION:** Short-hairy, taprooted annual. **Stems** unbranched, erect or ascending, 2-12 in (5-30 cm) tall. **Leaves** are basal and alternate, ⅜-4 in (1-10 cm) long, narrowly lanceolate and deeply to shallowly lobed. **Inflorescence** of solitary flowers in upper leaf axils. **Flowers** have a narrow, pink tube flaring to 4 white petals ¾-2 in (2-4 cm) long mounted on top of the slender ovary. **Fruit** a tubular, 4-angled capsule ¾-2 in (2-4 cm) long.

**HABITAT AND RANGE:** Sandy soil of dunes or stream terraces in the blackbrush, sagebrush and pinyon-juniper zones. Montana and North Dakota south to Mexico. Occurs in BEAR, BRCA, CANY, CARE, GLCA, GRST, HOVE, NABR, and ZION.

**NOTES:** Stem leaves are more deeply lobed and much narrower  than those at the base. A decoction of the root was used by Navajo to ease sore muscles. Rootstock evening-primrose (*O. coronopifolia*) has a similar inflorescence but is a perennial and lacks basal leaves.

Pale evening-primrose (*O. pallida*, below) has similar flowers and habitat but it is a rhizomatous perennial without basal leaves. It occurs in ARCH, BRCA, CANY, CARE, GLCA, GRST, HOVE, NABR, RABR, and ZION.

41

# San Rafael prickly poppy *(Argemone corymbosa)*
## Poppy Family (Papaveraceae)

**DESCRIPTION:** Prickly perennial with yellow sap. **Stems** erect, 8-24 in (20-60 cm) tall. **Leaves** are basal and alternate, thistle-like, oblanceolate and 1-6 in (3-16 cm) long with widely-spaced lobes and scattered prickles on the upper surface. **Inflorescence** of few stalked flowers in axils of upper leaf-like bracts. **Flowers** have 6 broad, white petals 1½ in (3-4 cm) long with numerous stamens. **Fruits** are ovoid, about 1 in (25-35 mm) long and prickly.

**HABITAT AND RANGE:** Usually sandy soil of desert shrub and blackbrush habitats, often along roads. Colorado Plateau of Utah and Arizona west to the Mojave Desert of California. Found in BEAR, CANY, GLCA, and GRST.

**NOTES:** Our plants are var. a*renicola* which is endemic to the Colorado Plateau. Armed prickly poppy (*A. munita*) has numerous small prickles on the upper leaf surface. Small prickly poppy (*A. parva*, lower right) has smaller flowers and leaves with short stalks. Prickly poppies are rarely attacked by insect pests due to chemical compounds and sap that make their foliage unpalatable.

# Alcove columbine (*Aquilegia micrantha*)
## Buttercup Family (Ranunculaceae)

**DESCRIPTION:** Sticky-hairy perennial with a stout root crown. **Stems** erect or ascending, often branched and 8-28 in (20-70 cm cm) high. **Leaves** are basal and alternate and three times pinnately divided into 3 or 9 stalked, ovate, lobed leaflets ⅜-1½ in (1-4 cm) long. **Inflorescence** of long, spreading branches with solitary, often nodding flowers at the tips. **Flowers** are white and yellow sometimes with a pink or blue tinge, consisting of 5 petals, each with a long tube pointing backward ½-1½ in (15-35 mm) long and 5 spreading, narrow, petal-like sepals ⅓-1 in (1-2 cm) long. **Fruit** a capsule ½-1 in (15-20 mm) long with 5 lobes, each spreading at the tip.

**HABITAT AND RANGE:** Hanging gardens and streambanks. Colorado Plateau of Arizona, Utah and Colorado north to the Wyoming border. Found in ARCH, BEAR, CANY, CARE, GLCA, GRST, NABR, and RABR.

**NOTES:** Our plants are var. *micrantha*. Flowers are pollinated by bumblebees. At least 13 species of columbine are recognized in southeast Utah, most being limited to inaccessible canyons of the Colorado River or in the Zion area. Hybrids between species are common where ranges overlap. Blue columbine (*A. coerulea*) has longer, white or blue and white flowers and is mostly in montane habitats. A red-flowered phase of alcove columbine is endemic to shady canyons in GRST.

# Red alumroot (*Heuchera rubescens*)
## Saxifragaceae (Saxifrage Family)

**DESCRIPTION:** Perennial with leafless stems 2-16 in (5-40 cm) high. **Leaves** basal, long-stalked; the blades are ⅜-1½ in (1-4 cm) long, glabrous to long-hairy and broadly ovate with a basal sinus and broadly-toothed margins. **Inflorescence** narrow with short, few-flowered side branches. **Flowers** have a pink, sticky, tubular calyx ¼ in (3-5 mm) long and 5 inconspicuous white petals as long as the stamens. **Fruit** an ovoid capsule 3-6 mm long, partly enclosed in the calyx.

**HABITAT AND RANGE:** Sandstone cliffs and rock outcrops in the sagebrush and pinyon-juniper zones. Oregon and Idaho south to California, Texas and Mexico. Found in CARE, GLCA, GRST, and ZION.

**NOTES:** Shoshoni used an infusion of the roots to treat diarrhea. Littleleaf alumroot (*H. parvifolia*) has a green calyx, petals longer than the stamens and grows in soil.

# Poison ivy (*Toxicodendron rydbergii*)
## Cashew Family (Anacardiaceae)

**DESCRIPTION:** Shrub to 3 ft (100 cm) high. **Stems** short-hairy, little-branched. **Leaves** alternate, palmately divided into 3 wavy-margined, glabrous leaflets, 1-5 in (2-12 cm) long. **Inflorescence** is a narrow, loose cluster of small flowers from leaf axils. **Flowers** have 5 yellowish-white petals ⅛ in (2-3 mm) long. **Fruits** are white to yellowish berries, ¼ in (4-7 mm) long in elongate clusters.

**HABITAT AND RANGE:** Sandy or gravelly soil along streams, on canyon walls and in hanging gardens at low elevations up through the pinyon-juniper zone. Throughout most of North America except the southeast states and California. Found in ARCH, CANY, CARE, GLCA, GRST, HOVE, NABR, RABR, and ZION.

**NOTES:** Even slight exposure to the oil of the leaves and stems can cause dermatitis in those who are allergic. Leaves turn red to purple in the fall. Box elder (*Acer negundo*, P. 17) is a tall shrub or tree with similar leaves that are opposite on the twigs.

## Greasebush (*Glossopetalon spinescens*)
### Crossosomataceae (Greasewood Family)

**DESCRIPTION:** Densely-branched, thorny shrub 4 in to 6 ft (10-200 cm) tall. **Twigs** green and ribbed. **Leaves** are alternate, oblanceolate, up to ½ in (3-12 mm) long and glabrous to sparsely hairy. **Flowers** arise from upper leaf nodes and have 5 spreading, narrow, twisted, white petals ¼ in (3-7 mm) long. **Fruit** is an asymmetrically globose capsule ⅛ in (2-3mm) long.

**HABITAT AND RANGE:** Rock outcrops and stony soil in canyons of desert shrub, sagebrush and pinyon-juniper habitats. Washington to southwest Montana and south to California, Texas and Mexico. Occurs in BEAR, CANY, CARE, GLCA, GRST, HOVE, NABR, and ZION.

**NOTES:** Two varieties or even two species are sometimes recognized, but the differences separating them seem trivial. The stems are highly flammable.

45

## **Fendlerbush** (*Fendlera rupicola*)
### Hydrangea Family (Hydrangeaceae )

**DESCRIPTION:** Densely-branched shrub 3-6 ft (1-2 m) tall. **Twigs** reddish or yellow, becoming gray with longitudinally-striped bark. **Leaves** are opposite or clustered on short branch tips, narrowly elliptic, ½-1 in (1-3 cm) long and sparsely hairy. **Flowers** occur on branch tips and have 4 spreading, white petals ⅜-¾ in (1-2 cm) long that taper to a very slender base. **Fruit** is a 4-lobed, ovoid capsule about ½ in (7-15 mm) long.

**HABITAT AND RANGE:** Rocky slopes and stony soil in desert shrub, blackbrush, sagebrush and pinyon-juniper habitats. Nevada to Colorado and south to Mexico and Texas. Occurs in ARCH, BEAR, CANY, and GLCA.

**NOTES:** The closely-related yerba desierto (*Fendlerella utahensis*) is also a shrub with opposite leaves, but the flowers are smaller and occur in flat-topped clusters. Both genus names honor August Fendler, one of the pioneer botanists of the southwestern U.S. Havasupai used vigorous stems of fendlerbush to make arrows.

46

## Littleleaf mock orange (*Philadelphus microphyllus*)
### Hydrangea Family (Hydrangeaceae)

**DESCRIPTION:** Highly branched shrub 3-6 ft (1-2 m) tall. **Twigs** brownish, becoming gray. **Leaves** are opposite, narrowly elliptic, up to 1 in (4-25 mm) long and short-hairy. **Flowers** are fragrant, occur on tips of short branches and have 4 spreading, white petals ¼-½ in (5-15 mm) long that are broad at the base. **Fruit** is an ovoid capsule ⅜ in (4-10 mm) long embedded in the calyx.

**HABITAT AND RANGE:** Stony soil or rock outcrops in canyons and on lowers slopes of pinyon-juniper communities. Southern Idaho and Wyoming south to California, Texas and Mexico. Found in ARCH, BEAR, CANY, CARE, and ZION.

**NOTES:** Littleleaf mock orange is variable in leaf shape and degree of hair on the leaves, and many forms were formerly recognized. Fendlerbush (p. 46) has petals that taper to the base.

## Desert mountain lilac (*Ceanothus greggii*)
### Buckthorn Family (Rhamnaceae)

**DESCRIPTION:** Highly-branched shrub to 6 ft (2 m) high. **Twigs** short-wooly. **Leaves** opposite and short-stalked; the blades elliptic, short-hairy and ¼-¾ in (5-16 mm) long. **Inflorescence** branched-ellipsoid with numerous stalked flowers. **Flowers** are cup-shaped with 5 fan-shaped white or blue petals 2-3 mm long and 5 exserted stamens. **Fruit** a 3-lobed capsule ¼ in (4-5) mm across.

**HABITAT AND RANGE:** Gravelly soil of blackbrush and pinyon-juniper habitats. California and Nevada east to Texas and south to Mexico. Found in BEAR, CANY and GLCA (var. *franklinii*) and ZION (var. *vestitus*).

**NOTES:** Two forms occur in our area; var. *franklinii* has blue flowers and is endemic to the Colorado Plateau, while var. *vestitus* (pictured here) has white flowers and occurs along the Colorado River. Utah mountain lilac (*C. martinii*) has alternate leaves and is found in BRCA, GRST, and ZION. Many *Ceanothus* species have symbiotic endophytic fungi that fix nitrogen.

# Utah serviceberry *(Amelanchier utahensis)*
## Rose Family (Rosaceae)

**DESCRIPTION:** Branched, deciduous shrub up to 6 ft (2 m) tall with grayish twigs. **Leaves** are alternate; the blades short-hairy, ovate with blunt, toothed tips and ½-1 in (1-3 cm) long. **Inflorescence** of several stalked flowers at the tips of short branches. **Flowers** have 10 to 20 stamens, 5 white petals ⅜ in (5-10 mm) long and 2-4 styles. **Fruit** is ¼-⅜ in (5-10 mm) long with persistent sepals on top, apple-like, and changes from green to red or deep purple when fully ripe.

**HABITAT AND RANGE:** Streambanks and lower canyon slopes in the sagebrush and pinyon-juniper zones. Washington to Montana and south to Mexico, Arizona and Texas. Known from ARCH, BEAR, BRCA, CANY, CARE, GLCA, GRST, HOVE, NABR, RABR, and ZION.

**NOTES:** Alder-leaf serviceberry (*A. alnifolia*) has larger leaves, larger flowers with 5 styles and usually is found at higher elevations. Havasupai dried the fruit for winter use and employed the twigs in making baskets.

## **Apache plume** (*Fallugia paradoxa*)
### Rose Family (Rosaceae)

**DESCRIPTION:** Diffusely-branched, deciduous shrub 3-5 ft (1-1½ m) tall with white twigs. **Leaves** are clustered, ¼-¾ in (4-16 mm) long, spatula-shaped with several finger-like lobes and are yellowish brown-wooly beneath. **Flowers** occur on tips of long, naked stems; each has 5 white, overlapping petals; male flowers have more than 50 stamens. **Fruit** is a cluster of hairy seeds, each with a persistent plume-like style ½-1 in (2-4 cm) long.

**HABITAT AND RANGE:** Streambanks and lower canyon slopes in the blackbrush, sagebrush and pinyon-juniper zones. California to Colorado, Texas and Mexico. Found in BEAR, BRCA, CANY, CARE, GLCA, GRST, and ZION.

**NOTES:** The "paradox" in *Fallugia paradoxa* is that the plants are dioecious with separate male and female individuals; thus only about half produce the feathery fruit. Hopi employed the stems for arrows, while the Navajo used Apache plume to induce insanity. Cliffrose (*Purshia stansburiana*, P. 52) has gland-dotted leaves and glabrous seeds.

50

# Wild crab apple (*Peraphyllum ramosissimum*)
## Rose Family (Rosaceae)

**DESCRIPTION:** Deciduous shrub 2-6 ft (0.5-2 m) tall with reddish to gray twigs. **Leaves** are clustered, short-stalked and ½-2 in (1-5 cm) long; the blades oblanceolate and short-hairy. **Flowers** arise from leaf clusters and have 5 white petals ⅜ in (6-9 mm) long and 15-20 stamens. **Fruit** globose, apple-like, yellow to red and about ⅝ in (8-15 mm) long with persistent sepals.

**HABITAT AND RANGE:** Streambanks, canyons and lower slopes in pinyon-juniper habitats. Columbia Plateau of Oregon and Idaho south to California and New Mexico. Occurs in BEAR, BRCA, GRST, NABR, and ZION.

**NOTES:** Fruits are acrid-tasting. Desert peach (*Prunus fasciculata*) has flowers with tiny petals and 1-seeded fruit; it is a species of the Great Basin and Mojave deserts west of the Colorado Plateau, but has been reported for ZION.

# Chokecherry (*Prunus virginiana*)
## Rose Family (Rosaceae)

**DESCRIPTION:** Deciduous shrub or small tree up to 12 ft (4 m) tall with white-dotted, purplish twigs. **Leaves** are stalked and alternate; the glabrous blades are 1-4 in (2-10 cm) long, elliptic and pointed with fine-toothed margins. **Inflorescence** cylindrical, 2-6 in (5-15 cm) long with numerous flowers. **Flowers** have 5 white petals ¼ in (4-6 mm) long and 20-30 stamens. **Fruit** is a 1-seeded, ovoid berry ¼-⅜ in (6-8 mm) long that matures from green to red to black when ripe.

**HABITAT AND RANGE:** Along streams and canyons and on lower slopes in the sagebrush and pinyon-juniper communities. Throughout most of temperate North America. Known from BEAR, BRCA, CANY, GLCA, GRST, HOVE, NABR, and ZION.

**NOTES:** Our plants are var. *melanocarpa* which occurs throughout the West. Navajo used an infusion of the fruit to treat stomachache and mixed them with meat to make pemmican. Fresh fruits are bitter to us, but loved by birds.

51

## Cliffrose  (*Purshia stansburiana*)
### Rose Family  (Rosaceae)

**DESCRIPTION:** Highly-branched, deciduous, aromatic shrub to 8 ft (2-3 m) tall with brown or gray twigs and gland-dotted foliage. **Leaves** are alternate, ¼-⅝ in (3-15 mm) long with 3 to 7 finger-like lobes and rolled margins; they are white-wooly beneath. **Flowers** arising from leaf bases have 5 white, shallowly-lobed petals and numerous stamens. **Fruit** is a cluster of glabrous seeds, each with a persistent plume-like style ¾-2¼ in (2-6 cm) long.

**HABITAT AND RANGE:** Stony soil of canyons and lower slopes in blackbrush and pinyon-juniper habitats. Deserts of California to Colorado and south to New Mexico and Mexico. Found in ARCH, BEAR, BRCA, CANY, CARE, GLCA, GRST, HOVE, NABR, RABR, and ZION.

**NOTES:** Seeds of Apache plume (*Fallugia paradoxa*, P. 50) also have a long plume but are hairy; the foliage is not gland-dotted but is yellowish-brown wooly beneath. Bitterbrush (*P. tridentata*) has hairy, obovate leaves with 3 shallow lobes at the tip and seeds that are not plumose. A decoction of cliffrose leaves was used by the Hopi to cleanse wounds.

# Furry desert-dogbane (*Amsonia tomentosa*)
## Dogbane Family (Apocynaceae)

**DESCRIPTION:** Perennial. **Stems** are 8-24 in (20-60 cm) high with alternate leaves. **Leaves** are narrowly lanceolate, tangled-hairy (rarely hairless) and 1-2 in (3-5 cm) long. **Flowers** clustered at stem tips are about ⅜-½ in (8-11 mm) long, vase-shaped with 5 reflexed lobes; purple in bud but white when open. **Fruits** occur in pairs, are bean-like and 2-3½ in (5-9 cm) long with several constrictions.

**HABITAT AND RANGE:** Sandy soil of terraces along streams and dry washes, occasionally along roads in desert shrub and blackbrush communities. Great Basin and Colorado Plateau south to California, New Mexico and west Texas. Found in ARCH, BEAR, CANY, CARE, GLCA, and NABR.

**NOTES:** Glabrous forms of the plant can be found in the same populations as typical hairy plants. Zuni used a poultice made from the root of this plant to treat snake bites. Jones' desert-dogbane (*Amsonia jonesii*) has wider leaves and shorter flowers.

# Indian hemp
## (*Apocynum cannabinum*)
## Dogbane Family (Apocynaceae)

**DESCRIPTION:** Rhizomatous perennial. **Stems** erect and 1-3 ft (30-100 cm) tall with milky sap. **Leaves** are opposite, lanceolate, glabrous or hairy, ascending and 2-4 in (5-10 cm) long. **Inflorescence** branched, stalked from leaf axils. **Flowers** are white, up to ¼ in (2-5 mm) long, bell-shaped with 5 spreading lobes. **Fruits** are tubular, 5-8 in (12-20 cm) long, drooping in pairs. **Seeds** have a tuft of white hair at the tip.

**HABITAT AND RANGE:** Moist soil of stream terraces, ditch banks and roadsides throughout North America. Found in ARCH, BEAR, BRCA, CANY, CARE, GLCA, GRST, NABR, RABR, and ZION.

**NOTES:** Native Americans used the fibers to make cord and to treat stomachache. Spreading dogbane (*A. androsaemifolium*) is similar but the leaves droop, and the flowers have pink lines. Milkweeds (*Asclepias* spp.) also have opposite leaves and milky sap but very different flowers.

# Jones' milkweed *(Asclepias labriformis)*
## Milkweed Family (Asclepiadaceae)

**DESCRIPTION:** Perennial. **Stems** are usually clustered and up to 20 in (50 cm) tall with milky sap. **Leaves** are glabrous to sparsely hairy, 2-6 in (5-15 cm) long with short petioles; the lowest opposite each other. **Flowers** are about ¼ in (7 mm) across and have 5 reflexed, greenish-white petals and 5 erect white hoods, each bearing a claw-like horn arching over the central column. **Fruits** are pear-shaped and ribbed, 2-3 in (5-7 cm) long and pendulous. **Seeds** have tufts of long hair at the tip.

**HABITAT AND RANGE:** Moist, sandy soil along streams and washes up to the pinyon-juniper zone. Endemic to the Colorado Plateau of Utah. Found in CANY, CARE, GLCA, and GRST.

**NOTES:** This is one of the most poisonous milkweeds. Spider milkweed (*A. asperula*, P. 210) has narrow, alternate leaves, and flowers are green and purple, not white. Whorled milkweed (*A. subverticillata*) also has narrow leaves but erect pods and smaller flowers and blooms in late summer and fall.

# Yellow-hair miner's candle
## (*Cryptantha fulvocanescens*)
### Borage Family (Boraginaceae)

DESCRIPTION: Perennial. **Stems** usually several, unbranched, 3-12 in (8-30 cm) tall. **Leaves** basal and alternate, oblanceolate, 1-3 in (2-7 cm) long and stiff-hairy. **Inflorescence** an open spike of small clusters that uncurl as the flowers bloom. **Flowers** are white, tubular, up to ½ in (8-12 mm) long with 5 spreading lobes and yellow centers. **Seeds** 1-4, are enclosed in the pear-shaped calyx that has minute pimple-like bumps and is about ¼ in (3-7 mm) long.

HABITAT AND RANGE: Sandy, clayey, or gravelly soil of desert shrub, blackbrush, sagebrush and pinyon-juniper habitats. Utah, Colorado, Arizona and New Mexico. Found in ARCH, BEAR, BRCA, CANY, CARE, GLCA, GRST, and NABR.

NOTES: Yellow-eye miner's candle (*C. flavoculata*) has small ridges rather than pimple-like bumps on the seeds; James' miner's candle (*C. cinerea*) has smooth ovoid seeds. Navajo used an infusion of yellow-hair miner's candle to treat snake bites.

# Slender cryptanth
## (*Cryptantha gracilis*)
### Borage Family (Boraginaceae)

DESCRIPTION: Annual. **Stems** branched, 4-8 in (10-20 cm) tall with spreading hairs. **Leaves** are mainly alternate on the stem, spreading-hairy and up to 1 in (15-30 mm) long. **Inflorescence** branched with flower clusters that expand to become curvilinear. **Flowers** are white, tubular with 5 spreading lobes and 1-2 mm across. **Seeds** usually solitary, smooth and hard-coated are enclosed in the bristly calyx.

Habitat and Range: Sandy or silty soil of desert shrub, sagebrush or pinyon-juniper habitats. Great Basin and Colorado Plateau, southern Oregon, Idaho and Wyoming south to California, Arizona and New Mexico. Occurs in BEAR, CANY, CARE, GLCA, GRST, NABR, RABR, and ZION.

NOTES: There are numerous species of annual cryptanths that have similar leaves and flowers but differ in the size, shape, and ornamentation of their seeds and the orientation of hairs on the stems and leaves. Plains cryptanth (*C. crassisepala*) has minutely bumpy seeds; prickly cryptanth (*C. kelseyana*) has 1 large and 3 small seeds in each calyx.

## Osterhout's miner's candle (*Cryptantha osterhoutii*)
### Borage Family (Boraginaceae)

**DESCRIPTION:** Perennial. **Stems** usually several, unbranched, 4-24 in (10-60 cm) tall. **Leaves** are basal and alternate on the stem, 3-5 in (7-12 cm) long, stiff-hairy and bristly. **Inflorescence** of small flower clusters on the upper stem that unfold and become linear as the flowers bloom. **Flowers** are ¼-⅜ in (6-9 mm) across, white and tubular with 5 spreading lobes and yellow centers. **Seeds** 1-4, are hard-coated and bumpy.

**HABITAT AND RANGE:** Sandy soil in desert shrub, blackbrush, sagebrush or pinyon-juniper habitats. Endemic to the Colorado Plateau of Utah, Arizona and Colorado. Found in ARCH, BEAR, CANY, CARE, GLCA, and HOVE.

**NOTES:** This species is named for George Osterhout, a Colorado lumberman and amateur botanist who collected many new plant species in the Rocky Mountains. James' miner's candle (*C. cinerea*) has smooth rather than bumpy seeds. Carbon miner's candle (*C. mensana*) also has bumpy seeds but is usually taller.

# Ives' phacelia (*Phacelia ivesiana*)
## Waterleaf Family
## (Hydrophyllaceae)

DESCRIPTION: Spreading-hairy annual. **Stems** branched, erect, 2-10 in (4-25 cm) high. **Leaves** are alternate, narrowly oblong, ½-2 in (1-5 cm) long with lobed margins. **Inflorescence** several-flowered, uncoiling from branch tips. **Flowers** are white, bell-shaped and ⅛ in (2-4 mm) long; the corolla barely longer than the calyx.

HABITAT AND RANGE: Usually sandy soil of desert shrub, sagebrush and pinyon-juniper habitats. Intermountain deserts from southern Idaho and Montana south to California through New Mexico. Occurs in ARCH, BEAR, CANY, CARE, GLCA, GRST, HOVE, NABR, RABR, and ZION.

NOTES: Twin phacelia (*P. affinis*) also has small flowers, but its stems have hairs with black glands at the tip. The seeds of Ives' phacelia look like miniature sea shells with 8-10 coils.

# Fragrant sand-verbena
## (*Abronia fragrans*)
## Four-o'clock Family
## (Nyctaginaceae)

DESCRIPTION: Sticky-hairy perennial. **Stems** usually several, 7-32 in (18-80 cm) tall. **Leaves** stalked, basal and opposite; the blades are lanceolate ½-3½ in (1-9 cm) long. **Inflorescence** umbrella-like at stem tips with 25 to 80 flowers. **Flowers** are white to pinkish, trumpet-shaped; the tube ½-1 in (10-25 mm) long with 5 two-lobed, wrinkled, spreading lobes. **Fruits** obovoid, up to ½ in (5-12 mm) long with 0 to 5 longitudinal wings.

HABITAT AND RANGE: Throughout our area on dunes and in other poorly-vegetated habitats with very sandy soil or sometimes gravel or clay. Plains and deserts from Montana and North Dakota south to Mexico. Occurs in ARCH, BEAR, BRCA, CANY, CARE, GLCA, GRST, HOVE, NABR, RABR, and ZION.

NOTES: Plants in our area are mostly var. *elliptica*, sometimes considered to be a separate species. Leaves were used by the Navajo to treat boils and insect bites. Dwarf sand-verbena (P. 174) has naked stems.

## **Wooly plantain** (*Plantago patagonica*)
### Plantain Family (Plantaginaceae)

**Description:** Long-hairy, taprooted annual 2-8 in (5-20 cm) tall. **Leaves** are all basal with grass-like, hairy, linear-oblanceolate blades ½-6 in (1-15 cm) long. **Inflorescence** narrow and dense with numerous sessile flowers, each subtended by a bract. **Flowers** are transparent-white and have a short tube and 4 spreading petals less than ⅛ in (2 mm) long. **Fruits** are ovoid, 2-seeded capsules ⅛ in (2-3 mm) long.

**Habitat and Range:** All soil types except heavy clay in blackbrush, sagebrush and pin-yon-juniper habitats throughout temperate North America. Known from ARCH, BEAR, CANY, CARE, GLCA, GRST, HOVE, NABR, RABR, and ZION.

**Notes:** Flower bracts are usually inconspicuous, but plants in some populations may have bracts longer than the flowers. Several perennial plantain species also occur in our area. Both the native wooly-foot plantain (*P. eriopoda*) and the introduced English plantain (*P. lanceolata*) have dense hair at the base of the plant; common plantain (*P. major*) has glabrous leaves and is also introduced. Our plantains bear little resemblance to the plantains of commerce, which are related to bananas.

# Small woolstar
## (*Eriastrum diffusum*)
## Phlox Family
## (Polemoniaceae)

**DESCRIPTION:** Low, diffusely-branched, sparsely-wooly annual. **Stems** prostrate or ascending, 1-6 in (3-15 cm) long. **Leaves** are basal and alternate and linear or with 1 to 2 pairs of lateral lobes. **Inflorescence** a head-like cluster of flowers and subtending wooly, leaf-like bracts. **Flowers** are white or light blue and ⅜ in (7-9 mm) long with a short tube, 5 spreading petals and a calyx with spine-tipped lobes. **Fruit** an ovoid capsule to ¼ in (3-4 mm).

**HABITAT AND RANGE:** Silty or sandy soil, often in riparian habitats in blackbrush, sagebrush and pinyon-juniper habitats. Warm and cold deserts in Nevada and California east to Texas and Colorado. Found in ARCH, GLCA, GRST, HOVE, and ZION.

**NOTES:** Plants of small woolstar are usually wider than high; Great Basin woolstar (*E. sparsiflorum*) has erect stems that are higher than wide.

# Spreading gilia (*Gilia polycladon*)
## Phlox Family (Polemoniaceae)

**Description:** Diffusely-branched at the base, long-hairy and sticky annual. **Stems** mostly naked, ascending, 1-10 in (3-24 cm) long. **Leaves** are basal and alternate, about ½ in (1-3 cm) long and linear to wedge-shaped with 2 to 4 pairs of lateral lobes. **Inflorescence** a head-like cluster of flowers subtended by leaf-like bracts. **Flowers** are white, ⅛-¼ in (3-6 mm) long with a short tube, 5 spreading petals and spine-tipped calyx lobes. **Fruit** an obovoid capsule ⅛-¼ in (3-5 mm) long with several seeds.

**Habitat and Range:** Sandy, silty or gravelly, sparsely-vegetated soil of desert shrub, blackbrush, sagebrush and pinyon-juniper communities.

Deserts from Oregon and California east to Wyoming through Texas. Found in ARCH, BEAR, CANY, CARE, GLCA, GRST, HOVE, RABR, and ZION.

**Notes:** Dwarf gilia (*G. pumila*) has longer, bluish flowers; Gunnison's gilia (P. 65) has unlobed leaves. The seeds of spreading gilia become sticky-slimy when moistened, allowing them to adhere to animals and be transported across the desert.

# Great Basin gilia (*Gilia leptomeria*)
## Phlox Family (Polemoniaceae)

**Description:** Branched, sticky-hairy, malodorous annual. **Stems** erect, mostly naked above, 1-10 in (4-25 cm) high. **Leaves** are basal and alternate, oblanceolate and ½-2 in (1-6 cm) long with several pairs of shallow, rounded lobes. **Inflorescence** broad and diffuse with stalked flowers. **Flowers** are white and up to ¼ in (2-7 mm) long with a tube and 5 spreading petals with pointed or lobed tips. **Fruit** an ovoid capsule.

**Habitat and Range:** All soil types except heavy clay throughout our area. Deserts from southern Washington and Montana to Arizona and northern New Mexico. Found in ARCH, BEAR, CANY, CARE, GLCA, GRST, HOVE, NABR, RABR, and ZION.

**Notes:** Two varieties of Great Basin gilia occur in our area: var. *micromeria* has smaller flowers than var. *leptomeria* (pictured here). Several annual gilia species occur in our area: spiny gilia (*G. latifolia*) has spiny-lobed, oak-like leaves; shy gilia (*G. inconspicua*) has glabrous stems and wooly hairs at the base of the lower leaves; broadlobe gilia (*G. hutchinsifolia*) has leaves that are twice lobed.

## **Ballhead gilia** (*Gilia congesta*)
### Phlox Family (Polemoniaceae)

**DESCRIPTION:** Malodorous, long-hairy perennial with a branched root crown. **Stems** usually several, erect, unbranched, 2-20 in (5-50 cm) tall. **Leaves** are basal and alternate, ½-2 in (1-4 cm) long and linear or with 1 to 3 pairs of linear lobes. **Inflorescence** a tight ball of flowers at stem tips. **Flowers** are white; the tube ¼ in (3-5 mm) long with 5 spreading lobes and spine-tipped sepals. **Fruit** a capsule about ⅛ in (2-4 mm) long.

**HABITAT AND RANGE:** Sandy, silty or gravelly soil of desert shrub, sagebrush and pinyon-juniper habitats, sometimes in hanging gardens. Washington to North Dakota south to California, Arizona and New Mexico. Known from BRCA, CARE, GLCA, GRST, NABR, and ZION.

**NOTES:** There are two forms in our area; var. *congesta* (pictured here) has lobed leaves and is rarely over 8 in (20 cm) tall; var. *frutescens* is taller and usually has unlobed leaves. Paiute people used a decoction of the plant to treat diarrhea. The foul-smelling flowers may be pollinated by flies.

## Prickly phlox (*Leptodactylon pungens*)
### Polemoniaceae (Phlox Family)

**DESCRIPTION:** Bristly and finely-hairy subshrub. **Stems** erect or ascending, branched, 4-32 in (10-80 cm) high. **Leaves** are alternate on upper stem, opposite or appearing whorled on middle and lower stem and about ⅜ in (5-12 mm) long; each is divided from the base into 3 to 9 linear, bristle-tipped lobes; many leaves have smaller leaves in their axils. **Inflorescence** of solitary flowers in the axils of upper leaves. **Flowers** are white with a tube ½-1 in (15-25 mm) long and 5 spreading lobes ⅜ in (6-11 mm) long. **Fruit** a cylindric capsule ¼ in (4-6 mm) long.

**HABITAT AND RANGE:** Sandy, silty or gravelly soil of sagebrush or pinyon-juniper communities. Deserts and steppe from British Columbia south to California through New Mexico. Found in ARCH, BEAR, BRCA, CANY, CARE, GLCA, GRST, HOVE, NABR, and ZION.

**NOTES:** Navajo used prickly phlox to treat snake bites. Matted prickly phlox (*L. caespitosum*) has 4 petals and a compact, phlox-like growth form. Watson's prickly phlox (*L. watsonii*) has 6 petals and deeply-divided opposite leaves and usually grows in cliff faces. Prickly phlox flowers open in late evening and close the following morning.

# Desert phlox (*Phlox austromontana*)
## Phlox Family (Polemoniaceae)

**DESCRIPTION:** Nearly glabrous, loosely mat-forming perennial. **Stems** are prostrate to ascending, branched and up to 4 in (10 cm) long. **Leaves** are needle-like, opposite, closely-spaced and ½-1 in (10-25 mm) long. **Flowers** are solitary at stem tips and white, pink or bluish with a tube ½ in (8-15 mm) long and 5 spreading lobes ¼ in (5-8 mm) long. **Fruit** an ellipsoid capsule with a style up to ¼ in (2-5 mm) long.

**HABITAT AND RANGE:** Gravelly or stony soil primarily of sagebrush and pinyon-juniper habitats but sometimes in drier habitats. Washington south to California, Arizona and New Mexico. Occurs in ARCH, BEAR, BRCA, CARE, GLCA, GRST, and ZION.

**NOTES:** Most of our plants are var. *autromontana*; however, var. *lutescens* with cream-colored flowers, occurs near the Colorado River in GLCA. Carpet phlox (*P. hoodii*, lower right) forms denser cushions and has tangled hairs in the leaf axils and smaller flowers. Cedar Canyon phlox (*P. gladiformis*) is sticky-hairy and ill-smelling and is found in BRCA. Havasupai peoples made a decoction of desert phlox roots and used it as a poultice to treat body aches.

## Flaxflower (*Linanthastrum nuttallii*)
### Phlox Family (Polemoniaceae)

**DESCRIPTION:** Nearly glabrous perennial with a woody base. **Stems** numerous, erect or ascending, unbranched, 3-12 in (8-30 cm) high. **Leaves** are opposite, about ½-¾ in (1-2 cm) long; each is divided from the base into 5 to 9 linear lobes creating the impression that the leaves are whorled; many leaves have smaller leaves in their axils. **Inflorescence** of loose flower clusters at stem tips. **Flowers** are white with a short, hairy tube and 5 spreading lobes about ¼ in (5-8 mm) long. **Fruit** an ellipsoid capsule ¼ in (4-6) mm long.

**HABITAT AND RANGE:** Usually sandy soil in sagebrush and pinyon-juniper habitats. Washington to western Montana south to northern Mexico. Found in BEAR, BRCA, CARE, GRST, and ZION.

**NOTES:** Flaxflower is more common at higher elevations. This plant has been placed in four different genera: *Linanthastrum, Linanthus, Leptodactylon* and *Leptosiphon*. Prickly phlox (*Leptodactylon pungens*, P. 62) has shorter and more prickly leaves and is woody at the base.

## Gunnison's gilia
### (*Gilia gunnisonii*)
### Phlox Family
### (Polemoniaceae)

**DESCRIPTION:** Variously hairy annual. **Stems** are erect, usually branched and 2-8 in (6-20 cm) tall. **Leaves** are alternate, widely-spaced, linear and not lobed, ¼-1½ in (5-40 mm) long with spine tips. **Inflorescence** of flower clusters at stem tips. **Flowers** are white to light blue with a tube ⅜ in (6-10 mm) long with 5 spreading lobes about ⅛ in (2-4 mm) long. **Fruit** a capsule about ⅛ in (2-4 mm) long.

**HABITAT AND RANGE:** Sandy soil of desert shrub, sagebrush and pinyon-juniper habitats, often on dunes or around sandstone outcrops. Endemic to the Colorado Plateau. Found in ARCH, BEAR, CANY, CARE, GLCA, GRST, NABR, and RABR.

**NOTES:** Dwarf gilia (*G. pumila*) has a similar growth form but the leaves have linear lobes and purple flowers. Spreading gilia (*G. polycladon*, P. 59) has wedge-shaped and toothed leaves.

## Bastard toadflax
### (*Comandra umbellata*)
### Sandalwood Family  (Santalaceae)

**DESCRIPTION:** Glabrous, rhizomatous perennial. **Stems** erect, branched, 3-12 in (8-30 cm) tall. **Leaves** are alternate, ½-1 in (1-3 cm) long, lanceolate to ovate and pale green with a waxy coat. **Inflorescence** composed of clusters of few flowers at branch tips. **Flowers** lack petals but have 5 white, petal-like sepals ¼ in (2-5 mm) long that are attached on top of a conical ovary. **Fruit** is a purplish berry ⅛ in (6-9 mm) thick with the old flower on top.

**HABITAT AND RANGE:** Often grassy areas in blackbrush, sagebrush and pinyon-juniper habitats. Throughout North America. Found in ARCH, BEAR, BRCA, CANY, CARE, GLCA, GRST, HOVE, NABR, RABR, and ZION.

**NOTES:** Bastard toadflax parasitizes neighboring plants through the root systems. It is our only member of this primarily tropical family. Navajo used the plant to treat sore eyes.

# Bush penstemon
## (*Penstemon ambiguus*)
### Figwort Family (Scrophulariaceae)

**Description:** Glabrous perennial with a woody base. **Stems** numerous, erect, often branched, 10-24 in (25-80 cm) high. **Leaves** are opposite, widely-spaced, thread-like and ½-2 in (1-4 cm) long. **Inflorescence** of widely-spaced pairs of stalked flowers along upper stems. **Flowers** are white to pinkish with a pink tube ½-1 in (15-25 mm) long with 5 unequal, spreading lobes and 4 fertile stamens and 1 sterile stamen within.

**Habitat and Range:** Sandy soil often on dunes or near sandstone outcrops in all habitat zones. Nevada east to Nebraska and south to Texas. Found in BEAR, CARE, GLCA, GRST, and RABR.

**Notes:** Navajo treated scorpion and eagle bites with a poultice made with bush penstemon. Bush penstemon is unique among our species in having the corollas twisted so that the lips are erect and flattened, forming a flower that resembles a phlox.

# Abajo penstemon
## (*Penstemon lentus*)
### Figwort Family
### (Scrophulariaceae)

**Description:** Waxy-glabrous perennial with erect stems 6-24 in (20-50 cm) tall. **Leaves** are basal and opposite, 1-4 in (2-11 cm) long; the basal have elliptic to ovate blades that become narrower and sessile above. **Inflorescence** has several stalked flowers in whorls above the upper leaves. **Flowers** are blue or white, ½-1 in (17-23 mm) long, conical with 5 unequal, spreading lobes, 4 fertile stamens and 1 hairy, sterile stamen.

**Habitat and Range:** Stony soil of sagebrush and pinyon-juniper habitats. Endemic to the Colorado Plateau of Utah, Colorado, Arizona and New Mexico. Found in BEAR, GLCA, HOVE, and NABR.

**Notes:** Both var. *albiflorus* (pictured here) with white flowers, and var. *lentus* with blue flowers occur in our area.

# Palmer's penstemon (*Penstemon palmeri*)
## Figwort Family (Scrophulariaceae)

**DESCRIPTION:** Waxy-glabrous perennial with erect stems 20-55 in (50-140 cm) tall. **Leaves** are opposite, ovate with toothed margins, 1-5 in (2-13 cm) long; the bases of the upper leaves are fused and cup-like. **Inflorescence** is often sticky and has several stalked flowers, all facing the same direction, in the axils of upper leaves and leaf-like bracts. **Flowers** are white to pink, 1-2 in (25-40 mm) long, balloon-like with 5 unequal, spreading lobes and 4 fertile stamens and 1 densely hairy, sterile stamen within.

**HABITAT AND RANGE:** Canyons, streambanks and roadsides in the desert shrub, black-brush, sagebrush and pinyon-juniper communities. Idaho and Wyoming south to California through New Mexico. Occurs in BEAR, CANY, CARE, GLCA, GRST, NABR, and ZION.

**NOTES:** Variety *eglandulosus* (pictured here) has a glabrous inflorescence while that of var. *palmeri* is sticky-glandular. A poultice of Palmer's penstemon was used by Navajo to treat snake bites. No other penstemon in our area has such bulbous flowers or has flowers with a strong, pleasing aroma; most penstemons are scentless. The large shape of the corolla accomodates bumblebees. The bushy sterile stamen acts like a lever when pushed and holds visiting bees in place so they can get more pollen dusted on their backs to take to the next blossom.

## Indian apple (*Datura wrightii*)
### Nightshade Family (Solanaceae)

**Description:** Gray-hairy perennial. **Stems** ascending or erect, branched and up to 2½ ft (70 cm) high. **Leaves** alternate and stalked; the blades are ovate, 2-8 in (5-20 cm) long with wavy or shallowly-lobed margins. **Flowers** are white, solitary in leaf axils, funnel-shaped and 5-8 in (12-20 cm) long. **Fruit** is a spiny, hemispheric capsule 1-2 in (3-4 cm) long.

**Habitat and Range:** Sandy, stony or silty soil, especially along streambanks and roadsides in sagebrush and pinyon-juniper communities. California east to Colorado, Texas and Mexico; introduced farther north and east. Known from ARCH, BEAR, CANY, CARE, GLCA, GRST, HOVE, NABR, RABR, and ZION.

**Notes:** All parts of the plant are poisonous and were used by Native Americans as a narcotic and to induce hallucinations. Indian apple has the largest flowers of any native plant species in the Colorado Plateau. Flowers open at night. Hawkmoths visiting the blossoms may become intoxicated by the plant's various hallucinogenic alkaloids and thus spend more time visiting and pollinating the flowers. Jimsonweed (*D. stramonium*) has smaller flowers and thimble-shaped capsules.

# Birch-leaf mountain mahogany
## (*Cercocarpus montanus*)
### Rose Family (Rosaceae)

**DESCRIPTION:** Branched, deciduous shrub up to 10 ft (4 m) tall with reddish to grayish twigs. **Leaves** are short-stalked, alternate, long-hairy, ½-1½ in (1-4 cm) long and obovate with rounded, toothed tips. **Inflorescence** of few short-stalked flowers at branch tips. **Flowers** have 20 to 40 stamens exserted from a reddish tube ⅜ in (6-11 mm) long with 5 white, wrinkled sepals 1-2 mm long; petals are absent. **Fruit** is a hairy seed with a long, plume-like tip 2-4 in (5-9 cm) long partly enclosed in the flower tube.

**HABITAT AND RANGE:** Outcrops or stony soil in sagebrush and pinyon-juniper communities. Oregon to South Dakota south to Mexico. Found in ARCH, BEAR, BRCA, CANY, CARE, GLCA, GRST, NABR, and ZION.

**NOTES:** Curl-leaf mountain mahogany (*C. ledifolius,* lower right) has nearly linear leaves, and is usually found at higher elevations. Littleleaf mountain mahogany (*C. intricatus*) has narrowly elliptic leaves and grows mainly on sandstone cliff faces. All species of mountain mahogany are browsed by ungulates during the winter.

## Pale wolfberry (*Lycium pallidum*)
### Nightshade Family (Solanaceae)

**DESCRIPTION:** Highly-branched, thorny shrub to 6 ft (2 m) high. **Leaves** are oblanceolate, waxy-glabrous, ½-1 in (1-4 cm) long and clustered at nodes. **Flowers** are white or greenish, purple-veined, funnel-shaped, about ½-⅞ in (1-2 cm) long with 5 lobes at the tip; one or few borne on stalks from leaf nodes. **Fruit** a red or blue, globose berry about ½ in (1 cm) long.

**HABITAT AND RANGE:** Canyon bottoms and along washes in blackbrush, sagebrush and pinyon-juniper habitats. California east to Colorado and Texas. Found in BEAR, CANY, GLCA, GRST, HOVE, NABR, and ZION.

**NOTES:** The leaves of wolfberry are usually shed during the heat of the summer. Havasupai and Hopi ate the berries, and Navajo made a poultice of the leaves to treat toothache. Dense thickets of wolfberry are often good indicators of archaeological sites. Flowers of Anderson's wolfberry (*L. andersonii*) and Torrey's wolfberry (*L. torreyi*) are usually less than ½ in (1 cm) long; the latter has a veiny calyx, but the former does not.

# Mojave brickellbush
## (*Brickellia oblongifolia*)
## Sunflower Family
## (Asteraceae)

**DESCRIPTION:** Perennial with a woody base. **Stems** unbranched, 4-24 in (10-60 cm) tall. **Leaves** are mostly alternate, ½-2 in (1-4 cm) long with short, sticky hairs. **Heads** slender, stalked, about ½ in (1-2 cm) high; involucral bracts overlap in several rows, each bract with prominent veins. **Disk flowers** dull white, inconspicuous. **Ray flowers** absent. **Seeds** have long bristles (pappus) at the tip.

**HABITAT AND RANGE:** Dry, gravelly soil of desert shrub, blackbrush and pinyon-juniper habitats. North American deserts from British Columbia and Montana south to California, Arizona and New Mexico. Found in ARCH, BEAR, BRCA, CANY, CARE, GLCA, GRST, HOVE, and ZION.

**NOTES:** Nearly all members of this genus occur exclusively in the West.

# Dwarf dusty maiden
## (*Chamaechaenactis scaposa*)
## Sunflower Family (Asteraceae)

**DESCRIPTION:** Perennial. **Stems** leafless, unbranched, ½-3 ½ in (1-9 cm) high. **Leaves** all basal, petiolate; blades ovate, about ¼-¾ in (4-18 mm) long, short-hairy. **Heads** solitary, about ½ in (7-17 mm) high; involucral bracts sticky, hairy and not overlapping. **Disk flowers** are few and white but turning pink with age). **Ray flowers** absent. **Seeds** with oblong scales (pappus) at the tip.

**HABITAT AND RANGE:** Gravelly or clayey soil of sagebrush and pinyon-juniper habitats. Colorado Plateau north to southern Wyoming. Found in CARE.

**NOTES:** This is a genus of only one species. It was discovered by Alice Eastwood who was one of the first female botanists to explore the West and rescued invaluable herbarium specimens from certain destruction by the 1906 San Francisco fire.

# Dusty maiden (*Chaenactis stevioides*)
## Sunflower Family (Asteraceae)

**DESCRIPTION:** Annual. **Stems** branched, 2-16 in (5-40 cm) high and often finely glandular. **Leaves** are basal and alternate, up to 4 in (10 cm) long and deeply divided into widely-spaced linear lobes. **Heads** about ⅜ in (5-10 mm) high on branch tips; involucral bracts not overlapping. **Disk flowers** are white; the marginal ones largest. **Ray flowers** absent. **Seeds** topped by a few opaque scales (pappus).

**HABITAT AND RANGE:** Sandy soil of desert shrub, blackbrush, sagebrush and pinyon-juniper habitats. Widespread in North American deserts from Oregon and Wyoming south into Mexico. Occurs in ARCH, BEAR, CANY, CARE, GLCA, GRST, HOVE, NABR, RABR, and ZION.

**NOTES:** Douglas dusty maiden (*C. douglasii*) is a biennial or short-lived perennial with white-wooly stems and leaves. Showy dusty maiden (*C. macrantha*, right) has larger heads and often pink-tinged disk flowers. Navajo used the sap of dusty maiden as a glue.

## Rose-heath (*Chaetopappa ericoides*)
### Sunflower Family (Asteraceae)

**Description:** Clump-forming perennial. **Stems** numerous, often branched, 2-6 in (5-15 cm) tall. **Leaves** are narrow, spine-tipped, ¼-¾ in (6-20 mm) long and appressed close to the stem. **Heads** about ¼ in (5-7 mm) high; involucral bracts overlap and are purple-tipped and short-hairy. **Disk flowers** yellow. **Ray flowers** 8 to 15, white with rounded tips, often with a pinkish tinge as they age. **Seeds** have numerous long bristles on the tip.

**Habitat and Range:** Sandy or gravelly, sometimes disturbed soil in desert shrub, black-brush or pinyon-juniper communities. Western Great Plains and intermountain deserts from southern Wyoming to Mexico. Known from ARCH, BEAR, BRCA, CANY, CARE, GLCA, GRST, HOVE, NABR, and ZION.

**Notes:** Navajo and Hopi used this plant to treat a sore nose. Taxonomists long debated whether this species was a daisy or an aster, and finally compromised and gave rose-heath its own genus of about a dozen species. The slender, somewhat overlapping stem leaves simulate the appearance of heather (Ericaceae), accounting for the common name and specific epithet.

# New Mexico thistle
*(Cirsium neomexicanum)*
Sunflower Family
(Asteraceae)

**DESCRIPTION:** Spiny, white-hairy biennial. **Stems** spindly, up to 6 ft (2 m) tall, branched mainly in the inflorescence. **Leaves** are deeply lobed with sharp teeth and long spines, lightly hairy, 4-14 in (10-35 cm) long. **Heads** about 1 in (2-3 cm) high and wide, solitary on leafless branch tips; involucral bracts spine-tipped, wooly, the outer reflexed. **Disk flowers** white. **Ray flowers** absent. **Seeds** have feathery bristles at the tip.

**HABITAT AND RANGE:** Poorly vegetated, sandy or clayey, often gravelly soil of blackbrush, sagebrush, desert scrub, and pinyon-juniper communities. Throughout most of the desert regions of western U.S. Occurs in ARCH, BRCA, CANY, CARE, GLCA, GRST, HOVE, NABR, RABR, and ZION.

**NOTES:** New Mexico thistle often occurs in barren habitats where it can be quite conspicuous. A phase of the species in Utah is called var. *utahense*, which might be translated as the "Utah New Mexico thistle" to really confuse people. The spindly stems sway in the slightest breeze. Yavapai ate the peeled stems. Wheeler's thistle (*C. wheeleri*) is a forest perennial with pink flowers and without reflexed involucral bracts.

# San Rafael daisy
## (*Erigeron compactus*)
## Sunflower Family
## (Asteraceae)

**Description:** Perennial, Cushion-forming. **Stems** are 1-4 in (2-10 cm) long and nearly leafless. **Basal leaves** are linear, up to 1½ in (4-20 mm) long and have short, appressed hairs. **Heads** solitary and about ¼ in (5-10 mm) high; involucral bracts are narrowly lance-shaped, barely overlapping and short- hairy. **Disk flowers** yellow. **Ray flowers** 30 to 55, white to pink. **Seeds** have long bristles at the tip.

**Habitat and Range:** Gravelly or clayey, sparsely-vegetated soil of desert shrub, salt desert shrub and pinyon-juniper communities. Southern Wyoming south to California, Arizona and New Mexico. Found in CARE.

**Notes:** Our plants are var. *consimilis*; var. *compactus* is more of a Great Basin plant. See basin daisy (P. 76). *Erigeron* is one of the larger plant genera in the Colorado Plateau region, with at least 32 species recorded.

# Spreading daisy (*Erigeron divergens*)
## Sunflower Family (Asteraceae)

**Description:** Annual or short-lived perennial covered with straight, spreading hairs. **Stems** 2-20 in (5-50 cm) high. **Leaves** are basal and alternate and stalked; the blades are narrowly oblong and ½-3 in (1-7 cm) long. **Heads** are ¼ in (4-5 mm) high, solitary on stem tips; involucral bracts linear, barely overlapping with long, spreading hairs. **Disk flowers** yellow. **Ray flowers** more than 70, white to blue. **Seeds** have long bristles at the tip.

**Habitat and Range:** Sandy soil of desert shrub to pinyon-juniper woodlands, often on stream terraces. Throughout most of western North America. Known from ARCH, BEAR, BRCA, CANY, CARE, GLCA, GRST, NABR, RABR, and ZION.

**Notes:** Navajo inhaled the ground plant to treat headache. Spreading daisy can be confused with pretty daisy (P. 189), which has curved rather than straight stem hairs, and hairy daisy (*E. aphanactis*) which also has spreading hairs, but lacks conspicuous ray flowers.

## Basin daisy (*Erigeron pulcherrimus*)
### Sunflower Family (Asteraceae)

**DESCRIPTION:** Grayish-hairy perennial with a stout root crown. **Stems** are unbranched and 2-14 in (5-35 cm) tall. **Leaves** are basal and alternate, linear and up to 3 in (7 cm) long. **Heads** solitary, ⅜ in (6-9 mm) high; involucral bracts overlap somewhat and are sticky and have long hairs. **Disk flowers** yellow. **Ray flowers** 25 to 60, white to violet. **Seeds** have long bristles at the tip, often mixed with shorter ones.

**HABITAT AND RANGE:** Sparsely-vegetated, gravelly, often clayey soils of salt desert shrub and pinyon-juniper communities. Wyoming south to Arizona and New Mexico. Found in ARCH and CARE.

**NOTES:** Basin daisy resembles members of the genus *Aster* by having overlapping involucral bracts, but can be distinguished by its earlier flowering time and slender stem leaves. Spreading daisy (P. 75) has narrowly oblong basal leaves; shaggy daisy (P. 77) has long, spreading hairs.

## Shaggy daisy
### (*Erigeron pumilus*)
### Sunflower Family (Asteraceae)

**DESCRIPTION:** Perennial covered with long, spreading hairs. **Stems** usually unbranched and up to 8 in (20 cm) tall. **Leaves** are basal and alternate, linear-oblong and up to 3 in (8 cm) long. **Heads** usually solitary, ¼ in (4-7 mm) high; involucral bracts are linear and barely overlapping. **Disk flowers** yellow. **Ray flowers** 30 to 50, white to violet. **Seeds** have a mixture of bristles and narrow scales at the tip.

**HABITAT AND RANGE:** Often sparsely-vegetated soil of sagebrush and pinyon-juniper habitats. Nearly throughout the western U.S. and southwest Canada. Occurs in ARCH, BEAR, BRCA, CANY, CARE, GLCA, GRST, NABR, and ZION.

**NOTES:** Shaggy daisy is a widespread and variable species with several named forms. The spreading hairs on the stems and leaves resemble those of spreading daisy (P. 75) but the latter is taller and lacks a basal tuft of leaves. These are the two most common low elevation daisies in southern Utah.

## Crustweed (*Glyptopleura marginata*)
### Sunflower Family (Asteraceae)

**DESCRIPTION:** Nearly stemless annual. **Leaves** all basal with milky sap; the lobed, oblong, blue-green blades are ½-1½ in (1-4 cm) long and have white, tiny sawtooth margins. **Heads** about ½ in (10-13 mm) high and usually shorter than the basal leaves; involucral bracts are green in 2 series, the outer with spiny margins. **Disk flowers** absent. **Ray flowers** 9-18, white with fringed tips. **Seeds** have a lumpy exterior but no pappus.

**HABITAT AND RANGE:** Usually sandy soil of desert shrub and sagebrush communities. Great Basin and Mojave deserts and Colorago Plateau of southern Oregon and Idaho to California and Utah. Known from CARE, GLCA, and RABR.

**NOTES:** Flowers are open only in the morning and early afternoon. Paiute ate the leaves and stems raw. The unusual scientific name of the genus translates from the Greek as "carved rib" for the distinctive ornamentation of the seeds.

## Tidytips  (*Layia glandulosa*)
### Sunflower Family (Asteraceae)

DESCRIPTION: Annual. **Stems** sometimes branched above, 2-12 in (5-30 cm) tall with gland-tipped hairs. **Leaves** are basal and alternate and ½-2 in (1-6 cm) long with lobed or smooth margins. **Heads** are ⅜ in (6-9 mm) high; involucral bracts barely overlap and are hairy and sticky. **Disk flowers** yellow. **Ray flowers** usually 5, white, pleated with 3-lobed tips. **Seeds** have about 10 narrow, long-hairy scales on the tip.

HABITAT AND RANGE: Often sandy soil of sagebrush and pinyon-juniper habitats. British Columbia south to California, Arizona and New Mexico. Found in GLCA, GRST, and ZION.

NOTES: The genus *Layia* is diverse in California (15 species), but only tidytips and one other species are found outside of the Golden State. Native Americans in southern California mixed the seeds with flour to make porridge.

## Low feverfew  (*Parthenium ligulatum*)
### Sunflower Family (Asteraceae)

DESCRIPTION: Stemless, mat-forming perennial. **Leaves** are all basal, less than 1 in (3-20 mm) long and short-hairy. **Heads** ¼ in (5-7 mm) high, solitary and embedded among the leaves; involucral bracts overlap, the inner broader and more rounded than the outer. **Disk flowers** white. **Ray flowers** inconspicuous, white with shallowly 2-lobed tips. **Seeds** are hairy with a persistent ray flower and small, pointed scales on top of each.

HABITAT AND RANGE: Sparsely-vegetated clay soils in salt desert shrub, sagebrush and pinyon-juniper habitats. Endemic to the Colorado Plateau of Utah and Colorado and disjunct in central Nevada. Known from CARE.

NOTES: In the Second World War, botanists investigated related species of *Parthenium* as an alternate source of natural rubber. Another member of the genus, guayule (*P. argentatum*), is a tall, leafy herb from Texas and Mexico which produces larger amounts of natural rubber and is being developed as a commercial crop.

## Silvery Easter-daisy (*Townsendia incana*)
### Sunflower Family (Asteraceae)

**Description:** Mat-forming perennial. **Stems** spreading, unbranched, 1-2 in (2-6 cm) long and densely white-hairy. **Leaves** are narrow, alternate, silvery-hairy and 1-1½ in (1-4 cm) long. **Heads** ⅜ in (7-11 mm) high; involucral bracts overlap and have purple margins. **Disk flowers** yellow. **Ray flowers** 8-22, white to pinkish with rounded tips. **Seeds** covered in clinging hairs with bristles on top.

**Habitat and Range:** Sandy or rarely clay soil of desert shrub, blackbrush, sagebrush and pinyon-juniper habitats. Intermountain region from southern Montana to Arizona and New Mexico. Occurs in ARCH, BEAR, BRCA, CANY, CARE, GLCA, GRST, NABR, RABR, and ZION.

**Notes:** Easter-daisies are named for their early blooming time (often around Easter). Undersides of rays often have a pale lavender tinge. Navajo employed the plant to facilitate childbirth. Jones' Easter-daisy (*T. jonesii*) also forms mats but is not so densely hairy. Annual Easter-daisy (*T. annua*, lower left) appears similar, but is obviously an annual with a slender central stem.

# Narrow-leaf woody-aster
### (*Machaeranthera confertifolia*)
### Sunflower Family (Asteraceae)

**DESCRIPTION:** Shrub-like perennial. **Stems** unbranched, 4-8 in (10-20 cm) tall. **Leaves** are alternate, linear, ½-2 in (10-45 mm) long and glabrous or sticky. **Heads** solitary, up to ½ in (8-12 mm) high; involucral bracts overlap and are sharp-pointed and sticky or sparsely hairy. **Disk flowers** yellow. **Ray flowers** 4 to 14, usually white with rounded tips. **Seeds** are hairy with bristles on top.

**HABITAT AND RANGE:** Barren, clay soil in salt desert shrub and pinyon-juniper habitats. Endemic to the Colorado Plateau of southern Utah. Found in CARE, GLCA, and GRST.

**NOTES:** Many species of woody-aster often occur in soils with high levels of selenium, indicating that forage plants growing with them may have high levels of this poisonous trace element in their tissue. Smooth woody-aster (*M. glabriuscula*) has narrowly lanceolate rather than linear leaves and is restricted to eastern Utah. Mojave woody-aster (P. 193) and Cisco woody-aster (P. 194) have pink to purple ray flowers.

# San Juan onion
## (*Allium macropetalum*)
## Lily Family (Liliaceae)

**DESCRIPTION:** Glabrous perennial. **Bulbs** often clustered with a fibrous coat. **Stems** erect or ascending, 2-8 in (5-20 cm) tall, shorter than the leaves. **Leaves** 2, linear, tubular. **Inflorescence** of several unequal-stalked flowers arising from the stem tip and subtended by 2 or 3 membranous bracts with obvious stripes. **Flowers** with 6 white, pink-veined petals ⅜ in (8-12 mm) long.

**HABITAT AND RANGE:** Sandy or silty soil of desert shrub or pinyon-juniper habitats. Colorado Plateau south to Mexico. Found in ARCH, BEAR, CANY, CARE, GLCA, GRST, NABR, and RABR.

**NOTES:** The stem of Nevada onion (*A. nevadense*) has a solitary long leaf. Onion flowers are edible and have a mild oniony flavor. Eating flowers and leaves prunes the plant while digging the bulb kills it.

# Textile onion (*Allium textile*)
## Lily Family (Liliaceae)

**DESCRIPTION:** Glabrous perennial. **Bulbs** often clustered with a fibrous coat. **Stems** erect or ascending, 1-10 in (3-26 cm) tall. **Leaves** 2, linear, U-shaped in cross-section, about as long as the stem. **Inflorescence** of several equal-stalked flowers arising from the stem tip and subtended by 3 membranous bracts with a single midvein. **Flowers** with 6 white petals ¼ in (5-9 mm) long.

**HABITAT AND RANGE:** Silty soil of sagebrush and pinyon-juniper communities. Great Plains and intermountain deserts from Alberta and Saskatchewan south to Arizona and New Mexico. Occurs in ARCH and GLCA.

**NOTES:** Native Americans used bulbs of most species to flavor food in a manner similar to many European cultures.

## Sego lily (*Calochortus nuttallii*)
### Lily Family (Liliaceae)

**DESCRIPTION:** Glabrous perennial. **Stems** erect, 3-20 in (8-50 cm) tall. **Leaves** linear, 2-3½ in (3-9 cm) long. **Flowers** few from stem tips; petals 1-2 in (2.5-6 cm) long, white or pale purple with a purple crescent over a yellow semicircle near the base. **Fruit** is an erect, narrowly elliptic, 3-angled capsule 1-2 in (3-5 cm) long.

**HABITAT AND RANGE:** Silty or gravelly soil of sagebrush and pinyon-juniper communities. Great Plains and intermountain deserts and grasslands from Montana and North Dakota south to Nevada, Arizona and New Mexico. Found in ARCH, BEAR, BRCA, CANY, CARE, GLCA, GRST, HOVE, NABR, RABR, and ZION.

**NOTES:** Sego lily is the state flower of Utah. Bulbs were eaten by Native Americans and early European settlers. Cisco mariposa (*C. ciscoensis*) is a recently described species from eastern Utah and western Colorado that differs in having solid-colored petals that are white or pink. It is common on clay soils north of Moab and along Interstate 70.

## Funnel lily (*Androstephium breviflorum*)
### Lily Family (Liliaceae)

**DESCRIPTION:** Glabrous perennial from a bulb. **Stems** erect, leafless, unbranched, 4-12 in (10-30 cm) high. **Leaves** linear, U-shaped in cross-section, about as long as the stem. **Inflorescence** of several equal-stalked flowers arising from the stem tip subtended by 3 membranous bracts. **Flowers** white to purplish with a dark central stripe, tubular with 6 spreading lobes up to ½ in (5-12 mm) long and stamens united into an inner petal-like tube.

**HABITAT AND RANGE:** Sandy, silty or stony soil of blackbrush, sagebrush and pinyon-juniper communities. Intermountain deserts from southern Wyoming to California through New Mexico. Found in ARCH, BEAR, CANY, CARE, GLCA, GRST, HOVE, NABR, RABR, and ZION.

**NOTES:** Onions (*Allium* spp.) have separate petals, and the leaves and bulbs have an onion-like odor. Blue-dicks (*Dichelostemma pulchellum*) also has stamens fused into a tube but has taller stems, longer leaves, and blue flowers.

## Sand lily  (*Eremocrinum albomarginatum*)
### Lily Family  (Liliaceae)

**DESCRIPTION:** Glabrous, fibrous-based perennial. **Stems** erect, leafless, unbranched and 4-14 in (10-35 cm) tall. **Leaves** are basal, linear and 4-16 in (10-40 cm) long. **Inflorescence** a terminal spike of numerous, overlapping flowers. **Flowers** are white; the 6 petals about ½ in (1-2 cm) long with green veins. **Fruit** an oblong, 3-lobed capsule ¼ in (4-6 mm) long.

**HABITAT AND RANGE:** Sandy soil of dunes, desert shrub, sagebrush and blackbrush communities. Endemic to the Colorado Plateau of Utah and Arizona. Known from ARCH, BEAR, CANY, CARE, GLCA, HOVE, NABR, and RABR.

**NOTES:** Navajo used the plant to treat snakebite. *Eremocrinum* is a monotypic genus distinguished by the short tube formed by fusion of the tepals. Species of death camas (P. 84) have smaller petals without green veins.

## **Foothills death camas** (*Zigadenus paniculatus*)
### Lily Family (Liliaceae)

**DESCRIPTION:** Glabrous perennial from bulbs. **Stems** erect, unbranched, 6-28 in (15-70 cm) high. **Leaves** are alternate, linear, 4-14 in (10-35 cm) long and longest near the base of the stem. **Inflorescence** narrow, branched below with long-stalked flowers. **Flowers** have 6 white petals with greenish bases; the outer ⅛ in (3-4 mm) long; the inner longer. **Fruits** are erect, 3-sectioned, narrowly ellipsoid capsules ⅔ in (15-20 mm) long.

**HABITAT AND RANGE:** Silty or sandy soil of sagebrush and pinyon-juniper communities. Washington to Montana south to California through New Mexico. Found in BEAR, BRCA, CANY, GLCA, GRST, HOVE, and ZION.

**NOTES:** Although the bulbs are considered poisonous, the Navajo were reported to have cooked and eaten them. Watson's death camas (*Z. venenosus*, lower right) is nearly identical and occurs in the same habitats but lacks a branched inflorescence and is much less common. Alcove death camas (*Z. vaginatus*) has larger petals and an unbranched inflorescence and occurs in hanging gardens.

# Comb Wash wild buckwheat (*Eriogonum clavellatum*)
## Knotweed Family (Polygonaceae)

**DESCRIPTION:** Long-hairy perennial forming loose clumps 4-8 in (10-20 cm) high. **Leaves** on the lower stem are wooly beneath, about ½ in (1-2 cm) long and linear with rolled-in edges. **Inflorescence** a hemispheric cluster of several bell-shaped involucres less than ¼ in (3-5 mm) long, each containing several stalked flowers. **Flowers** are cup-shaped with 6 white to pinkish petals about ⅛ in (3-4 mm) long. **Seeds** are glabrous.

**HABITAT AND RANGE:** Mainly shale-derived clay soil in salt desert shrub, blackbrush and pinyon-juniper habitats. Endemic to the Four Corners region of the Colorado Plateau. Found only in BEAR.

**NOTES:** Shortstem wild buckwheat (P. 197) is generally taller and does not usually form clumps. Shockley's wild buckwheat (*E. shockleyi*, left) forms small mats but has hairy foliage and shorter stature.

# Cushion wild buckwheat
## (*Eriogonum ovalifolium*)
## Knotweed Family (Polygonaceae)

**DESCRIPTION:** Small, white-hairy, clump-forming perennial with naked stems 2-12 in (5-30 cm) tall. **Leaves** are basal, stalked; the blades ovate and 1-2 in (2-6 cm) long. **Inflorescence** hemispheric, composed of several clusters of vase-shaped involucres each containing several short-stalked flowers. **Flowers** have 6 white to pink (rarely yellow), glabrous petals ¼ in (3-7 mm) long. **Seeds** are glabrous.

**HABITAT AND RANGE:** Sandy, silty or gravelly soil, primarily in sagebrush and pinyon-juniper habitats. British Columbia and Alberta south through most of the western U.S. Found in ARCH, BEAR, CANY, CARE, GLCA, GRST, HOVE, NABR, and ZION.

**NOTES:** The white-flowered form pictured here is var. *purpureum*. Shoshoni employed a decoction of the roots to treat colds. Panguitch wild buckwheat (*E. panguicense*) has linear-oblanceolate leaf blades and always occurs on limestone or other calcium-rich soils.

# Palmer's wild buckwheat (*Eriogonum palmerianum*)
## Knotweed Family (Polygonaceae)

**DESCRIPTION:** Wooly-hairy annual 2-12 in (5-30 cm) high. **Leaves** basal, stalked; the blades ovate to orbicular and ½-1 in (1-4 cm) long, often deciduous at flowering time. **Inflorescence** is branched from just above the leaves with sessile clusters of flowers along the branches. **Flowers** have 6 white to pink, glabrous petals 1-2 mm long. **Seeds** are hairy at the base.

**HABITAT AND RANGE:** Sandy, silty or gravelly soil of washes and flats in most habitats. Western deserts from southern Idaho south to California and Mexico. Found in BEAR, CANY, CARE, GLCA, GRST, HOVE, RABR, and ZION.

**NOTES:** Spreading wild buckwheat (*E. divaricatum*) has short-hairy leaves and yellow flowers.

# Slender wild buckwheat
## (*Eriogonum microthecum*)
### Knotweed Family (Polygonaceae)

**DESCRIPTION:** Small shrub 2-40 in (4-100 cm) high. **Leaves** are alternate, short-stalked; the blades linear-lanceolate, wooly beneath and up to 1½ in (4-35 mm) long, often with the margins inrolled. **Inflorescence** diffuse-hemispheric, composed of short-hairy, vase-shaped involucres at branch tips; each containing several short-stalked flowers. **Flowers** have 6 white, glabrous petals ⅛ in (2-3 mm) long. **Seeds** are glabrous.

**HABITAT AND RANGE:** Silty or gravelly soil in desert shrub, sagebrush and pinyon-juniper habitats. Throughout intermontane western U.S. Found in ARCH, BEAR, BRCA, CANY, CARE, GLCA, GRST, HOVE, NABR, and ZION.

**NOTES :** Fremont's wild buckwheat (*E. corymbosum*) has oblong leaves with rounded tips and flowers that are sometimes pink or yellow and bloom in late summer and fall. Sand wild buckwheat (*E. leptocladon*) has flowers along the length of inflorescence branches.

# Harriman's yucca
## (*Yucca harrimaniae*)
### Agave Family (Agavaceae)

**DESCRIPTION:** Clump-forming, evergreen perennial 14-28 in (35-70 cm) high. **Leaves** are linear, 4-20 in (10-50 cm) long and less than 2 in (1-4 cm) wide with curled fibers along the margin. **Inflorescence** unbranched, partially within the leaves. **Flowers** pendent; each with 6 white to pale purplish petals about 2 in (4-6 cm) long. **Fruits** are peanut-shaped capsules to 2 in (4-5 cm) long.

**HABITAT AND RANGE:** Bedrock or gravelly soil of desert shrub, sagebrush and pinyon-juniper habitats. Western Nevada east to Colorado and New Mexico. Found in ARCH, BEAR, BRCA, CANY, CARE, GLCA, GRST, NABR, and RABR.

**NOTES:** Narrow-leaved yucca (*Y. angustissima*) has an inflorescence completely above the leaves which are less than ½ in (1 cm) wide. Yuccas are pollinated by yucca moths which collect the plant's pollen and pack it onto the fertile stigma to ensure pollination, while also laying their eggs in the developing fruits. Yucca pods usually contain a high percentage of damaged seeds that were eaten by the developing moth larvae.

# Datil yucca (*Yucca baccata*)
## Agave Family (Agavaceae)

**DESCRIPTION:** Evergreen perennial 14-28 in (35-70 cm) tall. **Leaves** are all basal, swordlike, 12-28 in (30-70 cm) long and 1-2 in (3-5 cm) wide with scattered fibers along the margins. **Flowering stems** are branched, about as long as the leaves with numerous crowded flowers. **Flowers** are pendent and have 6 white petals 2-3 in (4-8 cm) long and tinged with purple. **Fruits** are obovoid, fleshy capsules 4-7 in (10-17 cm) long with 3 rows of flat seeds.

**HABITAT AND RANGE:** Sandy, silty or gravelly soil of sagebrush and pinyon-juniper habitats. California east to Colorado, Texas and Mexico. Found in BEAR, BRCA, CANY, GLCA, GRST, HOVE, NABR, and ZION.

**NOTES:** Native Americans baked the fleshy fruits or made them into drinks. Fresh petals are edible, but should be cooked. Bailey's yucca (*Y. baileyi*) also has leaves about as long as the inflorescence, but the leaves are up to ½ in (10 mm) wide and the fruits are not fleshy. Vespertine yucca (*Y. vespertina*) is a closely related form with longer, blue-green, inrolled leaves and flower stalks shorter than the leaves. It occurs primarily in southwestern Utah, including Zion.

# Plains spring-parsley (*Cymopterus acaulis*)
## Parsley Family (Apiaceae)

DESCRIPTION: Perennial. **Stems** leafless, 1-3 in (2-8 cm) long in flower, elongating to 10 in (25 cm) in fruit. **Leaves** are all basal, often sticky, 1½-6 in (4-14 cm) long and divided into 2 or 3 pairs of deeply-lobed leaflets. **Flowers** are small and yellow in an umbrella-shaped inflorescence with clusters subtended by green bracts forming an asymmetrical, star-like cup. **Fruits** are about ⅜ in (5-10 mm) long and ellipsoid with several wavy-margined purple wings up to ⅛ in (2 mm) wide.

HABITAT AND RANGE: Usually sandy soil in desert shrub, blackbrush, sagebrush or juniper woodlands. The species occurs on the Great Plains and cold deserts from southern Saskatchewan to Mexico. Found in ARCH, BEAR, CANY, CARE, GLCA, GRST, HOVE, NABR, RABR.

NOTES: Most plants in the Red Rock Desert are var. *fendleri*. A purple flowered form (var. *higginsii*) occurs on clay soils near Glen Canyon. Navajo dried the plants for winter food. Sticky spring-parsley (*C. newberryi*, below) has leaves with fewer and broader leaflets.

# Sticky spring-parsley
## (*Cymopterus newberryi*)
## Parsley Family (Apiaceae)

DESCRIPTION: Perennial. **Stems** leafless, up to 6 in (15 cm) long. **Leaves** are all basal, sticky, about 2 in (5 cm) long and composed of a large terminal leaflet with only 1 or 2 pairs of smaller, lobed leaflets. **Flowers** are yellow in an open inflorescence with clusters subtended by green, hand-like bracts with the "fingers" pointing out. **Fruits** are about ⅜ in (5-10 mm) long with several narrow wings, some of which may have wavy margins.

HABITAT AND RANGE: Usually on very sandy soil of desert shrub, blackbrush, sand sagebrush and pinyon-juniper communities. Southern Utah and adjacent Arizona, mainly on the Colorado Plateau. Found in ARCH, CANY, GLCA, GRST, HOVE, and ZION.

NOTES: Fine sand grains may coat the sticky leaves and stems. Plains spring-parsley (above) is similar but its leaves are more divided and the wings of its mature fruit are wider and wavier. The peeled roots were eaten by Hopi children.

# Canyonland spring-parsley (*Cymopterus macdougalii*)
## Parsley Family (Apiaceae)

**DESCRIPTION:** Perennial. **Stems** are leafless, up to 4 in (10 cm) long in flower, often longer in fruit. **Leaves** are all basal, dark green, 1-3½ in (3-9 cm) long with 7 to 9 widely-spaced, sharply-lobed leaflets. **Flowers** are yellow in a hemispheric inflorescence with clusters subtended by few, narrow, inconspicuous bracts. **Fruits** are about ¼ in (4-8 mm) long with several narrow, flattened wings along the margins.

**HABITAT AND RANGE:** Sandy soil or cracks in shady sandstone canyons at low elevations. Colorado Plateau of southeast Utah and adjacent Colorado and Arizona. Found in BEAR, GRST and NABR.

**NOTES:** Canyonland spring-parsley is fairly uncommon in southeast Utah, but can be readily observed along the main trails in Natural Bridges National Monument. The species is named for Daniel MacDougal, who was director of the Carnegie Desert Botanical Laboratory in Tucson, AZ in the early 20th century and was a leader in research on desert ecosystems of the southwest and Africa. The genus *Cymopterus* contains approximately 50 species, all found in the Great Plains and deserts of western North America. Foliage of aromatic spring-parsley (*C. terebinthinus*) has a turpentine-like odor and more finely divided leaflets. Canyon desert-parsley (*Lomatium latilobum*) has similar leaves but fruits with only 2 wings and longer flower bracts.

# Colorado Plateau spring-parsley

(*Cymopterus purpureus*) Parsley Family (Apiaceae)

**DESCRIPTION:** Perennial. **Stems** leafless, up to 8 in (20 cm) long. **Leaves** are all basal, smooth, sometimes shiny, 2-4 in (5-10 cm) long with 5 to 9 deeply lobed, sharp-pointed, fern-like leaflets. **Flowers** are yellow (rarely purple) in an umbrella-shaped inflorescence with clusters subtended by few, narrow, inconspicuous bracts. **Fruits** are green to purplish and less than ½ in (8-12 mm) long with several, broad, flat or slightly wavy wings about ⅛ in (2-4 mm) wide.

**HABITAT AND RANGE:** Clay soils from desert shrublands to pinyon-juniper woodlands. Colorado Plateau of Utah, Colorado, New Mexico and Arizona. Found in ARCH, BEAR, BRCA, CANY, CARE, GLCA, GRST, HOVE, NABR, and ZION.

**NOTES:** Occasionally this plant has purple flowers, more befitting its scientific name. The common phase in canyon country is var. *purpureus*; var. *rosei* occurs in the mountains of central and western Utah on clay or limestone talus, and var. *jonesii* is found in the Great Basin on sandy slopes. Navajo used the ground plant to season soup.

# Desert-parsley
## (*Lomatium foeniculaceum*)
## Parsley Family (Apiaceae)

DESCRIPTION: Perennial that is densely short-hairy, not aromatic. **Stems** leafless, as little as 3 in (5 cm) long in flower but to 12 in (30 cm) long in fruit. **Leaves** are all basal; the blades are 1-5 in (2-13 cm) long and finely dissected into tiny, parsley-like, finely gray-hairy leaflets less than ⅛ in (3 mm) long. **Inflorescence** umbrella-like with unequal stalks and yellow flowers. **Fruits** are elliptic to oval and little more than ¼ in (5-11 mm) long with short wings on the edges but with only low ribs between.

HABITAT AND RANGE: Gravelly or clayey soil of pinyon-juniper and sagebrush habitats. Widespread from southern Canada to California and Texas. Known from Kane Co. in our area. Found in GLCA and GRST.

NOTES: Aromatic spring-parsley (*Cymopterus terebinthinus*) has similar-shaped leaves, but they are green and glabrous. Spring-parsleys (*Cymopterus*) and desert-parsleys (*Lomatium*) are similar, but fruits of the former have wings on the margins and faces, while fruits of the latter have marginal wings only. The two genera are difficult to distinguish in flower. Nevada desert-parsley (*L. nevadense*) has white flowers.

# Parry's desert-parsley (*Lomatium parryi*)
## Parsley Family (Apiaceae)

DESCRIPTION: Perennial. **Stems** leafless and 3-15 in (8-40 cm) high. **Leaves** are glabrous and nearly as high as the stems, 3-10 in (7-24 cm) long with 5 to12 widely-spaced pairs of deeply lobed, short leaflets. **Inflorescence** hemispheric, umbrella-like with equal stalks and yellow flowers. **Fruits** are elliptic and about ½ in (9-18 mm) long with wide lateral wings and indistinct ribs between.

HABITAT AND RANGE: Sandy soil and sandstone outcrops; common in blackbrush and pinyon-juniper habitats; less common in desert shrub communities. Colorado Plateau of Utah, Colorado and Arizona west to California. Found in ARCH, BEAR, BRCA, CANY, CARE, GLCA, GRST, and NABR.

NOTES: Leaves are just beginning to expand at the time the elongated stems are flowering. This desert-parsley was named for Charles Parry who was born in England but lived most of his life in the U.S. He became a doctor and served with the U.S.-Mexico Boundary Survey during which time he collected many plants new to science.

# Rushy desert-parsley (*Lomatium junceum*)
## Parsley Family (Apiaceae)

**DESCRIPTION:** Perennial. **Stems** are leafless, 4-10 in (10-25 cm) long and partly hidden among the leaves. **Leaves** are all basal and glabrous; the blades are up to 7 in (17 cm) long and divided into few, linear, petiole-like lobes, giving the plant a grass-like appearance. **Inflorescence** hemispheric with equal stalks and yellow flowers. **Fruits** are elliptic and about ½ in (10-15 mm) long with wide lateral wings and distinct longitudinal ribs between.

**HABITAT AND RANGE:** Shaley or clayey soil of desert shrub or pinyon-juniper habitats. Endemic to the area in and around the San Rafael Swell on the Colorado Plateau of Utah. Found in CARE.

**NOTES:** The grass-like appearance is unique among members of the Parsley Family on the Colorado Plateau. The species name means rush-like. This and other desert-parsleys often have pleasantly fragrant foliage if rubbed between fingers. There are 23 species and varieties of *Lomatium* in southern Utah, of which 12 occur in our area. Rushy desert-parsley was not discovered until the late 1970s.

# Western tansymustard
## (*Descurainia pinnata*)
## Mustard Family (Brassicaceae)

**DESCRIPTION:** Annual. **Stems** often branched, 3-16 in (8-40 cm) tall. **Leaves** are basal and alternate and stalked; the blades are twice pinnately lobed, fern-like, hairy and 1-4 in (2-10 cm) long. **Flowers** have 4 pale yellow petals 1-3 mm long. **Fruits** linear, many-seeded ascending pods, up to ½ in (3-15 mm) long on widely-spaced spreading stalks.

**HABITAT AND RANGE:** Sparsely-vegetated or disturbed soil of sagebrush, blackbrush and pinyon-juniper habitats. Throughout temperate North America. Found in ARCH, BEAR, BRCA, CANY, CARE, GLCA, GRST, HOVE, NABR, RABR, and ZION.

**NOTES:** A dizzying array of intergrading forms have been described for this variable species and two close relatives (*D. incana* and *D. incisa*). Native Americans ate the leaves of tansymustard as greens and ground the tiny seeds into an edible meal. Flixweed (*D. sophia*), with longer fruits and more divided leaves, is introduced from Europe.

# Flaxleaf plainsmustard
## (*Schoenocrambe linifolia*)
## Mustard Family (Brassicaceae)

**DESCRIPTION:** Glabrous perennial. **Stems** branched, 8-28 in (20-70 cm) tall. **Leaves** are linear, alternate and ½-4 in (1-10 cm) long. **Flowers** have 4 pale yellow petals up to ½ in (7-12 mm) long. **Fruits** are ascending, linear pods 1-3 in (3-7 cm) long with numerous seeds in rows.

**HABITAT AND RANGE:** Silty or clayey soils of sagebrush or pinyon-juniper habitats. Intermountain region from British Columbia and Alberta south to Arizona and New Mexico. Known from BEAR, BRCA, CARE, GLCA, and GRST.

**NOTES:** Tumble mustard (*Sisymbrium altissimum*), an introduced weed of disturbed habitats, has a similar habit and fruits, but the leaves are lobed, and lower stems have straight hairs.

94

# Western wallflower (*Erysimum capitatum*)
## Mustard Family (Brassicaceae)

**DESCRIPTION:** Biennial or short-lived perennial. **Stems** usually several, unbranched, 2-20 in (5-50 cm) tall. **Leaves** narrow, ½-4 in (1-10 cm) long with minute T-shaped hairs; the basal are stalked, while those of the stem are alternate and without stalks. **Flowers** have 4 yellow petals up to 1 in (13-25 mm) long. **Fruits** are linear, 1-4 in (2-10 cm) long, many-seeded, ascending pods on spreading stalks.

**HABITAT AND RANGE:** Sandy or silty soil of desert shrub, sagebrush and pinyon-juniper habitats. British Columbia to Montana and south to Mexico. Occurs in ARCH, BEAR, BRCA, CANY, CARE, GLCA, GRST, NABR, and ZION.

**NOTES:** Pretty wallflower (*E. asperum*, right) is a Great Plains species with nearly horizontal fruits; it is rare in our area. Navajo inhaled the odor of crushed leaves to relieve a headache. "Wallflower" seems a misnomer for such a showy species, but is derived from a relative in Europe that often grows out of cracks in masonry walls.

## Rydberg's twinpod (*Physaria acutifolia*)
### Mustard Family (Brassicaceae)

**DESCRIPTION:** Silvery-hairy, multi-stemmed perennial. **Stems** lax, unbranched, 1-8 in (3-20 cm) long. **Leaves** are basal and alternate, 1-4 in (2-9 cm) long; the blades are elliptic, sometimes basally lobed. **Flowers** have 4 yellow petals up to ½ in (6-11 mm) long. **Fruits** are borne on S-shaped, spreading stalks and have 2 inflated, ellipsoid lobes ⅜ in (6-10 mm) long with a style less than ¼ in (5 mm) long between the lobes.

**HABITAT AND RANGE:** Sandy or silty soil of desert shrub, sagebrush and pinyon-juniper communities. Intermountain region from southern Montana to the Colorado Plateau of Arizona and New Mexico. Found in ARCH, BEAR, CANY, CARE, GLCA, GRST, HOVE, and NABR.

**NOTES:** Two forms are recognized in our area; var. *acutifolia* (pictured here) has entire-margined basal leaves, while var. *purpurea* has some lobed basal leaves. Newberry's twinpod (*P. newberryi*) has a shorter style between the lobes of the four-angled fruit.

96

# Watson's bladderpod (*Physaria intermedia*)
## Mustard Family (Brassicaceae)

**DESCRIPTION:** Bunch-forming, silvery-hairy perennial. **Stems** unbranched, 2-10 in (5-20 cm) tall. **Leaves** are alternate, linear and up to 1 in (1-3 cm) long. **Flowers** have 4 yellow petals ⅜ in (6-9 mm) long. **Fruits** borne on spreading stalks, are silvery-hairy, pear-shaped and up to ¼ in (3-6 mm) long with a linear style on top.

**HABITAT AND RANGE:** Sandy, silty or gravelly soil of sagebrush and pinyon-juniper habitats. Utah, Arizona and New Mexico. Found in BEAR, BRCA, CARE, GRST, and ZION.

**NOTES.** Navajo ingested an infusion of this plant to counteract spider bites. Fendler's bladderpod (*P. fendleri*, lower right) is similar but has broader leaves and glabrous, orbicular fruits. Bladderpods (formerly *Lesquerella* spp.)with unlobed fruits have recently been combined with twinpods (*Physaria*) because intermediate forms occur.

# Colorado Plateau bladderpod (*Physaria rectipes*)
## Mustard Family (Brassicaceae)

**DESCRIPTION:** Short-lived, silvery-hairy perennial. **Stems** unbranched, 4-12 in (10-30 cm) tall. **Leaves** are basal and alternate, linear-oblong and ½-3 in (1-8 cm) long. **Flowers** have 4 yellow petals about ⅜ in (5-10 mm) long. **Fruits** on spreading stalks are globose, less than ¼ in (3-5 mm) long with a linear style on top.

**HABITAT AND RANGE:** Usually sandy, sparsely-vegetated soil of sagebrush and pinyon-juniper habitats. Endemic to the Colorado Plateau of the Four Corners region. Occurs in BEAR, BRCA, CANY, CARE, GLCA, GRST, NABR, RABR, and ZION.

**NOTES:** Silvery bladderpod (*P. ludoviciana*) has the same stature but the leaves are more linear, and the fruit stalks are recurved; King's bladderpod (*P. kingii*, right) has spoon-shaped basal leaves.

# Prince's plume  (*Stanleya pinnata*)
## Mustard Family  (Brassicaceae)

**DESCRIPTION:** Nearly glabrous, perennial with a woody base. **Stems** sometimes branched, 1-4 ft (30-120 cm) tall. **Leaves** are alternate, 2-7 in (5-18 cm) long; those near the base are usually lobed. **Flowers** have 4 yellow petals about ½ in (10-16 mm) long and 6 yellow, linear stamens about twice as long. **Fruits** are spreading, linear pods 2-3 in (4-8 cm) long with numerous seeds in rows.

**HABITAT AND RANGE:** Stony outcrops and sparsely-vegetated silty or clayey soil of desert shrub, salt desert shrub, sagebrush and pinyon-juniper communities. Montana and North Dakota south to California through Texas. Occurs in ARCH, BEAR, BRCA, CANY, CARE, GLCA, GRST, HOVE, NABR, and ZION.

**NOTES:** Prince's plume concentrates selenium in its tissue. Selenium is required in mammalian diets in small quantities but is poisonous in larger doses. Crushed leaves of prince's plume give off a scent of selenium which smells a bit like a rotten egg stored in a dirty gym sock. Havasupai would eat the leaves after boiling two or three times to remove the selenium. Desert plume (*S. viridiflora*, right) also has long-exserted stamens, but there are basal leaves and stem leaves that are not lobed.

# Colorado Plateau stinkweed (*Cleomella palmeriana*)
## Spider-flower Family (Cleomaceae)

**DESCRIPTION:** Glabrous, malodorous annual. **Stems** often branched, 2-12 in (6-30 cm) high. **Leaves** are alternate, petiolate with 3 leaflets up to 1 in (1-2 cm) long. **Inflorescence** a cluster of numerous flowers that elongates with flowering. **Flowers** have 6 long-exserted stamens and 4 yellow, asymmetrically disposed petals up to ¼ in (3-5 mm) long. **Fruits** are rhomboidal capsules, up to ¼ in (3-5 mm) wide, with a straight projection (style) on top and borne on long, spreading to recurved stalks.

**HABITAT AND RANGE:** Barren, clay or silty soils in salt desert shrub and clay barren habitats. Endemic to the Colorado Plateau of Utah, Colorado, Arizona and New Mexico. Found in BRCA, CARE, GLCA, and GRST.

**NOTES:** Colorado Plateau stinkweed can turn gray clay barrens yellow for a few weeks following a wet winter, but then will be essentially absent in dry years. Yellow beeplant (P. 101) has elongated, drooping pods and taller stems.

100

# Yellow beeplant (*Cleome lutea*)
## Spider-flower Family (Cleomaceae)

**DESCRIPTION:** Mostly glabrous annual. **Stems** 1-5 ft (30-150 cm) tall, often branched. **Leaves** alternate and petiolate with mostly 5 leaflets 1-2 in (2-5 cm) long arranged like fingers on a hand. **Inflorescence** a terminal, expanding, linear cluster. **Flowers** are yellow with 4 petals ⅜ in (5-10 mm) long and 6 long-exserted stamens. **Fruits** are tubular pods 1-2 in (2-4 cm) long on pendulous stalks.

**HABITAT AND RANGE:** Sparsely-vegetated soil of desert shrub, salt desert shrub and pinyon-juniper habitats, sometimes along roads. Washington to Montana, south to Mexico. Found in ARCH, BEAR, BRCA, CANY, CARE, GLCA, GRST, NABR, and ZION.

**NOTES:** Navajo used the plant to treat ant bites. Rocky Mountain beeplant (*C. serrulata*) has purple petals. See Colorado Plateau stinkweed (P. 100).

# Shorthorn spurge (*Euphorbia brachycera*)
## Spurge Family (Euphorbiaceae)

**DESCRIPTION:** Perennial with milky sap. **Stems** numerous, 4-16 in (10-40 cm) tall. **Leaves** are alternate below the inflorescence, ovate, glabrous or short-hairy and ¼-1 in (7-25 mm) long. **Inflorescence** is branched and composed of small yellowish-green flowers closely subtended by opposite, leaf-like bracts. **Fruits** are short-stalked, nodding, 3-ribbed, 3-seeded, globose capsules ⅛ in (3-5 mm) long.

**HABITAT AND RANGE:** Sandy or gravelly, often moist soil of sagebrush and pinyon-juniper communities; sometimes in hanging gardens. Montana south to Arizona, New Mexico and Texas. Found in ARCH, BEAR, BRCA, CANY, CARE, GLCA, GRST, NABR, and ZION. A narrow-leaved form occurs in deep canyons in GRST and may be an unnamed variety.

**NOTES:** Navajo drank an infusion of the plant for purging. This benign, native species is sometimes confused with the aggressive invasive weed, leafy spurge (*E. esula*), which has broader bracts in the inflorescence and narrower stem leaves.

# Creeping rush-pea (*Caesalpinia repens*)
## Pea Family (Fabaceae)

**DESCRIPTION:** Low-growing, rhizomatous perennial. **Stems** prostrate. **Leaves** are basal, sparsely-hairy and 1-4 in (2-10 cm) long with 5 to 9 pairs of overlapping leaflets. **Inflorescence** ascending to erect, 2-8 in (5-20 cm) tall with 7 to 26 flowers. **Flowers** have 5 separate yellow petals ½ in (10-12 mm) long, the uppermost broader and red-dotted, old flowers are drooping. **Pods** pendulous, oblong, flattened, 1-2 in (2-5 cm) long.

**HABITAT AND RANGE:** Sandy soil of desert shrub communities, dunes and gravelly roadsides. Endemic to the Colorado Plateau of Utah. Occurs in ARCH and GLCA.

**NOTES:** Although creeping rush-pea is in the Pea Family, the five petals are almost identical in size and shape, unlike typical pea flowers. This species is distantly related to bird-of-paradise, a showy, yellow-flowered shrub that is sometimes cultivated in southern Utah.

102

# Long-bract trefoil
(*Lotus plebeius*)
Pea Family (Fabaceae)

DESCRIPTION: Appressed-hairy, prawling, perennial. **Stems** usually prostrate, branched, 6-14 in (15-35 cm) long. **Leaves** are alternate, ¼-1¼ in (5-30 mm) long with 3 to 4 leaflets on a short stalk. **Inflorescence** ascending from leaf axils with 1 or 2 flowers. **Flowers** are yellow with a blush of red or orange, pea-like and ½-¾ in (12-17 mm) long with a showy banner petal. **Pods** are linear, about 1 in (17-32 mm) long, slightly flattened and hairy.

HABITAT AND RANGE: Sandy or gravelly soil of riparian, blackbrush or pinyon-juniper habitats. Nevada and Utah south to Mexico and Texas. Found in GRST and ZION.

NOTES: The size and shape of the leaflets varies greatly; those lower on the stem often rounded, while those higher on the stem are linear. Utah trefoil (*L. utahensis*) is also a perennial but has sessile leaves and larger inflorescences.

# Yellow Sweetclover (*Melilotus officinalis*)
Pea Family (Fabaceae)

DESCRIPTION: Nearly glabrous biennial. **Stems** erect, branched, 1-5 ft (40-150 cm) tall. **Leaves** are alternate, widely-spaced, stalked with 3 finely-toothed leaflets up to 1½ in (4 cm) long. **Inflorescence** spike-like from leaf axils, 1-4 in (2-11 cm) long with 20 to 65 flowers. **Flowers** are yellow, pea-like and ¼ in (4-7 mm) long. **Pods** ovoid, glabrous, ⅛-¼ in (3-5 mm) long.

HABITAT AND RANGE: Riparian areas, fields and roadsides. Introduced from Europe throughout North America. Found in ARCH, BEAR, BRCA, CANY, CARE, GLCA, GRST, HOVE, NABR, and ZION.

NOTES: Yellow sweetclover has a distinctive, sweet odor from coumarin, a chemical used industrially in perfumes and to enhance flavor. Plants stay low to the ground during their first year and then bolt and flower the second year. White sweetclover (*M. alba*) is vegetatively similar but has white flowers and often occurs in moister sites.

# Golden pea (*Thermopsis montana*)
## Pea Family (Fabaceae)

**DESCRIPTION:** Nearly glabrous, rhizomatous perennial. **Stems** erect, mostly unbranched, 8-32 in (20-80 cm) tall. **Leaves** are alternate with 3 leaflets and a pair of leaflet-like stipules at the base of the stalk. **Inflorescence** narrow with 7 to 30 flowers at stem tips. **Flowers** yellow, pea-like, about 1 in (20-28 mm) long. **Pods** are linear, erect, about 2 in (4-5 cm) long, short-hairy and becoming black.

**HABITAT AND RANGE:** Moist riparian areas and mountain meadows. Intermountain valleys from Washington and Montana south to Arizona and New Mexico. Found in BEAR, CARE, GRST, NABR, and ZION.

**NOTES:** Navajo used the plant to treat sore eyes and throat. Foraging on golden pea foliage can induce muscle degeneration in cattle. Circle-pod pea (*T. rhombifolia*, right) has similar flowers and leaves, but it occurs in drier habitats, and the fruits are curved and pendant; these two species are sometimes combined into one.

# Golden corydalis (*Corydalis aurea*)
## Fumitory Family (Fumariaceae)

**DESCRIPTION:** Glabrous, annual or biennial. **Stems** ascending or prostrate, 2-16 in (6-40 cm) long. **Leaves** alternate; the blades are parsley-like, deeply 2- to 4-times divided into narrow segments. **Inflorescence** several-flowered from leaf axils. **Flowers** are yellow, pea-like, at least ½ in (12-18 mm) long, elongate, with upper and lower petals longer than the lateral 2 and a pouch-like spur at the base. **Fruits** linear, bean-like, ½-1 in (15-30 mm) long, constricted between the seeds, curved and pendulous at maturity.

**HABITAT AND RANGE:** Silty or gravelly soil of desert shrub, sagebrush and pinyon-juniper habitats. Throughout temperate North America except the southeast and Pacific slope. Found in ARCH, BEAR, BRCA, CANY, CARE, GLCA, GRST, HOVE, NABR, and ZION.

**NOTES:** Navajo used the plant to treat diarrhea, and a lotion made from the plant was used to treat backache and sores. The seeds of golden corydalis have oily bodies that attract ants which then transport the seeds underground to their nests to store for food, but some will be forgotten and grow into new plants. While edible to ants, the oily bodies repel deer mice, which might otherwise forage on the seeds. Golden corydalis may be toxic to livestock, which explains why this colorful plant is often one of the few wildflowers present in heavily grazed pastures.

## Broom flax (*Linum aristatum*)
### Flax Family (Linaceae)

**DESCRIPTION:** Glabrous, taprooted annual. **Stems** erect, branched near the base, 9-16 in (8-40 cm) high. **Leaves** are alternate, linear, up to ½ in (3-15 mm) long, appressed to the stem. **Flowers** are solitary at stem tips; each has 5 separate, yellow petals up to ½ in (8-12 mm) long with orange bases. **Fruits** are ellipsoid capsules less than ¼ in (3-5 mm) long.

**HABITAT AND RANGE:** Dunes and other sandy habitats in blackbrush, sand sagebrush and pinyon-juniper communities. Utah and Colorado south to Arizona through Texas. Found in ARCH, BEAR, CANY, CARE, GLCA, GRST, HOVE, NABR, and ZION.

**NOTES:** There are several species of yellow flax in our area: small yellow flax (*L. australe*) is also an annual, but is not usually branched at the base; Utah yellow flax (*L. subteres*) is a short-lived perennial with larger flowers and capsules subtended by the persistent calyx; and perennial yellow flax (*L. kingii*) is a perennial usually found in clay soils. Flax petals fall off the flower with even the slightest touch, thus museum specimens almost never have fully intact blossoms.

## White-stem blazingstar (*Mentzelia albicaulis*)
### Blazingstar Family (Loasaceae)

**DESCRIPTION:** Taprooted annual. **Stems** erect, glabrous, whitish, 4-16 in (10-40 cm) tall and often branched. **Leaves** are alternate, 1-4 in (3-10 cm) long, deeply divided into numerous, narrow, well-spaced pinnate lobes and covered with curved hairs. **Flowers** occur in terminal clusters or upper leaf axils and have 5 separate, yellow petals ¼ in (3-7 mm) long with a thick base that is the ovary. **Fruits** are hairy, cylindrical capsules ⅓-1 in (8-22 mm) long with sepals on top.

**HABITAT AND RANGE:** Desert, sagebrush and pinyon-juniper habitats. Throughout western North America. Known from ARCH, BEAR, CANY, CARE, GLCA, GRST, HOVE, RABR, and ZION.

**NOTES:** Other blazingstars with pinnately lobed leaves have larger flowers. Crushed seeds were used by Hopi and Navajo to treat toothache. Research in Nevada showed that white-stem blazingstar was one of the first species to recolonize after nuclear tests.

106

# Desert stickleaf
## (*Mentzelia multiflora*)
## Blazingstar Family
## (Loasaceae)

**DESCRIPTION:** Taprooted biennial or perennial. **Stems** erect, short-hairy, whitish, 6-32 in (15-80 cm) tall and usually branched. **Leaves** are alternate, narrow, 1-5 in (3-12 cm) long, with numerous rounded lobes and covered with curved hairs. **Flowers** are solitary in axils of leaf-like bracts and apparently have 10 separate, yellow petals ½ in (12-18 mm) long and a thick base that is the ovary. **Fruits** are hairy, conical capsules ½-1 in (11-25 mm) long with sepals on top.

**HABITAT AND RANGE:** Usually sandy soils in desert shrub and sagebrush communities. Deserts and western Great Plains from California east to Nebraska and Texas. Found in ARCH, BEAR, BRCA, CANY, CARE, GLCA, GRST, NABR, and RABR.

**NOTES:** The fishhook-like hairs on the foliage cause them to cling like velcro. Flowers of desert stickleaf have 5 petals and usually 5 petal-like stamens that are narrower than the true petals. Cronquist's stickleaf (*M. marginata*, right), endemic to the Colorado Plateau, is similar but has reddish bark underneath the white outer bark and hairy petals. Wing-seed stickleaf (*M. pterosperma*) has more bowl-shaped capsules.

107

# Lavender evening-primrose (*Calylophus lavandulifolius*)
## Evening-primrose Family  (Onagraceae)

**DESCRIPTION:** Hairy perennial with a woody base. **Stems** numerous, unbranched, erect or ascending, 1-8 in (2-20 cm) tall. **Leaves** are alternate on the stem, ¼-1½ in (5-35 mm) long and narrowly oblanceolate. **Inflorescence** of solitary flowers in upper leaf axils. **Flowers** have a narrow, reddish tube 1-3 in (3-8 cm) long, flaring to 4 wrinkled, yellow petals ½-1 in (15-25 mm) long mounted on top of the slender ovary. **Fruits** a narrowly ellipsoid capsule about ½ in (1-2 cm) long.

**HABITAT AND RANGE:** Great Basin east through the deserts to the western Great Plains of South Dakota through Texas. Found in BEAR, BRCA, CANY, CARE, GLCA, GRST, and NABR.

**NOTES:** The flowers fade to orange or purple. The stigmas of true evening primroses (e.g., bronze evening-primrose, P. 110) are 4-cleft, while those of lavender evening primrose are square or disk-shaped.

# Alice's suncup (*Camissonia eastwoodiae*)
## Evening-primrose Family (Onagraceae)

**DESCRIPTION:** Mostly glabrous annual. **Stems** erect, 2-12 in (6-30 cm) tall. **Leaves** are mainly basal and have an ovate blade ½-3 in (1-7 cm) long with several small, wing-like leaflets on the stalk. **Inflorescence** of stalked flowers becomes narrow as it expands upward. **Flowers** have a narrow tube expanding to 4 yellow and red-spotted petals ¼-½ in (6-13 mm) long mounted on top of the ovary. **Fruits** a tubular capsule 1-1½ in (2-4 cm) long.

**HABITAT AND RANGE:** Heavy clay soil of barren flats in salt-tolerant desert shrub communities. Endemic to the Colorado Plateau of Utah and adjacent Colorado and Arizona. Found in ARCH, CARE, GLCA, and GRST.

**NOTES:** Several species are vegetatively similar to Alice's suncup: scapose suncup (*C. scapoidea*) has smaller flowers but is about the same height; Walker's suncup (*C. walkeri*) also has smaller flowers but is usually taller; showy suncup (*C. brevipes*) has longer fruits. Many species pairs in *Camissonia* include one large-flowered, outcrossing species that requires an insect pollinator and a small-flowered relative that is capable of self-pollination.

109

# Bronze evening-primrose (*Oenothera howardii*)
## Evening-primrose Family (Onagraceae)

**DESCRIPTION:** Glabrous or short-hairy, stemless, clump-forming perennial. **Leaves** are all basal, 1-8 in (2-20 cm) long and narrowly lanceolate. **Flowers** arise from axils of leaves; each has a narrow tube 2-4 in (5-10 cm) long expanding to 4 yellow petals 1-3 in (3-7 cm) long with the ovary below. **Fruits** hidden among the basal leaves are woody, ovoid, capsules 1-2 in (3-5 cm) long with 4 wings.

**HABITAT AND RANGE:** Gravelly or clay soil of slopes and stream terraces in desert shrub and pinyon-juniper habitats. Nevada east to Kansas and Texas. Found in BEAR, BRCA, CANY, CARE, GRST, and ZION.

**NOTES:** Yellow evening-primrose (*O. flava*) is also common, but has smaller flowers and ragged-margined leaves. Tufted evening-primrose (*O. caespitosa*, P. 40) has white to pink flowers and warty fruits without wings.

110

# Skunkbush sumac
## (*Rhus aromatica*)
## Cashew Family
## (Anacardiaceae)

**DESCRIPTION:** Much-branched shrub 1-6 ft (½ -2 m) high. **Stems** supple, brown, becoming gray with age. **Leaves** are alternate and mostly glabrous; the blades are undivided or with 1 or 3 shallowly-lobed leaflets ½-2 in (1-5 cm) long. **Inflorescence** of small flowers clustered near branch tips before the leaves have expanded. **Flowers** have 5 pale yellow petals about ⅛ in (1-3 mm) long. **Fruits** are red, finely-hairy berries ¼ in (5-8 mm) long in globose clusters.

**HABITAT AND RANGE:** Usually gravelly or stony soil, often along streams or on sandstone canyon walls and rims in blackbrush, sagebrush and especially pinyon-juniper habitats. Throughout most of North America. Occurs in ARCH, BEAR, BRCA, CANY, CARE, GLCA, GRST, HOVE, NABR, RABR, and ZION.

**NOTES:** The form with undivided leaves (var. *simplicifolia*) is more common in dry, exposed habitats. Ripe fruits have a refreshing lemony taste, but are better sucked than eaten. The foliage is foul-smelling.

# Fremont's barberry *(Mahonia fremontii)*
## Barberry Family (Berberidaceae)

**DESCRIPTION:** Evergreen shrub up to 10 ft (3 m) tall. **Stems** have brown to grayish bark. **Leaves** composed of 5 to 9 rigid, waxy-blue leaflets that are holly-like and up to 1 in (1-3 cm) long with spiny-toothed margins. **Inflorescence** a small cluster of 3 to 6 flowers. **Flowers** have 9 yellow sepals and 6 smaller yellow petals ⅛ in (4 mm) long. **Fruit** is a bluish, few-seeded berry ½ in (12-18 mm) long.

**HABITAT AND RANGE:** Stony, gravelly, or clay soil of desert shrub and pinyon-juniper habitats. Intermountain deserts of Nevada to California and New Mexico. Occurs in ARCH, BEAR, BRCA, CANY, CARE, GLCA, GRST, NABR, and ZION.

**NOTES:** Navajo and Havasupai used the roots to make a yellow dye and Yavapai ate the berries. Apaches used the purple berries to dye their skin in ceremonies. Oregon grape (*M. repens*) is a low-growing shrub common in higher-elevation forested habitats.

# Roundleaf buffaloberry *(Shepherdia rotundifolia)*
## Oleaster Family  (Elaeagnaceae)

**Description:** Evergreen shrub to 7 ft (2 m) high. **Stems** branched; the twigs whitish with flake-like hairs. **Leaves** are opposite, stalked; the blades ovate, ¼-2 in (5-45 mm) long, silvery-gray above and whitish beneath. **Flowers** are solitary or few in leaf axils, small and yellowish with 4 petals. **Fruits** are ellipsoid berries up to ⅜ in (5-8 mm) long, roughly covered with gray, flakey hairs and with the remains of the calyx on top.

**Habitat and Range:** Sandy or stony soil of blackbrush and pinyon-juniper habitats. Endemic to the Colorado Plateau of Utah and Arizona. Known from BEAR, BRCA, CANY, CARE, GLCA, GRST, NABR, RABR, and ZION.

**Notes:** Havasupai believed that dust from the leaf undersides would cause blindness. Silver buffaloberry (*S. argentea*) has narrow leaves, thorny twigs and red berries.

# Birchleaf buckthorn *(Rhamnus betulifolia)*
## Buckthorn Family  (Rhamnaceae)

**Description:** Mostly glabrous shrub to 6 ft (2.5 m) high with deciduous leaves. **Leaves** are alternate and stalked; the blades 1-6 in (2-15 cm) long, obovate, sometimes with a blunt tip. **Inflorescence** many-flowered, hemispheric on stalks from leaf axils. **Flowers** are tiny, cup-shaped with 5 yellow-green sepals less than ⅛ in (1-3) mm long and 5 brownish petals smaller than the sepals. **Fruit** a black, ellipsoid berry ⅓ in (7-10 mm) long.

**Habitat and Range:** Moist canyon walls and hanging gardens, usually on sandstone. Nevada and Arizona east to Texas and south to Mexico. Found in ARCH, BEAR, CANY, CARE, GLCA, GRST, NABR

**Notes:** Birds eat the berries and spread the seeds.

## Blackbrush (*Coleogyne ramosissima*)
### Rose Family (Rosaceae)

**DESCRIPTION:** Highly branched, thorny, deciduous shrub 1-4 ft (30-120 cm) high with gray bark. **Leaves** have star-like hairs, are oblanceolate, up to ½ in (3-12 mm) long and occur in clusters at nodes. **Flowers** occur on tips of short branches, lack petals and have four yellow, fringed petal-like sepals ¼ in (5-8 mm) long with 20 to 40 stamens. **Fruit** is a glabrous seed ⅛ in (3-4 mm) long with a persistent style at the top.

**HABITAT AND RANGE:** Silty to sandy, usually stony soil of alluvial plains in blackbrush or pinyon-juniper habitats. Mojave Desert and Colorado Plateau from California to Arizona and Colorado. Found in ARCH, BEAR, CANY, CARE, GLCA, GRST, NABR, RABR, and ZION.

**NOTES:** Blackbrush can form unbroken stands across large areas of nearly level terrain. It is especially important at the boundary between the cold deserts of the Colorado Plateau and the Mojave and Sonoran deserts. The species is long-lived and has infrequent episodes of seedling establishment following rare events when winter precipitation is sufficient and seedling predation is low. After a rainstorm, the stems and foliage of blackbrush are very dark, accounting for its common name. Deer browse the plants in winter.

## Pallid milkweed (*Asclepias cryptoceras*)
### Milkweed Family (Asclepiadaceae)

**DESCRIPTION:** Lax perennial. **Stems** are 4-12 in (10-30 cm) long with milky sap. **Leaves** are smooth, blue-green, opposite, broadly ovate and 2-4 in (4-9 cm) long with short stalks. **Inflorescence** umbrella-like. **Flowers** are ⅜ in (8 mm) across with 5 yellow-green, spreading to reflexed petals and 5 purple, semi-circular hoods clustered around a central axis. **Fruits** are oblong and ribbed, 2-3 in (4-7 cm) long and borne erect on S-shaped stalks. Seeds have tufts of long hair at the tip.

**HABITAT AND RANGE:** All types of soil from desert shrub to pinyon-juniper habitats. Great Basin and Colorado Plateau north to southeast Washington and southern Wyoming. Found in ARCH, BEAR, CARE, GLCA, GRST, and NABR.

**NOTES:** Native Americans used the root to relieve headaches and the milky sap for ringworm. Ruth's milkweed (*A. ruthiae*, P. 163) is similar but has hairy, more lance-shaped leaves and purple flowers.

## Big-seed milkweed (*Asclepias macrosperma*)
### Milkweed Family (Asclepiadaceae)

**DESCRIPTION:** Prostrate perennial with milky sap. **Stems** clustered and 2-10 in (6-25 cm) long. **Leaves** are opposite, lanceolate, 1-2 in (3-6 cm) long and wooly with wavy, upturned margins. **Inflorescence** hemispheric. **Flowers** are ⅜ in (about 8 mm) across and have 5 greenish-yellow, spreading to reflexed petals and 5 sausage-shaped hoods, each with a curved horn projecting out over the central column. **Fruits** are egg-shaped, 2-3 in (4-7 cm) long and borne erect on S-shaped stalks. Seeds have tufts of long hair at the tip.

**HABITAT AND RANGE:** Sandy soil of blackbrush, sagebrush and pinyon-juniper communities. Endemic to the Colorado Plateau of Utah, Colorado, Arizona and New Mexico. Found in ARCH, BEAR, CANY, CARE, GLCA, GRST, and RABR.

**NOTES:** This species is sometimes considered to be a variety of dwarf milkweed (*A. involucrata*), but the latter is found farther to the south and east. Big-seed milkweed and the rare Welsh's milkweed (*A. welshii*) have winged, saucer-like seeds that sail over their sand dune habitat in the wind.

# Yellow miner's candle (*Cryptantha flava*)
## Borage Family (Boraginaceae)

**DESCRIPTION:** Perennial. **Stems** usually several, unbranched, 4-16 in (10-40 cm) tall. **Leaves** are basal and alternate, 1-4 in (2-9 cm) long and stiff-hairy. **Inflorescence** of small clusters that unfold wand-like as the flowers bloom. **Flowers** are ⅜ in (8-10 mm) across, yellow and tubular with 5 spreading lobes. **Seeds** 1 or 2, smooth and hard-coated with sharp edges.

**HABITAT AND RANGE:** Sandy to silty soil of desert shrub, sagebrush and pinyon-juniper communities. Intermountain deserts from Wyoming to Arizona and New Mexico. Found in ARCH, BEAR, BRCA, CANY, CARE, GLCA, GRST, NABR, and RABR.

**NOTES:** Hopi used this species to treat throat cancer, and the Navajo powdered it to treat sore eyes. Golden miner's candle (*C. confertiflora,* pictured right) also has yellow flowers but usually 4 seeds per flower rather than 1 or 2. Although producing fewer seeds seems counter-productive, researchers have found that the surviving seeds of yellow miner's candle are larger and better protected (they are dispersed inside the spiny calyx) than other miner's candles, and so have a higher probability of germination. The seeds within each flower compete for resources, and only the fittest one or two survives to maturity.

# Narrowleaf puccoon (*Lithospermum incisum*)
## Borage Family (Boraginaceae)

**DESCRIPTION:** Perennial. **Stems** several, branched, 4-16 in (10-40 cm) tall. **Leaves** are alternate, linear, appressed-hairy and ½-2 in (1-5 cm) long. **Inflorescence** of several short-stalked flowers in upper leaf axils. **Flowers** are yellow with a long, narrow tube ½-1 in (15-35 mm) long and up to ¾ in (9-18 mm) across the 5 spreading, ruffled lobes. **Seeds** 4 per flower, smooth and shiny-gray.

**HABITAT AND RANGE:** Sagebrush and pinyon-juniper habitats. Great Plains and intermountain region from across southern Canada south to Mexico. Occurs in ARCH, BEAR, BRCA, CANY, CARE, GLCA, GRST, NABR, and ZION.

**NOTES:** Smaller, self-pollinated flowers are sometimes produced below the showier flowers. These so-called cleistogamous flowers tend to produce more seed than the showy blooms of early spring. Navajo chewed the plant to treat colds. Southwest stoneseed (*L. multiflorum*) has shorter flower tubes and produces a purple dye from the roots (museum specimens are often stained from the dye).

117

# Clustered broomrape *(Orobanche fasciculata)*
## Broomrape Family (Orobanchaceae)

**DESCRIPTION:** Yellowish to purple, sticky-hairy, leafless perennial 2-4 in (5-10 cm) high. **Inflorescence** of several long-stalked flowers at the end of the short, thick stem. **Flowers** are purple or yellow, about 1 in (15-30 mm) long, curved-tubular with 5 lanceolate lobes at the mouth. **Fruit** an obovoid, many-seeded capsule, ½ in (10-13 mm) long.

**HABITAT AND RANGE:** Most often silty soil from desert shrub to pinyon-juniper habitats. Throughout most of temperate North America, rare farther east. Found in ARCH, BEAR, BRCA, CANY, CARE, GLCA, GRST, and ZION.

**NOTES:** The yellow phase of clustered broom-rape (shown here) is uncommon compared to the purple phase. The plants are parasitic on the roots of neighboring plants, often members of the sagebrush genus. Germinated seeds first produce specialized stems called haustoria that attach to the roots of their host and then send shoots above ground.

# Redstem monkeyflower *(Mimulus rubellus)*
## Figwort Family (Scrophulariaceae)

**DESCRIPTION:** Sticky-hairy annual. **Stems** erect, sometimes branched, ½-8 in (1-20 cm) high. **Leaves** are opposite, well-spaced, lanceolate, up to ½ in (3-15 mm) long. **Flowers** are stalked and arise from upper leaf nodes; the yellow or red corolla is tubular and about ⅜ in (6-10 mm) long with 5 unequal lobes at the mouth. **Fruit** is an ovoid capsule about ¼ in (4-7 mm) long, hidden in the calyx.

**HABITAT AND RANGE:** Sites that are vernally moist but become dry later in the year in blackbrush, sagebrush and pinyon-juniper habitats. Wyoming south to California through Texas and Mexico. Found in BEAR, BRCA, CANY, GLCA, GRST, HOVE, NABR, and ZION.

**NOTES:** Ciliate hairs along the upper margins of the calyx teeth help distinguish redstem monkeyflower from other annual monkeyflowers. Suksdorf's mon-keyflower (*M. suksdorfii*) is a more compact plant with overlapping leaves. Seep monkeyflower (*M. floribundus*) has stalked leaves and often occurs in more perennially moist sites.

# Goldenhead (*Acamptopappus sphaerocephalus*)
## Sunflower Family (Asteraceae)

**DESCRIPTION:** Branched, hemispheric shrub to 2 ft (60 cm) high. **Leaves** are alternate, erect, linear-oblanceolate, glabrous and ¼-1 in (5-25 mm) long. **Heads** on branch tips, ¼ in (4-7 mm) high. Involucral bracts overlap and are oval and scale-like with yellow-green centers and membranous margins. **Disk flowers** yellow, about ⅛ in (2-5 mm) long. **Ray flowers** absent. **Seeds** white-wooly topped by coarse bristles.

**HABITAT AND RANGE:** Sandy or clayey soil of desert shrub and blackbrush habitats. Arizona and California to southern Utah and adjacent Nevada. Found at lower elevations in GLCA, GRST, and ZION.

**NOTES:** More common in the Mojave and Sonoran deserts. Goldenhead superficially resembles rabbitbrush (*Chrysothamnus*) and goldenbush (*Haplopappus*), but blooms in the early spring rather than late summer or fall. A recent study found that goldenhead seedlings are more likely to be established on the north side of other shrubs where they are partially shaded.

# Noddinghead
## (*Enceliopsis nutans*)
## Sunflower Family (Asteraceae)

**DESCRIPTION:** Perennial. **Stems** leafless, 4-10 in (10-25 cm) tall. **Leaves** all basal; the rounded blades are sparsely short-hairy and 1-3 in (2-8 cm) long. **Heads** solitary, about ½ in (1-2 cm) high and 1½ in (2-3.5 cm) wide. Involucral bracts are narrowly lance-shaped and overlapping. **Disk flowers** yellow. **Ray flowers** absent. **Seeds** are covered with long, stiff, erect hairs but lack a pappus.

**HABITAT AND RANGE:** Sandy or more often clay soils of desert shrub and salt desert shrub habitats. Endemic to the Colorado Plateau of Utah and Colorado. Occurs in ARCH.

**NOTES.** Stems flop to the ground once the flowers have been pollinated, suggesting that the seeds may be distributed by ants.

# Nakedstem (*Enceliopsis nudicaulis*)
## Sunflower Family (Asteraceae)

**DESCRIPTION:** Perennial. **Stems** leafless, 4-20 in (10-50 cm) high. **Leaves** are all basal; the blades 1-4 in (2-9 cm) long, rounded, grayish with dense, short hair. **Heads** solitary and ½-1 in (13-22 mm) high. Involucral bracts overlap and are narrowly lance-shaped. **Disk flowers** orange. **Ray flowers** 11 to 28, yellow, shallowly 3-lobed at the tip. **Seeds** have stiff, long hairs and are flat with 2 small spurs at the tip.

**HABITAT AND RANGE:** Sparsely-vegetated, gravelly, sandy or clay soil of desert shrub, salt desert shrub, blackbrush, sagebrush and pinyon-juniper communities. Colorado Plateau, Great Basin and Mojave deserts from Idaho south to California and Arizona. Found in ARCH, CANY, CARE, and GLCA.

**NOTES:** The heads often nod after the rays have withered. Nakedstem is relatively common and easy to spot against the brick-red badland soils near the west entrance of Capitol Reef National Park. Noddinghead (P. 119) is similar, but the heads have no rays and the flower heads droop to the ground at maturity.

# Stinking blanket-flower *(Gaillardia flava)*
## Sunflower Family (Asteraceae)

**DESCRIPTION:** Short-hairy perennial with resin glands. **Stems** often branched near base, 8-20 in (20-50 cm) high, leafless above. **Leaves** stalked; the blades oblong, up to 4 in (2-10 cm) long and deeply divided into widely-spaced, linear lobes. **Heads** about ½ in (15 mm) high. Overlapping involucral bracts are long-hairy. **Disk flowers** are light yellow and long-hairy. **Ray flowers** 8 to 12, are yellow, deeply 3-lobed at the tip. **Seeds** have 5 to 10, stiff, long-pointed membranous scales at the tip.

**HABITAT AND RANGE:** Mostly restricted to the Mancos shale or sandy alluvial soil along streams in desert shrub and salt desert shrub habitats. Endemic to the Colorado Plateau of Utah.

**NOTES:** The glands on the leaves produce a malodorous, bitter exudate. Hopi blanket-flower (*G. pinnatifida*) has broader and more crowded leaf lobes and purplish disk flowers. Hopi blanket-flower is the most common of the six native *Gaillardia* species found on the Colorado Plateau. Although all are very showy, the highway department prefers planting the introduced Indian blanket (*G. pulchella*) in its seed mixes, and this bright-orange species is becoming established on roadsides outside of Moab.

121

# Canyonlands blanket-flower (*Gaillardia spathulata*)
## Sunflower Family (Asteraceae)

**DESCRIPTION:** Perennial. **Stems** 2-14 in (5-35 cm) tall, are usually branched at the base. **Leaves** are alternate, stalked; the blades unlobed, pitted, resinous and up to 2 ½ in (6 cm) long. **Heads** are about ½ in (15 mm) high. Involucral bracts are lanceolate, overlapping and long-hairy. **Disk flowers** are yellow, long-hairy. **Ray flowers** 8 to 12, are yellow, deeply 3-lobed at the tip. **Seeds** have 5 to 10, stiff, needle-tipped scales at the tip.

**HABITAT AND RANGE:** Sparsely-vegetated, sandy, stony or clay soils of dry washes in salt desert shrub, desert shrub, blackbrush and sagebrush habitats. Endemic to the Colorado Plateau of Utah and Colorado. Occurs in ARCH, CANY, CARE, GLCA, and GRST.

**NOTES:** Leaves sometimes have broadly toothed margins. The rays often look a little scruffy. The closely related Parry's blanket-flower (*G. parryi*) is also endemic to the Colorado Plateau in southern Utah and northern Arizona and differs in having leaves only at the base.

# Erect gumweed *(Grindelia fastigiata)*
## Sunflower Family (Asteraceae)

**DESCRIPTION:** Perennial, branched above. **Stems** clustered, 1-3 ft (30-100 cm) tall. **Leaves** are alternate with toothed margins; those at the base are petiolate but those of the stem often without petioles; the blades 1½-3 in (4-7 cm) long. **Heads** are ⅜-½ in (8-11 mm) high on branch tips. Involucral bracts are resinous and overlapping; the outer with strongly recurved tips. **Disk flowers** yellow. **Ray flowers** absent. **Seeds** with 2 to 3 stiff, needle-like bristles at the tip.

**HABITAT AND RANGE:** Mostly sandy soil that receives a little extra moisture such as in canyons, on stream terraces or roadsides in desert shrub communities. Endemic to the Colorado Plateau of Utah and Colorado. Found in ARCH, CANY, and GLCA.

**NOTES:** The plant's native predilection for disturbed soil with extra moisture predisposes it to occupy roadsides. Rydberg's gumweed (*G. apahanactis*) is also rayless but is an annual or biennial. Curly-cup gumweed (*G. squarrosa,* right) has rays and is reported to hybridize with erect gumweed. Pueblo tribes in New Mexico used this plant to treat stomachache. The sticky resins produced in the hairs and involucral bracts of gumweeds have potential use in the manufacture of soap, varnish, paint, roofing, and lubricants.

# Prairie sunflower
## (*Helianthus petiolaris*)
## Sunflower Family
## (Asteraceae)

**Description:** Taprooted annual. **Stems** often branched, up to 3 ft (100 cm) tall. **Leaves** are alternate and sparsely stiff-hairy; the blades ½-3 in (1-8 cm) long. **Heads** are about ¾ in (18 mm) high. Involucral bracts overlap and are narrowly lanceolate and short-hairy. **Disk flowers** purplish with dark scales in between; the central scales have white hairs that give the disk a bi-colored appearance. **Ray flowers** yellow with rounded tips. **Seeds** have 2 stiff, pointed scales on top.

**Habitat and Range:** Sandy or disturbed soil of desert shrub and pinyon-juniper habitats. Throughout most of North America, especially in the West. Found in ARCH, BEAR, BRCA, CANY, CARE, GLCA, GRST, HOVE, NABR, and ZION.

**Notes:** Common sunflower (*H. annuus*) is often taller with wider leaves, and the scales between the disk flowers lack white hairs. It is more common on roadsides than prairie sunflower and has been cultivated for food and dye since pre-Columbian times.

# Hairy golden-aster
## (*Chrysopsis villosa*)
## Sunflower Family (Asteraceae)

**Description:** Long-hairy perennial. **Stems** branched, 6-20 in (15-50 cm) tall. **Leaves** are alternate, sometimes glandular; the blades up to 2 in (5 cm) long. **Heads** ⅜ in (5-10 mm) high. Involucral bracts are of different lengths. **Disk flowers** yellow. **Ray flowers** yellow with rounded tips. **Seeds** have long and short bristles at the tip.

**Habitat and Range:** Often sandy, sometimes disturbed soil of blackbrush, sagebrush and pinyon-juniper habitats. Throughout western and central North America. Occurs in ARCH, BEAR, BRCA, CANY, CARE, GLCA, GRST, HOVE, NABR, RABR, and ZION.

**Notes:** Hairy golden-aster is composed of numerous forms recognized by differences in the leaf shape and hairs of the stems and leaves. Navajo used this plant as a sweathouse emetic and a toothache remedy. Hairy golden-aster contains high concentrations of humulene, an essential oil useful for treating inflammatory diseases.

# Hyalineherb
## (*Hymenopappus filifolius*)
### Sunflower Family (Asteraceae)

DESCRIPTION: Wooly to nearly glabrous perennial. **Stems** often branched near the base, 4-24 in (10-60 cm) tall. **Leaves** are basal and alternate, 1-8 in (3-20 cm) long and pinnately divided to the midrib into widely-spaced linear lobes. **Heads** are up to ½ in (4-12 mm) high, few or several on each stem. Involucral bracts overlap and are wooly and ovate with rounded tips. **Disk flowers** yellow with small glands. **Ray flowers** absent. **Seeds** are hairy with several membranous scales at the tip.

HABITAT AND RANGE: Gravelly or sandy soil of desert shrub, blackbrush, sagebrush and pinyon-juniper communities. Great Plains and intermountain region of North America. Occurs in ARCH, BEAR, BRCA, CANY, CARE, GLCA, GRST, HOVE, NABR, RABR, and ZION.

NOTES: Numerous forms of this species have been recognized; most of our plants can be referred to var. *cinereus*. Hopi baked the leaves in bread, while Navajo treated coughs with a decoction of the plant. Hyalineherb is an important pollen source for beetles.

# Colorado rubberweed
## (*Hymenoxys richardsonii*)
### Sunflower Family (Asteraceae)

DESCRIPTION: Perennial. **Stems** are clustered, 4-16 in (10-40 cm) tall, unbranched and densely hairy at the base. **Leaves** are glabrous or nearly so, up to 5 in (2-12 cm) long, deeply divided into widely-spaced, crystal-dotted, linear lobes. **Heads** several, ¼ in (4-8 mm) high in a terminal, open inflorescence. Involucral bracts are crystal-dotted and form 2 rows; the outer is thickened. **Disk flowers** dark yellow. **Ray flowers** 9 to14, yellow with a shallowly 3-lobed tip. **Seeds** are densely hairy with several membranous, long-pointed scales at the tip.

HABITAT AND RANGE: Sparsely-vegetated soil of desert shrub, salt desert shrub, sagebrush or pinyon-juniper habitats. Western Great Plains and intermountain deserts from Canada to Arizona. Occurs in BEAR, BRCA, CANY, CARE, GLCA, and GRST.

NOTES: The plant is poisonous to livestock. Over a century ago a Colorado prospector discovered rubber in the roots of this species, but attempts to develop commercial rubber were unsuccessful due to its low quality. It was used by the Navajo as a ceremonial emetic and to make a lotion for ant bites.

# Four-nerve daisy (*Hymenoxys acaulis*)
## Sunflower Family (Asteraceae)

**DESCRIPTION:** Clump-forming perennial. **Stems** leafless, up to 16 in (40 cm) tall, often densely wooly at the base. **Leaves** are mostly glabrous, pitted, narrow, all basal and ½-4 in (1-10 cm) long. **Heads** solitary, about ⅜ in (5-9 mm) high. Involucral bracts are lance-shaped, overlapping and wooly at the base. **Disk flowers** dark yellow. **Ray flowers** 5 to 13, light yellow with a 3-lobed tip. Seeds are hairy with several membranous spine-tipped scales on top.

**HABITAT AND RANGE:** Sandy or gravelly, usually sparsely-vegetated soil of desert shrub, sagebrush and pinyon-juniper habitats. Great Plains and deserts of western U.S. and southern Canada. Known from ARCH, BRCA, CARE, GRST, and ZION.

**NOTES:** A dwarf form of four-nerve daisy (var. *nana*, pictured below) with leaves and stems only to 1 in (2 cm) long is endemic to the San Rafael Swell and found in CARE. Perky Sue (*H. argentea*) is similar to four-nerve daisy but differs by having a few leaves on the lower stem and is more restricted to the pinyon-juniper zone. Sundancer daisy is a commercially available cultivar of four-nerve daisy that is becoming popular with native plant gardeners in the west because it blooms profusely and requires little watering.

## Ragged rustlers (*Hymenoxys cooperi*)
### Sunflower Family (Asteraceae)

**DESCRIPTION:** Biennial. **Stems** unbranched below, 8-32 in (20-80 cm) tall. **Leaves** are glabrous to white-hairy, up to 4 in (10 cm) long and deeply divided into 3 to 7 widely-spaced linear lobes. **Heads** several, ¼ in (5-8 mm) high in a terminal, open inflorescence. Involucral bracts are hairy and of 2 lengths. **Disk flowers** orangish-yellow. **Ray flowers** 7 to 13, yellow with a shallowly 3-lobed tip. **Seeds** are densely hairy with several membranous, long-pointed scales at the tip.

**HABITAT AND RANGE:** Sandy or gravelly soil on slopes and ridges in sagebrush and pinyon-juniper communities. Deserts from southern Oregon and Idaho to California, Arizona and New Mexico. Found in GLCA, GRST, and ZION.

**NOTES:** This plant was used by Hopi to make a tea and a dye. Plants may live for more than two years but only rarely flower more than once before dying. Ragged rustlers differs from Colorado rubber-plant (*H. richardsonii*, P. 125) by having a single stem that lacks dense, white wool at the base.

# Gumweed tansy-aster (*Machaeranthera grindelioides*)
## Sunflower Family (Asteraceae)

**DESCRIPTION:** Perennial. **Stems** clustered, unbranched below, 1-12 in (2-30 cm) tall. **Leaves** are basal and alternate, sparsely short-hairy, spiny-margined and ½-2 in (1-5 cm) long. **Heads** ⅜ in (7-10 mm) high. Involucral bracts overlap and are sticky with whitish bases. **Disk flowers** yellow. **Ray flowers** absent. **Seeds** are hairy and have numerous long bristles on the tip.

**HABITAT AND RANGE:** Stony or clayey soils of blackbrush, sagebrush and pinyon-juniper communities. Western Great Plains and intermountain deserts from Canada south to Arizona and New Mexico. Occurs in ARCH, BRCA, CANY, CARE, GLCA, GRST, and NABR.

**NOTES:** A decoction of the roots was used by Hopi to treat coughs. Hoary tansy-aster (*M. canescens*) has white or blue ray flowers and smooth or blunt-lobed rather than spiny leaf margins.

# Basin daisy
## (*Bahia nudicaulis*)
## Sunflower Family (Asteraceae)

**DESCRIPTION:** Perennial forming small clumps. **Stems** branched, 6-22 in (15-55 cm) tall. **Leaves** are alternate and stalked; the blades sparsely short-hairy and 1-4 in (2-10 cm) long. **Heads** ⅜ in (7-11 mm) high are on long, naked stems. Involucral bracts overlap, often with stalked glands. **Disk flowers** orangish-yellow. **Ray flowers** yellow, veiny, 3-lobed at the tip. Seeds short-hairy with whitish scales at the tip.

**HABITAT AND RANGE:** Sparsely-vegetated, sometimes disturbed, sandy to clayey soil of salt desert shrub, desert shrub and pinyon-juniper habitats. Southern Montana south to northern Arizona and New Mexico. Found in ARCH, CANY, CARE, and GLCA.

**NOTES:** This species is divided into several forms based on involucral bract and leaf characters; most of our plants belong to var. *desertorum* which is a Colorado Plateau endemic. Basin daisy can accumulate toxic selenium and serve as an indicator of desert rangelands that are poorly suited for grazing.

# Narrow-leaf desert dandelion
## (*Malacothrix glabrata*)
## Sunflower Family (Asteraceae)

**DESCRIPTION:** Annual. **Stems** often branched, up to 16 in (40 cm) tall. **Leaves** are mainly basal, nearly glabrous, up to 2-5 in (5-12 cm) long and pinnately divided into widely-spaced linear lobes. **Heads** are about ½ in (8-13 mm) high. Involucral bracts are of 2 lengths; the outer much shorter than the inner. **Disk flowers** absent. **Ray flowers** numerous, yellow with toothed tips. Seeds have numerous long bristles at the tip, most of which easily fall off.

**HABITAT AND RANGE:** Sandy soil, often on stream terraces or mesa tops, of desert shrub, blackbrush and pinyon-juniper communities. North American deserts from southern Oregon and Idaho to Mexico. Known from ARCH, CANY, CARE, GLCA, GRST, NABR, and RABR.

**NOTES:** Leaves of sowthistle desert dandelion (P. 130) and Torrey's desert dandelion (P. 130) are much broader with closely-spaced lobes. Although distantly related to weedy dandelions (*Taraxacum* sp.), desert dandelions are native and have narrower and more deeply lobed leaves. In wet springs, desert-dandelion can turn the mesa tops bordering Lake Powell yellow with its abundant flowers.

129

# Sowthistle desert dandelion (*Malacothrix sonchoides*)
## Sunflower Family (Asteraceae)

**DESCRIPTION:** Annual. **Stems** often branched, 2-16 in (6-40 cm) tall. **Leaves** are mainly basal, glabrous, up to 5 in (12 cm) long and closely divided into wavy-toothed lobes.

**Heads** are ⅜ in (7-10 mm) high. Involucral bracts are of 2 lengths; the outer much shorter than the inner. **Disk flowers** absent. **Ray flowers** numerous, yellow with toothed tips. **Seeds** have numerous long bristles that easily fall off the top.

**HABITAT AND RANGE:** Sandy soil of desert shrub, blackbrush, sagebrush and pinyon-juniper habitats. Southern Oregon to Wyoming and south to Mexico. Found in ARCH, CANY, CARE, GLCA, GRST, and HOVE.

**NOTES:** Navajo used this plant to treat vomiting. Torrey's desert dandelion (*M. torreyi*, pictured left) is similar, but the heads are taller and often have gland-tipped hairs.

130

# Greenstem paperflower
## (*Psilostrophe sparsiflora*)
### Sunflower Family (Asteraceae)

DESCRIPTION: Perennial. **Stems** branched, 6-20 in (15-50 cm) tall. **Leaves** alternate, petiolate; the blades are 2-5 in (4-12 cm) long and sparsely short-hairy. **Heads** numerous, few-flowered, ¼ in (4-6 mm) high. Involucral bracts barely overlapping. **Disk flowers** 5 to12, yellow. **Ray flowers** 3 to 4, broad, reflexed, 3-lobed at the tip, becoming white and papery. **Seeds** with several long-pointed scales on top.

HABITAT AND RANGE: Sandy, silty or gravelly soil of desert shrub, sagebrush and pinyon-juniper communities. Mainly the Colorado Plateau of Utah, Arizona and New Mexico. Occurs in BRCA, CARE, GLCA, and GRST.

NOTES: Navajo used greenstem paperflower to treat diarrhea and as a poultice for wounds. It is poisonous to sheep and is unusual in having the ray flowers persist on the flower head long after seeds have ripened.

# Threadleaf groundsel
## (*Senecio flaccidus*)
### Sunflower Family (Asteraceae)

DESCRIPTION: Perennial with a woody base. **Stems** numerous, branched, wand-like, up to 3 ft (1 m) tall. **Leaves** are alternate, linear or linear-lobed, soft-hairy and 1-4 in (2-10 cm) long. **Heads** numerous, about ⅜ in (7-11 mm) high. Involucral bracts are soft-hairy, barely overlapping. **Disk flowers** yellow. **Ray flowers** 4 to 8 and sharply rounded at the tip. **Seeds** have numerous long bristles on top.

HABITAT AND RANGE: Sandy or gravelly soil of desert shrub, sagebrush and pinyon-juniper habitats. Southwestern Great Plains, Great Basin and Colorado Plateau from South Dakota and Wyoming to California, Arizona, New Mexico and Texas. Occurs in ARCH, CANY, CARE, and ZION.

NOTES: Both shrubby butterweed (*S. douglasii*) and broom groundsel (*S. spartioides*) have leaves with widely-spaced, needle-like lobes, but both have glabrous or nearly glabrous foliage.

# Basin butterweed
## (*Senecio multilobatus*)
## Sunflower Family (Asteraceae)

**DESCRIPTION:** Perennial. **Stems** branched at the base, 4-24 in (10-60 cm) tall. **Leaves** stalked, basal and alternate; the blades are deeply lobed, glabrous and up to 5 in (12 cm) long. **Heads** numerous, about ¼ in (4-9 mm) high. Involucral bracts glabrous, barely overlapping. **Disk flowers** yellow. **Ray flowers** 7 to 13, blunt at the tip. **Seeds** with numerous long bristles on top.

**HABITAT AND RANGE:** Gravelly or sandy soil of desert shrub, blackbrush, sagebrush and pinyon-juniper communities. Intermountain region from Idaho and Wyoming south to California and New Mexico. Found in ARCH, BRCA, CANY, CARE, GLCA, GRST, HOVE, NABR, and ZION.

**NOTES:** Yavapai used a decoction of the root to treat stomachache. Basin butterweed is common and widespread in the Colorado Plateau. Wooly butterweed (*S. canus*) has wooly, unlobed leaves and occurs on roadsides and pinyon-juniper habitats.

# Indian tea
## (*Thelesperma subnudum*)
## Sunflower Family (Asteraceae)

**DESCRIPTION:** Glabrous perennial. **Stems** 2-16 in (5-40 cm) tall, sometimes branched. **Leaves** mostly basal, are 1-4 in (2-9 cm) long and linear or divided into narrow lobes. **Heads** ¼-½ in (6-14 mm) high on long stalks. Involucral bracts few; the outer short; the inner veiny with white margins. **Disk flowers** yellow. **Ray flowers** about 8 or absent, yellow with toothed tips. **Seeds** with tiny scales on top.

**HABITAT AND RANGE:** Stony or gravelly, often sparsely-vegetated soil of desert shrub and pinyon-juniper communities. Great Plains, intermountain valleys, Great Basin and Colorado Plateau from southern Canada to Arizona and New Mexico. Known from ARCH, CANY, CARE, GLCA, and GRST.

**NOTES:** Rayed and rayless plants can often be found intermixed in the same population. Hopi used the leaves for tea, and both Hopi and Navajo used the leaves and flowers for a dye.

# Thrifty goldenweed (*Haplopappus armerioides*)
## Sunflower Family (Asteraceae)

**DESCRIPTION:** Tufted perennial. **Stems** unbranched, nearly leafless, 2-8 in (5-20 cm) tall. **Leaves** are resinous, linear-oblong, 1-3 in (3-8 cm) long. **Heads** are about ½ in (8-13 mm) high. Involucral bracts overlap and are resinous and rounded at the tip with a dark green spot. **Disk flowers** yellow. **Ray flowers** 4 to13, yellow, toothed at the tip. **Seeds** have numerous bristles at the tip.

**HABITAT AND RANGE:** Sandy or gravelly soil of desert shrub, sagebrush, blackbrush and pinyon-juniper habitats often on sandstone outcrops. Great Plains and Colorado Plateau from Saskatchewan south to Arizona and New Mexico. Known from ARCH, BRCA, CANY, CARE, GRST, HOVE, and NABR.

**NOTES:** Stemless goldenweed (*H. acaulis*, pictured right) is similar but usually has narrower leaves and pointed involucral bracts without a prominent green spot, and frequently occurs at higher elevations. Goldenweeds were originally described by Thomas Nuttall, the premier North American plant taxonomist of the early 19th century, and given the genus name *Stenotus*. Recent studies suggest that Nuttall was right, and his original name is employed by some authors.

# Five-needle pricklyleaf (*Thymophylla pentachaeta*)
## Sunflower Family (Asteraceae)

**DESCRIPTION:** Shrub-like, aromatic perennial. **Stems** are highly branched, 3-12 in (8-30 cm) tall. **Leaves** are nearly glabrous, opposite, ¼-1 in (5-20 mm) long and divided into few, widely-spaced linear lobes. **Heads** up to ¼ in (4-6 mm) high, on long stalks. Involucral bracts barely overlap, are all the same height and have dark, scattered, malodorous spots. **Disk flowers** yellow. **Ray flowers** about 13, yellow, up to ¼ in (4-6 mm) long with rounded tips. **Seeds** have 10 bristle-tipped scales on top.

**HABITAT AND RANGE:** Sandy or silty, sparsely-vegetated soil of desert shrub and blackbrush communities. Deserts from California and Nevada to west Texas and disjunct in Argentina. Found in CANY, CARE, GLCA, GRST, RABR, and ZION.

**NOTES:** Navajo ate the plant to hide their scent from deer. Pricklyleaf has relatively high concentrations of anti-oxidant chemicals in its foliage and might be useful as a dietary supplement. Dogweed (*T. acerosa*) also has linear leaves and dotted involucral bracts, but the heads have very short stalks.

## Salsify (*Tragopogon dubius*)
### Sunflower Family (Asteraceae)

**DESCRIPTION:** Biennial with milky sap. **Stems** 1-3 ft (30-100 cm) tall, inflated and hollow just below the head. **Leaves** are alternate, linear, nearly glabrous and 2-10 in (5-25 cm) long. **Heads** solitary, narrow, 1-2 in (25-40 mm) high. Involucral bracts barely overlap and are equal in height and have long-tapered tips. **Disk flowers** absent. **Ray flowers** numerous, yellow with blunt or rounded tips, shorter than the involucre bracts. **Seeds** have tapered tips that end in numerous feather-like bristles that spread apart.

**HABITAT AND RANGE:** Moist soil of fields, roadsides and riparian areas throughout the area. Introduced from Europe to most of North Ameria. Found in ARCH, BRCA, CANY, CARE, GLCA, GRST, HOVE, NABR, and ZION.

**NOTES:** The cooked roots are edible. Oyster plant (*T. porrifolius*) is vegetatively similar but has purple rays. The long beaks on the seeds of goatsbeard disperse by wind and by catching in the fur of animals or in our pant legs.

## Tropic goldeneye (*Viguiera soliceps*)
### Sunflower Family (Asteraceae)

**DESCRIPTION:** Annual. **Stems** 6-16 in (15-40 cm) tall, often branched below. **Leaves** are on the lower stem, petiolate, opposite or alternate; the diamond-shaped blades ½-2 in (1-5 cm) long and sparsely short-hairy. **Heads** ⅜ in (6-8 mm) high on long stalks. Involucral bracts overlap and are of similar length. **Disk flowers** oragnish-yellow. **Ray flowers**

10 to 13, yellow with rounded tips. **Seeds** are black, glabrous and without pappus at the tip.

**HABITAT AND RANGE:** Barren, clay soil derived from Tropic Shale in salt desert shrub communities. Known only from south-central Utah. Occurs in GLCA and GRST.

**NOTES:** Although this plant has a limited geographic and ecological range, it is abundant where it does occur in years with good winter rainfall. Southern goldeneye (*Viguiera annua* var. *longifolia*) has linear leaves and grows on Chinle barrens.

# Rough mule's-ears (*Wyethia scabra*)
## Sunflower Family (Asteraceae)

**DESCRIPTION:** Shrub-like perennial. **Stems** whitish, numerous, branched, 6-24 in (15-60 cm) tall. **Leaves** are alternate, linear-lanceolate, and 3-7 in (8-18 cm) long with scratchy surfaces. **Heads** ½-2 in (15-40 mm) high, solitary on branch tips. Involucral bracts overlap and spread out from the head. **Disk flowers** yellow. **Ray flowers** 10 to 20, yellow with pointed or toothed tips. **Seeds** are smooth with tiny scales on top.

**HABITAT AND RANGE:** Sandy or silty, sparsely-vegetated soil of desert shrub and pinyon-juniper habitats. Colorado Plateau of Arizona and New Mexico north to south-central Montana. Found in ARCH, CARE, GLCA, GRST, NABR, and RABR.

**NOTES:** Hopi and Navajo used the plant as a potentially lethal emetic. This plant flowers even in dry years. Arizona mule's-ears (*W. arizonica*) has basal leaves with elliptic blades and tends to occur in montane habitats.

# Brittlebush (*Encelia frutescens*)
## Sunflower Family (Asteraceae)

DESCRIPTION: Shrub to 3.5 ft (1 m) high. **Stems** branched, brittle and spreading-ascending. **Leaves** alternate, stalked; blades are about 1 in (2.5 cm) long, oval to triangular, and sparsely short-hairy. **Heads** are solitary on long stalks and ⅜ in (6-10 mm) high. Involucral bracts are narrow, overlapping and sometimes sticky. **Disk flowers** orange-yellow. **Ray flowers** 5 to 13, yellow, scalloped at the tip. **Seeds** have spreading hairs but no bristles at the tip.

HABITAT AND RANGE: Stony soil, often in washes within blackbrush, salt desert shrub, and pinyon-juniper habitats. Southern Nevada and Utah south to Mexico. Known from ARCH, CANY, GLCA, GRST, RABR, and ZION.

NOTES: The foliage can be mildly aromatic. Plants from the Colorado Plateau usually have green leaves with rough or glandular hairs, while those from the Mojave Desert have gray-green leaves covered by felt-like hairs and sometimes lack ray flowers. Brittlebush is drought deciduous, shedding some leaves (though rarely all of them at once) when soil moisture levels become too low.

# Spiny horsebrush
## (*Tetradymia spinosa*)
## Sunflower Family
## (Asteraceae)

DESCRIPTION: Shrub 1-4 ft (30-120 cm) tall. **Twigs** branched, spiny and wooly. **Leaves** are glabrous, about ½ in (1 cm) long and clustered alternately on the twigs. **Heads** up to ½ in (8-12 mm) high, 1 or 2 from leaf axils. Involucral bracts few, all the same height, wooly. **Disk flowers** 5 to 8, yellow. **Ray flowers** absent. **Seeds** are long-hairy with bristles at the tip.

HABITAT AND RANGE: Gravelly or stony soil of desert shrub, sagebrush and pinyon-juniper habitats. Intermountain region from southern Montana to California, Utah and New Mexico. Found in ARCH and CARE.

NOTES: The twigs of littleleaf horsebrush (*T. glabrata*) are short-hairy instead of wooly, and there are often more than 2 heads per leaf axil. Common horsebrush (*T. canescens*) is gray-hairy and lacks spines. Horsebrush species can be toxic to sheep.

# Golden mariposa (*Calochortus aureus*)
## Lily Family (Liliaceae)

**DESCRIPTION:** Glabrous perennial. **Stems** erect to ascending, sometimes branched above, 4-14 in (10-35 cm) tall. **Leaves** 2 to 4, linear, 3-8 in (8-20 cm) long. **Flowers** 1 to 5 from stem tips. Petals are yellow, 1-2 in (25-45 mm) long with a purple crescent above a yellow semicircle on the inner surface. **Fruit** is an erect, narrowly ovoid, 3-angled capsule 1-2 in (3-5 cm) long.

**HABITAT AND RANGE:** Silty, clay or gravelly soils in salt desert shrub, blackbrush and pinyon-juniper habitats. Endemic to the Colorado Plateau of Utah, Colorado, Arizona and New Mexico. Occurs in CANY, CARE, GLCA, GRST, and ZION.

**NOTES:** Golden mariposa can grow intermixed with the white-flowered sego lily (P. 82) in the Kanab area and occasionally plants intermediate in color are found. Bulbs were eaten by the Hopi and Navajo, but such use should be discouraged today or limited to visual feasting.

138

# Winged wild buckwheat (*Eriogonum alatum*)
## Knotweed Family (Polygonaceae)

**DESCRIPTION:** Short-hairy biennial or short-lived perennial. **Stems** 1-5 ft (30-150 cm) tall, unbranched below. **Leaves** are basal, linear-oblong, 1-8 in (3-20 cm) long. **Inflorescence** has clusters of short-stalked flowers in cup-shaped involucres toward the tips of long, spreading, naked branches. **Flowers** are cup-shaped with 6 yellow petals ⅛-¼ in (2-6 mm) long. **Seeds** are ⅜ in (5-9 mm) long with 3 longitudinal wings.

**HABITAT AND RANGE:** Gravelly or sandy soil primarily of sagebrush or pinyon-juniper habitats. Western North America from Wyoming south to Mexico. Known from ARCH, BRCA, CANY, CARE, GLCA, GRST, NABR, and ZION.

**NOTES:** In most cases plants flower once and then die. Navajo used the plant to prepare a lotion to treat rashes, and an infusion of the roots was employed to treat coughs. Redroot wild buckwheat (*E. racemosum*) is as tall as winged wild buckwheat but has white or pink flowers and wider leaf blades.

# Bent two-whorl buckwheat
## (*Stenogonum flexum*)
## Knotweed Family
## (Polygonaceae)

**DESCRIPTION:** Nearly glabrous annual 2-12 in (5-30 cm) tall. **Leaves** are basal and stalked; the blades orbicular and ½-1 in (1-4 cm) long. **Inflorescence** diffusely branched with small clusters of flowers at the end of naked, flexuous stems that point upward. **Flowers** have 6 yellow, short-hairy petals ⅛ in (1-4 mm) long. **Seeds** are glabrous.

**HABITAT AND RANGE:** Heavy clay soil of salt desert shrub, blackbrush and pinyon-juniper communities. Endemic to the Colorado Plateau and adjacent Uinta Basin. Known from CARE, GLCA, GRST, and RABR.

**NOTES:** Smooth two-whorled buckwheat (*S. salsuginosum*) has a basal rosette and linear leaves on the stem.

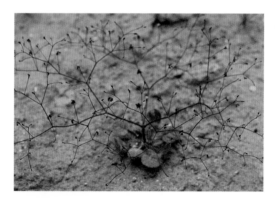

# Wetherill wild buckwheat (*Eriogonum wetherillii*)
## Knotweed Family (Polygonaceae)

**DESCRIPTION:** Long-hairy annual 2-12 in (5-30 cm) tall. **Leaves** are basal and stalked; the blades orbicular and ½-1 in (1-4 cm) long. **Inflorescence** reddish, diffusely branched with small clusters of flowers at the end of naked stems. **Flowers** have 6 yellow, glabrous petals less than ⅛ in (about 1 mm) long. **Seeds** are glabrous.

**HABITAT AND RANGE:** Sandy, silty or clayey soils in desert shrub, salt desert shrub, clay barrens, blackbrush and pinyon-juniper communities. Endemic to the Colorado Plateau. Found in ARCH, CANY, CARE, GLCA, GRST, NABR, and RABR.

**NOTES:** Bent two-whorl buckwheat (*Stenogonum flexum*, above) is nearly glabrous with larger flowers. Stokes wild buckwheat (*E. subreniforme*) has glabrous leaves and white or pink flowers.

140

# Desert trumpet (*Eriogonum inflatum*)
## Knotweed Family (Polygonaceae)

**Description:** Annual or biennial. **Stems** are glabrous, greenish-yellow to brownish, erect, 3-40 in (8-100 cm) high, inflated and hollow just below the inflorescence. **Leaves** are basal, stalked; the blades short-hairy, broadly ovate and ½-1 in (1-3 cm) long. **Inflorescence** diffusely branched with small clusters of flowers at the end of naked stems. **Flowers** have 6 yellow, short-hairy petals ⅛ in (2-4 mm) long. **Seeds** are glabrous.

**Habitat and Range:** Sandy to clayey or gravelly soils, often on alluvial plains or gentle slopes in desert shrub, salt desert shrub, blackbrush and pinyon-juniper communities. Southwest deserts from California to Colorado and south to Mexico. Known from ARCH, CANY, CARE, GLCA, GRST, HOVE, RABR, and ZION.

**Notes:** The size of the stem swelling is variable. Annual plants with greenish-yellow stems occurring on clay soils have been segregated as var. *fusiforme*. Havasupai boiled young leaves for food. The inflated stems are sometimes thought to be caused by insects, much like galls. However, the stems are always hollow, whereas galls are filled with cottony plant tissue and often a wriggling insect larva. Rather, the hollow stems may be a clever mechanical adaptation to reduce the weight of the stem and help keep the top-heavy branches aloft. Several other buckwheats, including the Zion wild buckwheat (*E. racemosum* var. *zionis*) have similarly inflated stems.

141

# Spindlestem
## (*Caulanthus crassicaulis*)
## Mustard Family (Brassicaceae)

**DESCRIPTION:** Glabrous-waxy perennial. **Stems** inflated, nearly leafless, 1-3 ft (30-100 cm) tall. **Leaves** are basal, petiolate; the blades 1-4 in (3-10 cm) long, lobed near the base but linear above. **Flowers** have 4 curved, purple petals almost completely enclosed by glabrous to long-hairy sepals up to ½ in (9-13 mm) long. **Fruits** are narrow, ascending to erect pods 3-6 in (8-14 cm) long with numerous seeds in rows.

**HABITAT AND RANGE:** Silty or stony soil in desert shrub, blackbrush and pinyon-juniper habitats. Colorado Plateau and Great Basin and Mojave deserts, Oregon to Wyoming south to California and Arizona. Occurs in BRCA, CARE, GLCA, GRST, NABR, and ZION.

**NOTES:** There are two forms of spindlestem; var. *crassicaulis* (pictured here) has long, spreading hairs on the calyx and a more inflated stem; var. *glaber* has a nearly glabrous calyx and a less inflated stem. The Panamint Indians prepared spindlestem by washing the leaves five or six times and then boiling like cabbage.

# Blue mustard (*Chorispora tenella*)
## Mustard Family (Brassicaceae)

**DESCRIPTION:** Annual. **Stems** branched, 4-16 in (10-40 cm) tall with sticky tack-like hairs. **Leaves** basal and alternate are stalked and ½-3 in (1-8 cm) long; the narrowly elliptic blades have wavy or toothed margins. **Flowers** have 4 pink to blue petals up to ½ in (9-12 mm) long. **Fruits** are ascending to erect, sickle-shaped pods 1-2 in (2-5 cm) long.

**HABITAT AND RANGE:** Disturbed soil of pastures, fields and roadsides in all vegetation types. Native to Asia and introduced to the western two-thirds of the U.S. Found in ARCH, BRCA, CANY, CARE, GRST, HOVE, and ZION.

**NOTES:** Plants have a mild musky odor produced by the tack-like glandular hairs. African mustard (*Malcolmia africana*, below) has branched rather than tack-like hairs. Blue mustard is a serious agricultural pest.

# African mustard
## (*Malcolmia africana*)
## Mustard Family
## (Brassicaceae)

**DESCRIPTION:** Annual, branched at the base. **Stems** 1-12 in (3-30 cm) tall, silvery with non-sticky branched hairs. **Leaves** are petiolate, alternate, and ½-4 in (1-9 cm) long with toothed margins. **Flowers** have 4 pink to violet petals about ⅜ in (6-10 mm) long. **Fruits** are widely spreading, linear pods, silvery with branched hairs and 1-3 in (4-6 cm) long.

**HABITAT AND RANGE:** Sparsely-vegetated, usually disturbed sites, especially on flats or canyon terraces. Introduced from Africa throughout the intermountain region. Occurs in ARCH, BRCA, CANY, CARE, GLCA, GRST, NABR, and ZION.

**NOTES:** African mustard has been increasing in recent years and is better able to colonize dry and relatively undisturbed sites than Blue mustard (above).

# Twistflower (*Streptanthus cordatus*)
## Mustard Family (Brassicaceae)

**DESCRIPTION:** Glabrous perennial. **Stems** unbranched, 6-24 in (15-60 cm) tall. **Leaves** basal and alternate; the basal are 1-4 in (3-10 cm) long and stalked with toothed margins; the stem leaves have smooth margins and clasp the stem at the base. **Flowers** have 4 narrow, purple petals surrounded by 4 yellow to purple sepals. **Fruits** are linear, flattened, slightly curved pods, 2-4 in (5-10 cm) long and up to ¼ in (6 mm) wide.

**HABITAT AND RANGE:** Silty or stony soil of sagebrush and pinyon-juniper habitats. Intermountain region from Oregon to Wyoming and south to California, Arizona and New Mexico. Known from ARCH, BRCA, CANY, CARE, GLCA, GRST, HOVE, NABR, and ZION.

**NOTES:** Navajo used the juice from the roots of twistflower as eye drops. Hare's-ear mustard (*Conringia orientalis*) is an introduced species with clasping stem leaves but yellow flowers, fruits that are round in cross-section and untoothed basal leaves.

144

# Crescent milkvetch (*Astragalus amphioxys*)
## Pea Family (Fabaceae)

**DESCRIPTION:** Silvery-hairy annual or more often perennial. **Stems** are up to 14 in (35 cm) long and nearly leafless. **Leaves** mostly basal, 1-5 in (2-13 cm) long with 9 to 21 obovate leaflets up to 1 in (2 cm ) long. **Inflorescence** up to 2 ½ in (60 mm) long, with 4 to 12 ascending flowers. **Flowers** pea-like, ½-1 in (10-30 mm) long, purple. **Pods** curved and slipper-shaped, 1-2 in (2-5 cm) long, green or sometimes purplish-spotted (when fresh), weakly 2-chambered.

**HABITAT AND RANGE:** Often sandy soil of desert shrub, blackbrush and pinyon-juniper communities. Nevada to Colorado, south to Arizona and New Mexico. Found in ARCH, BRCA, CANY, CARE, GLCA, GRST, NABR, RABR, and ZION.

**NOTES:** Two forms occur in our area, var. *amphioxys* and var. *vespertinus*; the latter has larger flowers. Cicada milkvetch (*A. chamaeleuce*) and Fisher milkvetch (*A. piscator*) are similar vegetatively, but the former has consistently purple-mottled pods, while the latter has pods that are distinctly 1-chambered. Like many milkvetchs, crescent milkvetch is poisonous to livestock, though rarely eaten due to its low stature.

# Milkweed milkvetch
## (*Astragalus asclepiadoides*)
## Pea Family (Fabaceae)

**DESCRIPTION:** Glabrous perennial. **Stems** are 3-24 in (7-60 cm) tall, unbranched and erect or ascending. **Leaves** are alternate, ovate, ½-2 in (15-60 mm) long with bases that clasp the stem. **Inflorescence** stalked, erect from leaf axils with 5 to 12 flowers. **Flowers** pea-like, ½-1 in (15-25 mm) long, light purple with a yellow upper petal. **Pods** ellipsoid, 1-2 in (2-4 cm) long, green with purple speckles.

**HABITAT AND RANGE:** Silty or clay, often saline soils in salt desert shrub and clay barren communities. Endemic to the Colorado Plateau of Utah and Colorado. Found in CARE and GRST.

**NOTES:** Milkweed milkvetch usually is associated with clay that contains selenium. It is uniq' among Utah *Astragalus* species in having simple, oval leaves.

# Bicknell milkvetch
## (*Astragalus consobrinus*)
## Pea Family (Fabaceae)

**DESCRIPTION:** Silvery, short-stemmed perennial up to 3 in (8 cm) tall. **Leaves** are basal and ½-2 in (1-6 cm) long with 5 to 11 obovate leaflets. **Inflorescence** is prostrate to ascending and has 2 to 7 flowers. **Flowers** are pea-like, pinkish with purplish tips and about ½ in (12-18 mm) long. **Pods** are about ½ in (11-19 mm) long, appressed-hairy and ovoid with a triangular beak.

**HABITAT AND RANGE:** Sandy or gravelly soil of sagebrush and pinyon-juniper habitats. Endemic to the Colorado Plateau of south-central Utah. Occurs in CARE.

**NOTES:** Bicknell milkvetch is locally common within a very small geographic area. Cicada milkvetch (*A. chamaeleuce*) has glabrous, often mottled pods; crescent milkvetch (P. 145) has curved, 2-lobed pods.

# Painted milkvetch (*Astragalus ceramicus*)
## Pea Family (Fabaceae)

**DESCRIPTION:** Silvery-hairy, rhizomatous perennial. **Stems** prostrate to ascending, wiry with few leaves, 1-16 in (3-40 cm) long. **Leaves** are alternate, 1-7 in (2-17 cm) long with 3 to 13 linear leaflets. **Inflorescence** ascending from leaf axils, 1-3 in (2-8 cm) long with 2 to 15 flowers. **Flowers** are pea-like, pinkish, less than ½ in (6-11 mm) long. **Pods** pendulous, inflated-ovoid, purple-mottled and ½-2 in (1- 3 cm) long with a short stalk hidden by the calyx.

**HABITAT AND RANGE:** Sandy soil of dunes, stream terraces and below sandstone outcrops. Great Plains of Montana and North Dakota south to Arizona and Texas. Occurs in ARCH, CANY, CARE, GLCA, GRST, NABR, and ZION.

**NOTES:** Hopi ate the sweet roots. Plants are difficult to detect when flowers and fruits are absent. Lesser rushy milkvetch (P. 34) has similar leaves but whitish flowers, linear pods and usually taller stems. The name '*ceramicus*' is a clever reference to the porcelain-like appearance of the spotted fruit pods.

147

# Rimrock milkvetch
## (*Astragalus desperatus*)
## Pea Family (Fabaceae)

**DESCRIPTION:** Nearly stemless perennial up to 8 in (20 cm) tall. **Leaves** basal, up to 5 in (12 cm) long with 5 to 15 sparsely-hairy leaflets. **Inflorescence** ascending with 3 to 15 flowers. **Flowers** are pea-like, purple, about ½ in (7-15 mm) long. **Pods** spreading, about ½ in (6-16 mm) long, bristly-hairy, purple-mottled, ellipsoid and usually curved.

**HABITAT AND RANGE:** Sandy or gravelly, often shallow soil in desert shrub or pinyon-juniper habitats. Endemic to the Colorado Plateau in the Four Corners region. Found in ARCH, BRCA, CANY, CARE, GLCA, and GRST.

**NOTES:** Two forms occur in our area: var. *desperatus* has larger inflorescences and curved pods; var. *petrophilus* has nearly straight pods and is found only in the San Rafael Swell. Monument Valley milkvetch (*A. monumentalis*) is vegetatively similar but has more linear pods.

# Yellow milkvetch
## (*Astragalus flavus*)
## Pea Family (Fabaceae)

**DESCRIPTION:** Perennial. **Stems** numerous, erect, 2-12 in (5-30 cm) tall. **Leaves** are alternate, 1-6 in (3-15 cm) long with 11 to 19 narrow leaflets covered with silvery, appressed hairs. **Inflorescence** erect with 6 to 30 crowded flowers. **Flowers** are pea-like, nearly erect, about ½ in (9-15 mm) long, yellowish and light purple with white to pink-purple centers. **Pods** erect, hairy, ellipsoid and up to ½ in (7-13 mm) long.

**HABITAT AND RANGE:** Clay or silty soil derived from marine shales or sandstones in desert shrub, salt desert shrub and pinyon-juniper habitats. Intermountain region from Southern Wyoming to Nevada, Arizona and New Mexico. Known from ARCH, CANY, CARE, GRST, and ZION.

**NOTES:** There are three forms of yellow milkvetch. Variety *flavus* has pale yellow to creamy white flowers; var. *argillosus* (pictured here) has pink to purple flowers; and var. *higginsii* has white flowers. Plants often have the ill-smelling scent of selenium.

148

# Hopi milkvetch
### (*Astragalus fucatus*)
### Pea Family (Fabaceae)

**DESCRIPTION:** Appressed-hairy perennial from a subterranean root-crown. **Stems** ascending, 2-14 in (5-35 cm) tall. **Leaves** are alternate, 1-5 in (2-13 cm) long with 9 to 17 narrow leaflets. **Inflorescence** erect with 9 to 25 ascending flowers. **Flowers** are pea-like, purple, up to ⅜ in (6-9 mm) long. **Pods** are about 1 in (17-30 mm) long, pendulous, appressed-hairy, inflated-ellipsoid, and purple-mottled.

**HABITAT AND RANGE:** Sandy soil of desert shrub and pinyon-juniper communities. Colorado Plateau of the Four Corners, disjunct in southern New Mexico. Occurs in CANY and GLCA.

**NOTES:** Growth form and fruits closely resemble painted milkvetch (*A. ceramicus*, P. 147), but Hopi milkvetch has basally attached hairs instead of T-shaped hairs.

# Freckled milkvetch
### (*Astragalus lentiginosus*)
### Pea Family (Fabaceae)

**DESCRIPTION:** Sparsely-hairy perennial. **Stems** ascending to erect and 6-24 in (15-60 cm) tall. **Leaves** are alternate, 1-6 in (3-15 cm) long with 13 to 23 leaflets. **Inflorescence** erect or ascending with 10 to 25 flowers. **Flowers** are pea-like, purple with white centers, pale pinkish-white, or whitish-yellow and just over ½ in (14-18 mm) long. The keel petal usually has a prominent purple spot. **Pods** are pendulous, ½-2 in (1-4 cm) long, purple-mottled and inflated-ellipsoid to recurved with a flattened triangular beak.

**HABITAT AND RANGE:** Silty or clay soils of desert shrub, salt desert shrub, sagebrush and pinyon-juniper habitats. Throughout the intermountain region from interior British Columbia south to California to west Texas and Mexico. Occurs in ARCH, BRCA, CANY, CARE, GLCA, GRST, RABR, and ZION.

**NOTES:** Although the plants are considered poisonous, the Zuni are reported to have eaten the pods. Freckled milkvetch is one of the most variable species of flowering plant in the western U.S. with over two dozen varieties recognized.

# Kaiparowits milkvetch
## (*Astragalus malacoides*)
## Pea Family (Fabaceae)

**DESCRIPTION:** Low-growing, short-hairy perennial. **Stems** prostrate to ascending, 3-10 in (7-26 cm) long. **Leaves** are alternate, 2-6 in (4-14 cm) long with 15 to 25 broad, blunt-tipped leaflets. **Inflorescence** ascending with 10 to 24 flowers. **Flowers** are pea-shaped, pale-purple and ⅜-1 in (7-21 mm) long. **Pods** pendulous, crescent-shaped, flattened, and 1-2 in (25-40 mm) long.

**HABITAT AND RANGE:** Clay barrens or silty soils of salt desert shrub, black-brush, sagebrush or pinyon-juniper habitats. Endemic to the Colorado Plateau of Utah. Found in CARE, GLCA, and GRST.

**NOTES:** Kaiparowits milkvetch was first discovered by B.F. Harrison in 1939 in the remote Kaiparowits Plateau of southern Utah.

# Preuss' milkvetch
## (*Astragalus preussii*)
## Pea Family (Fabaceae)

**DESCRIPTION:** Short-lived, mostly glabrous perennial. **Stems** are erect, branched and 4-16 in (10-40 cm) tall. **Leaves** alternate and 1-5 in (3-13 cm) long with 7 to 25 leaflets. **Inflorescence** erect with 4 to 25 flowers. **Flowers** face upward and are pink to purple (rarely white) and ½-1 in (13-24 mm) long. **Pods** erect, inflated-ellipsoid, short-stalked, ½-1½ in (12-34 mm) long.

**HABITAT AND RANGE:** Silty, gravelly or clay soils of desert shrub, salt desert shrub and blackbrush habitats. Mojave Desert and Colorado Plateau from California to Utah and New Mexico. Occurs in ARCH, CANY, GLCA, and GRST.

**NOTES:** Preuss' milkvetch has a strong ill-smelling odor of selenium. Stinking milkvetch (P. 35) has similar fruit pods, but whitish flowers. Birds, such as the verdin, have been observed sipping nectar from Preuss' milkvetch.

# Wooly locoweed (*Astragalus mollissimus*)
## Pea Family (Fabaceae)

**DESCRIPTION:** Long-hairy perennial with leafless stems 2-18 in (6-45 cm) tall. **Leaves** basal, 2-11 in (5-28 cm) long with 15 to 35 ovate leaflets. **Inflorescence** ascending with 10 to 25 flowers. **Flowers** are pea-like, spreading, purple and nearly 1 in (18-25 mm) long. **Pods** ascending, curved-ellipsoid, ½-1 in (11-25 mm) long and densely long-hairy.

**HABITAT AND RANGE:** Mostly sandy or gravelly soil, often along washes, on stream terraces or along roads, in desert shrub and pinyon-juniper communities. Western Great Plains and intermountain deserts from Wyoming and South Dakota south to Mexico and west to northern Arizona. Found in ARCH, BRCA, CANY, CARE, GLCA, GRST, HOVE, NABR, and ZION.

**NOTES:** This is a common, distinctive species that is addictive as well as poisonous to livestock. Ours is var. *thompsoniae*, yet another Colorado Plateau endemic named for pioneer botanist Ellen Powell Thompson. It is often one of the first plants to bloom, producing flowers even in January.

# Newberry's milkvetch
## (*Astragalus newberryi*)
## Pea Family (Fabaceae)

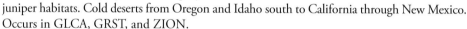

**DESCRIPTION:** Stemless perennial 1-5 in (2-12 cm) tall. **Leaves** are basal, spreading-hairy, 1-5 in (2-13 cm) long with 3 to 11 elliptic leaflets. **Inflorescence** ascending with 2 to 8 flowers. **Flowers** light purple and ½-1½ in (17-32 mm) long. **Pods** are ovoid, about 1 in (18-23 mm) long and densely spreading-hairy.

**HABITAT AND RANGE:** Sandy, silty or gravelly soil of desert shrub, sagebrush and pinyon-juniper habitats. Cold deserts from Oregon and Idaho south to California through New Mexico. Occurs in GLCA, GRST, and ZION.

**NOTES:** Ferron milkvetch (*A. musiniensis*) is also stemless but usually has fewer leaflets and more appressed-hairy foliage and pods. Cicada milkvetch (*A. chamaeleuce*) has purple-mottled pods. Crescent milkvetch (P. 145) has slipper-shaped pods with thin hairs.

# Sandstone milkvetch
## (*Astragalus sesquiflorus*)
## Pea Family (Fabaceae)

**DESCRIPTION:** Appressed-hairy, often mat-forming perennial. **Stems** are prostrate to ascending and up to 6 in (15 cm) long. **Leaves** alternate, ½-2 in (1-4 cm) long with 7 to 13 narrow leaflets. **Inflorescence** ascending with 1 to 4 flowers. **Flowers** are about ¼ in (6-8 mm) long and purple with white centers. **Pods** are oblong, flattened, ⅜ in (8-10 mm) long and purple-speckled.

**HABITAT AND RANGE:** Sandy soil and sandstone ledges in desert shrub and pinyon-juniper communities. Endemic to the Colorado Plateau of Utah, Colorado and Arizona. Found in CANY, CARE, GLCA, and GRST.

**NOTES:** Ground-cover milkvetch (*A. humistratus*) is vegetatively similar but has inflorescences with more flowers that are white- or cream-colored; rimrock milkvetch (P. 148) lacks leafy stems.

# Woodruff's milkvetch
## (*Astragalus woodruffii*)
## Pea Family (Fabaceae)

**DESCRIPTION:** Silvery-hairy, sparsely-leafy perennial. **Stems** numerous, erect, 10-24 in (25-60 cm) tall. **Leaves** are alternate, ½-3 in (1-7 cm) long, linear or with 2 to 9 linear leaflets. **Inflorescence** erect, with 8 to 45 flowers. **Flowers** about ¾ in (13-18 mm) long and pink to purple with white lower petals. **Pods** are erect, ellipsoid, flattened and about as long as the flowers.

**HABITAT AND RANGE:** Sandy or silty, barren soil of desert shrub and sand sagebrush habitats. Endemic to the Colorado Plateau of Utah. Occurs in CARE.

**NOTES:** This plant grows only on soils rich in selenium. San Rafael milkvetch (*A. rafaelensis*) is vegetatively similar but has pendulous pods and a more diffuse growth form.

# Fort Wingate milkvetch
## (*Astragalus wingatanus*)
## Pea Family (Fabaceae)

DESCRIPTION: Short-hairy perennial. **Stems** usually several, ascending, 6-18 in (15-45 cm) tall. **Leaves** are alternate and 1-3 in (2-7 cm) long with 3 to 17 narrow leaflets. **Inflorescence** ascending with 7 to 35 widely-spaced flowers. **Flowers** are ¼ in (5-8 mm) long and light purple with white lower petals. **Pods** are flattened, linear-elliptic, drooping, green or purple-spotted and about ½ in (9-15 mm) long.

HABITAT AND RANGE: Gravelly or clay soil of desert shrub or pinyon-juniper habitats. Colorado Plateau of Utah, Colorado, Arizona and New Mexico. Found in GLCA and NABR.

NOTES: Pliant milkvetch (*A. flexuosus*) has similar flowers and vegetation, but the fruits are nearly round in cross-section.

# Zion milkvetch (*Astragalus zionis*)
## Pea Family (Fabaceae)

DESCRIPTION: Silvery-hairy perennial up to 9 in (23 cm) tall with leafless stems. **Leaves** basal and 1¼-6 in (3-15 cm) long with 13 to 25 leaflets. **Inflorescence** ascending with 2 to 11 flowers.

**Flowers** purple, ¾-1 in (1-2 cm) long. **Pods** are spreading, crescent-shaped, often purple-mottled, ½-1½ in (1-4 cm) long and 2-lobed in cross-section.

HABITAT AND RANGE: Sandy soil of dunes or around sandstone outcrops in desert shrub, blackbrush or pinyon-juniper habitats. Endemic to the Colorado Plateau of Utah, Arizona and New Mexico. Found in CARE, GLCA, GRST, RABR, and ZION.

NOTES: Wooly locoweed (*A. mollissimus*, P. 151) also has many leaflets, but these are wider and covered with twisted hairs. Other milkvetch species in our area usually have fewer or wider leaflets.

# Northern sweetvetch (*Hedysarum boreale*)
## Pea Family (Fabaceae)

**DESCRIPTION:** Glabrous to silvery-hairy perennial. **Stems** ascending to erect, 6-24 in (15-60 cm) tall. **Leaves** are alternate, pinnately compound, 1-5 in (3-12 cm) long with 5 to 15 elliptic leaflets. **Inflorescence** erect from upper leaf axils with 5 to 45 well-spaced flowers. **Flowers** pinkish-purple, ½-¾ in (1-2 cm) long, pea-like with a blunt keel (lower petals) longer than the lateral petals. **Pods** pendulous, ½-3 in (1-8 cm) long, strap-like with indentations between each of the 2 to 8 segments.

**HABITAT AND RANGE:** Sandy or stony soil of desert shrub and pinyon-juniper communities. Across Canada south to Arizona through Texas. Occurs in ARCH, BRCA, CANY, CARE, GLCA, and GRST.

**NOTES:** The segmented pods are called loments and separate this genus from species of milkvetch (*Astragalus*). Flowers of western sweetvetch (*H. occidentale*) have at least one triangular, short sepal rather than 5 linear sepals as in northern sweetvetch. Northern sweetvetch is pollinated by at least 37 bee species. Because it is a nitrogen fixer and produces palatable forage, sweetvetches are potential candidates for use in rangeland restoration projects.

155

# Rydberg's sweetpea
## (*Lathyrus brachycalyx*)
## Pea Family (Fabaceae)

**DESCRIPTION:** Finely-hairy, vining perennial. **Stems** prostrate to ascending or climbing, 4-16 in (10-40 cm) long. **Leaves** are alternate, 1-4 in (2-9 cm) long with 3 to 6 pairs of leaflets and a terminal coiling tendril. **Inflorescence** erect from leaf axils with 2 to 5 flowers. **Flowers** are pea-like, pinkish-purple, ½-1 in (1-3 cm) long. **Pods** narrowly oblong, flattened, 1-2 in (3-5 cm) long, spreading to pendulous.

**HABITAT AND RANGE:** Sandy or gravelly soil along streams and in desert shrub or pinyon-juniper habitats. Intermountain cold deserts from southern Idaho to Arizona and New Mexico. Found in ARCH, BRCA, CANY, CARE, GLCA, GRST, NABR, and ZION.

**NOTES:** Seemly sweetpea (*L. eucosmus*) has a similar growth form but occurs in clay soils and has a 10-veined rather than 5-veined calyx. American vetch (*Vicia americana*, below) is another pea-like plant that has a tuft of small hair on the tip of the style, while sweetpeas have a line of hairs.

# American vetch
## (*Vicia americana*)
## Pea Family (Fabaceae)

**DESCRIPTION:** Nearly glabrous, vining perennial. **Stems** prostrate to ascending or climbing, 5-48 in (12-120 cm) long. **Leaves** are alternate, about 1 in (2-3 cm) long with 4 to 8 pairs of leaflets and a terminal coiling tendril. **Inflorescence** stalked from leaf axils, erect with 3 to 8 flowers. **Flowers** are pea-like, pinkish-purple, ½-1 in (13-22 mm) long. **Pods** narrowly elliptic, flattened, 1-1½ in (20-35 mm) long, spreading to pendulous.

**HABITAT AND RANGE:** Streambanks and other moist sites in sagebrush or pinyon-juniper communities. All of temperate North America except the southeastern U.S. Found in BRCA, CARE, GRST, and ZION.

**NOTES:** The pods are edible. The shape and pubescence of leaflets are variable. Dearpea vetch (*V. ludoviciana*) is an annual with smaller flowers. See Rydberg's sweetpea (above).

# Silvery lupine (*Lupinus argenteus*)
## Pea Family (Fabaceae)

**DESCRIPTION:** Short-hairy perennial. **Stems** erect, 6-32 in (15-80 cm) tall, often branched. **Leaves** are alternate and long-stalked with 6 to 9 leaflets ½-4 in (1-9 cm) long. **Inflorescence** erect, spike-like with 15 to 90 short-stalked flowers. **Flowers** are pea-like, blue with white centers and ½ in (8-14 mm) long. **Pods** are strap-shaped, flattened, hairy and about 1 in (2-3 cm) long.

**HABITAT AND RANGE:** Sandy, silty or gravelly soil in all habitats. Western Canada south to Mexico. Found in ARCH, BRCA, CANY, CARE, GLCA, NABR, and ZION.

**NOTES:** Two forms of silvery lupine occur in our area. Variety *moabensis* has flowers 12-14 mm long, while those of var. *argenteus* are smaller. Variety *rubricaulis* is found in the mountains of southern Utah and differs in lacking hairs on the upper surface of the leaflets. Showy lupine (*L. polyphyllus*, lower right) is also a perennial but has flowers with a more reflexed upper petal (banner) than silvery lupine.

157

# Short-stemmed lupine
## (*Lupinus brevicaulis*) Pea Family (Fabaceae)

**DESCRIPTION:** Low-growing, long-hairy annual. **Stems** up to 1 in (2 cm) long. **Leaves** basal, long-stalked with 4 to 8 leaflets up to ½ in (ca. 1 cm) long. **Inflorescence** is shorter than the longest leaves and has 4 to 12 flowers in a head-like cluster. **Flowers** pea-like, blue and white and ¼ in (5-7 mm) long. **Pods** are flattened-ellipsoid, hairy and about ½ in (ca. 1 cm) long.

**HABITAT AND RANGE:** Sandy or gravelly soil in salt desert shrub, blackbrush, sagebrush and pinyon-juniper communities. Intermountain deserts of southern Oregon to Wyoming and south to California and New Mexico. Found in ARCH, CANY, GRST, and ZION.

**NOTES:** Dwarf lupine (*L. pusillus*, below) and King's lupine (*L. kingii*) are also annuals but have longer and more erect stems and more elongated inflorescences.

# Dwarf lupine (*Lupinus pusillus*)
## Pea Family (Fabaceae)

**DESCRIPTION:** Long-hairy annual up to 10 in (24 cm) tall. **Leaves** are alternate, long-stalked with 3 to 9 leaflets ½-3 in (1-9 cm) long. **Inflorescence** erect, spike-like with 4 to 40 flowers. **Flowers** pea-like, blue with a white center, up to ½ in (8-12 mm) long. **Pods** are oblong and flattened, hairy and nearly 1 in (15-20 mm) long.

**HABITAT AND RANGE:** Sandy or gravelly soil of dunes and desert shrub, blackbrush and pinyon-juniper habitats. Western Great Plains and inter-mountain deserts from southern Canada south to California through New Mexico. Found in ARCH, CANY, CARE, GLCA, GRST, NABR, RABR, and ZION.

**NOTES:** The seed leaves (cotyledons) are unusual in that they persist at maturity, rather than shriveling shortly after germination as in most flowering plant species.

# Alfalfa (*Medicago sativa*)
## Pea Family (Fabaceae)

**DESCRIPTION:** Nearly glabrous perennial. **Stems** numerous, branched, erect, up to 3 ft (1m) tall. **Leaves** are alternate and short-stalked with 3 leaflets up to 1½ in (4 cm) long. **Inflorescences** borne in leaf axils are stalked, ellipsoid, ½-1½ in (1-4 cm) long and 10- to 40-flowered. **Flowers** usually blue or purple (rarely white), pea-like, ⅜ in (7-11 mm) long. **Pods** are coiled-circular and ¼ in (3-9 mm) across.

**HABITAT AND RANGE:** Moist riparian areas, irrigated fields and roadsides. Introduced from Eurasia. Occurs in ARCH, BRCA, CANY, CARE, GLCA, GRST, NABR, and ZION.

**NOTES:** Alfalfa is the most common broad-leaved hay crop in North America. The flowers can be white. Yellow alfalfa (*M. falcata*) has yellow flowers but is otherwise similar.

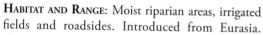

# Dune scurf-pea
## (*Psoralidium lanceolatum*)
## Pea Family (Fabaceae)

**DESCRIPTION:** Rhizomatous perennial with gland-dotted foliage. **Stems** erect, branched, 6-28 in (15-70 cm) tall. **Leaves** are alternate and stalked with 3 leaflets ½-2 in (15-50 mm) long. **Inflorescence** erect, spike-like with 5 to 40 flowers. **Flowers** white to blue, pea-like and ¼ in (5-6 mm) long. **Pods** are globose, hairy, gland-dotted and about ¼ in (4-5 mm) across.

**HABITAT AND RANGE:** Dunes or sandy soil of sand sagebrush or desert shrub habitats. Western Great Plains and intermountain deserts from southern Canada south to California through Texas. Found in ARCH, CANY, CARE, GLCA, GRST.

**NOTES:** Navajo used a lotion of the plant for sores. Prairie scurf-pea (*P. tenuiflorum*) is similar in most respects but has hairless ellipsoid pods and deeper purple flowers.

# Lambert's locoweed
## (*Oxytropis lambertii*)
## Pea Family (Fabaceae)

**DESCRIPTION:** Long-hairy perennial 6-20 in (14-50 cm) tall. **Leaves** are all basal, 2-8 in (5-20 cm) long with 7 to 15 pinnate leaflets. **Inflorescence** erect, long-stalked and spike-like, up to 8 in (20 cm) long with 6 to 30 flowers. **Flowers** are purple, pea-like and up to 1 in (17-25 mm) long. **Pods** erect, narrowly ellipsoid, ½-1 in (15-28 mm) long.

**HABITAT AND RANGE:** Sandy, silty or gravelly soil of desert shrub, sagebrush and pinyon-juniper habitats. Found in BRCA, CARE, and GRST.

**NOTES:** Silky locoweed (*O. sericea*) is vegetatively similar but has whitish or yellow flowers. Locoweeds could be mistaken for milkvetches (*Astragalus* spp.), but the former have nipple-tipped lower petals, while they are rounded in the latter.

# Rushy scurf-pea
## (*Psoralidium junceum*)
## Pea Family (Fabaceae)

**DESCRIPTION:** Nearly leafless, appressed-hairy perennial. **Stems** branched, whip-like, numerous with sunken dots, 18-36 in (45-90 cm) tall. **Leaves** are mainly basal, with 3 leaflets 1-2 in (20-45 mm) long. **Inflorescence** erect, linear with 7 to 20 widely-spaced, often paired flowers. **Flowers** are purple, pea-like and ¼ in (4-6 mm) long. **Pods** globose, long-hairy, up to 4 mm long.

**HABITAT AND RANGE:** Dunes or very sandy soil of sand sagebrush or blackbrush communities. Endemic to the Colorado Plateau of Utah and Arizona. Occurs in CARE, GLCA, and GRST.

**NOTES:** This plant is often locally abundant in its limited range in the Glen Canyon, Paria and San Juan river basins. From a distance the plant resembles a tall bunchgrass due to the slender, grass-like stems and narrow leaves.

## Blue sophora *(Sophora stenophylla)*
### Pea Family (Fabaceae)

**DESCRIPTION:** Rhizomatous, silky-hairy perennial. **Stems** erect, 6-16 in (15-40 cm) tall, often branched near the base. **Leaves** are alternate, ¾-2 in (2-6 cm) long with 7-15 linear, pinnate leaflets. **Inflorescence** erect, with 12 to 35 short-stalked flowers. **Flowers** light blue to dark purple, pea-like, ½-1 in (15-27 mm) long. **Pods** are linear, spreading on short stalks, 1-2 in (2-6 cm) long and constricted between the seeds.

**HABITAT AND RANGE:** Sandy soil of dunes and desert shrub or sand sagebrush habitats. Colorado Plateau of Utah and Arizona east through most of New Mexico. Occurs in ARCH, CANY, GLCA, and GRST.

**NOTES:** Blue sophora produces a number of alkaloid compounds that make it potentially toxic to livestock. White sophora (*S. nuttalliana*) has ovate leaflets, white flowers and ascending fruits, but is uncommon in southeast Utah.

161

# Stork's-bill
## (*Erodium cicutarium*)
## Geranium Family
## (Geraniaceae)

**DESCRIPTION:** Sticky-hairy annual. **Stems** prostrate to ascending, branched, 2-32 in (5-80 cm) long. **Leaves** are opposite, 1-5 in (2-12 cm) long; the blades with 9 to 17 sharply lobed leaflets. **Inflorescence** long-stalked from leaf axils with 2 to 8 flowers. **Flowers** have 5 pink petals ¼ in (3-7 mm) long. **Fruits** are 5-lobed capsules enclosed in the calyx with a beak 1-2 in (25-45 mm) long that eventually splits into 5 coiled or twisted needles.

**HABITAT AND RANGE:** Sandy, silty or gravelly, usually disturbed soil of roadsides and fields in all habitats. Probably introduced from Eurasia to all of temperate North America, but there is paleobotanical evidence suggesting that a form of the species is native. Known from ARCH, BRCA, CANY, CARE, GLCA, GRST, HOVE, NABR, RABR, and ZION.

Notes: Texas stork's-bill (*E. texanum*) has 3-lobed leaves; it is a native, warm desert annual occasionally found on the Colorado Plateau.

# Blue flax (*Linum lewisii*)
## Flax Family (Linaceae)

**DESCRIPTION:** Glabrous perennial. **Stems** numerous, erect, 6-24 in (15-80 cm) high and branched above. **Leaves** are alternate, linear, ½-1¼ in (1-3 cm) long and pointed upward. **Inflorescence** of several spreading to nodding, stalked flowers. **Flowers** have 5 separate, blue petals ½-1 in (1-2 cm) long with darker veins. **Fruits** are globose capsules ⅜ in (6-8 mm) long.

**HABITAT AND RANGE:** Higher desert communities, sagebrush and pinyon-juniper woodlands. Southern Canada south through the western U.S. to Mexico. Found in ARCH, BRCA, CANY, CARE, GLCA, GRST, HOVE, NABR, and ZION.

**NOTES:** Blue flax can occur as high as the lower alpine zone and is often used to landscape roadsides. Navajo used the plant to treat headaches, and farther north the stems were used to make baskets. Flax petals are only weakly attached.

# Pygmy fameflower
## (*Phemeranthus brevifolius*)
## Purslane Family
## (Portulacaceae )

**DESCRIPTION:** Succulent perennial. **Stems** ascending, branched, ½-2 in (1-5 cm) high. **Leaves** alternate, crowded, sausage-like, up to ½ in (4-13 mm) long. **Inflorescence** of short-stalked flowers from leaf axils. **Flowers** have 2 sepals and 5 pink petals ⅜ in (8-11 mm) long. **Fruit** an ovoid capsule 3-4 mm long.

**HABITAT AND RANGE:** Sandy or gravelly soil, often near sandstone outcrops in pinyon-juniper woodlands. Endemic to the Colorado Plateau. Occurs in ARCH, CANY, CARE, GLCA, GRST, and NABR.

**NOTES:** Navajo used an infusion of root bark to make a lotion. Small-flowered fameflower (*P. confertiflorus*) occurs in similar habitats as pygmy fameflower, but the flowers are borne at the top of a naked stem.

# Ruth's milkweed
## (*Asclepias ruthiae*)
## Milkweed Family
## (Asclepiadaceae)

**DESCRIPTION:** Low-growing perennial. **Stems** have milky sap and are only 2-6 in (5-15 cm) long. **Leaves** ½-2 in (1-5 cm) long, are short-wooly and blue-green with whitish veins. **Flowers** few, about ¼ in (about 6 mm) across and have 5 purple, reflexed petals and 5 reddish-purple, cup-shaped hoods each with a tiny horn in the open mouth. **Fruits** are smooth, ovoid, 1-2 in (3-6 cm) long, and borne erect on S-shaped stalks.

**HABITAT AND RANGE:** Sandy or clayey soil, usually in low-elevation desert shrub habitats. Endemic to the Colorado Plateau of Utah and Arizona. Found in ARCH, CANY, and CARE.

**NOTES:** Bassett Maguire, former professor of botany at Utah State University and an expert on tropical botany, named this species to honor his wife, Ruth. All 16 of the native milkweed species of Utah occur in the southern half of the state. See pallid milkweed (P. 115).

# Bare-stem larkspur
## (*Delphinium scaposum*)
## Buttercup Family
## (Ranunculaceae)

**DESCRIPTION:** Perennial with fibrous roots. **Stems** erect, glabrous, 8-24 in (20-60 cm) tall, unbranched. **Leaves** are mostly basal and stalked; the blades nearly orbicular, ½-1½ in (1-3 cm) long with obovate lobes like the fingers of a hand. **Inflorescence** narrow with stalked flowers along the upper stem. **Flowers** consist of 5 blue, spreading, petal-like sepals about ½ in (8-15 mm) long with a backward-pointing spur-like tube on the uppermost; petals are smaller, the upper 2 white, the lower 2 blue. **Fruit** a capsule ½-1 in (1-3 cm) long with 3 spreading lobes.

**HABITAT AND RANGE:** Silty, sandy or gravelly soil of blackbrush, sagebrush or pinyon-juniper habitats. Great Basin south through the Colorado Plateau. Found in ARCH, BRCA, CANY, CARE, GLCA, GRST, HOVE, NABR, RABR, and ZION.

**NOTES:** Our plants are var. *scaposum*. Plants were eaten by Navajo women to enhance fertility. Nuttall's larkspur (*D. nuttallianum*) has tuberous roots and leaves divided into more linear lobes. The "spur" on each flower of larkspur vaguely resembles the dorsal fin of a dolphin, which may help explain the genus name. Some larkspur populations vary in the amount of nectar provided to pollinators, with some plants producing large amounts ("bonanzas") and others offering little or none ("blanks"). Hummingbirds can be fooled by such plants into visiting many individuals searching for bonanza flowers (and dispersing pollen in the process), but bees are less likely to be fooled and tend to seek out other flowers instead.

# Cushion milkwort
## (*Polygala subspinosa*)
## Polygalaceae
## (Milkwort Family)

**DESCRIPTION:** Intricately-branched, thorny, low, mound-forming shrub 2-8 in (5-20 cm) high. **Leaves** are alternate, narrowly oblanceolate, short-hairy and ½-1 in (1-3 cm) long. **Inflorescence** of several flowers borne in the axils of leaf-like bracts toward the stem tips. **Flowers** are less than ½ in (8-12 mm) long and pea-like with a purple lower keel petal, 2 purple lateral petals and 2 united yellowish upper petals. **Fruit** is an ovoid capsule ¼ in (5-8 mm) long.

**HABITAT AND RANGE:** Gravelly or stony soil primarily in pinyon-juniper but also sagebrush and blackbrush habitats. Great Basin and Colorado Plateau deserts. Known from ARCH, CARE, GLCA, and GRST.

**NOTES:** Plants usually have some stiff, dead, thorny year-old stems mixed in with the flexuous green stems of the year. Thorny milkwort (*P. acanthoclada*) has white or yellowish-green flowers and is a shrub greater than 1 ft (30 cm) high.

# Glen Canyon hedgehog
## (*Echinocereus engelmannii*)
## Cactus Family (Cactaceae)

**DESCRIPTION: Stems** are cylindrical with 10 to 13 ribs, often solitary and 4-12 in (10-30 cm) tall, and succulent. **Central spines** 2 to 6 per cluster, 1-2 in (2-6 cm) long, whitish, flattened or angled, slightly curved. **Flowers** are borne below the apex on side branches. Petals pale to dark purple or pink, about 1½ in (3.5 cm) long and pointed at the tip.

**HABITAT AND RANGE:** Sandy or stony soil of blackbrush and pinyon-juniper habitats. Nevada, Utah, California and Arizona. Found in CANY, GLCA, GRST, and RABR.

**NOTES:** Yavapai ate the fresh fruit. Glen Canyon hedgehog is pollinated by bees seeking pollen rather than nectar. The stamens shed their pollen before the stigmas of the same flower are mature to promote outcrossing.

# Beavertail cactus
## (*Opuntia basilaris*)
### Cactus Family (Cactaceae)

**DESCRIPTION: Stems** 4-12 in (10-30 cm) tall, are composed of one or a series of several flattened, obovate segments (pads) that often form clumps or mats. **Spines** are all small, brown and bristle-like (glochids); true spines absent. **Flowers** are borne around the top of the pad. Petals deep rose, about 2 in (4-5 cm) long.

**HABITAT AND RANGE:** Sandy or gravelly soils of desert shrub communities. Colorado Plateau and Great Basin and Sonoran deserts from Nevada and Utah south to Mexico. Found in CANY, CARE, and GLCA.

**NOTES:** Pipe Spring prickly pear (*Opuntia aurea*) is also spineless but normally has yellow flowers. Although its range is restricted, it is locally common and frequently crosses with other *Opuntia* species (especially in Zion), producing plants with pink to red flowers.

# Small-flowered fishhook cactus (*Sclerocactus parviflorus*)
### Cactus Family (Cactaceae)

**DESCRIPTION: Stems** are globose, 2-18 in (5-45 cm) tall composed of nipple-like protuberances (tubercles) forming 8 to 15 longitudinal ribs. **Spines** brown to white, numbering 8 to 17, and up to 3 in (7 cm) long, occur on the tips of tubercles; at least one of the central spines is usually curved. **Flowers** are borne around the stem tip. Petals are rose to magenta or yellow and about 1 in (25 mm) long.

**HABITAT AND RANGE:** Gravelly or stony soil or rock outcrops in desert shrub and pinyon-juniper habitats. Endemic to the Colorado Plateau of Utah and Arizona. Found in ARCH, BRCA, CANY, CARE, GLCA, GRST, NABR, and RABR.

**NOTES:** Most fishhook cactus plants have hooked spines. Hedgehog cacti (*Echinocereus* spp.) differ in having straight spines and flowers on short side branches. Several fishhook cacti species are critically endangered due to over-collection, trampling, and herbivory by beetles.

# Common pricklypear
## (*Opuntia polyacantha*)
## Cactus Family (Cactaceae)

**DESCRIPTION:** **Stems** 2-10 in (5-25 cm) tall, are composed of one or many flattened, obovate segments (pads) that often form clumps or mats. **Spines** of several lengths, usually up to 4 in (9 cm) long, mostly straight and black to white. **Flowers** are borne at the apex of the pads. Petals yellow (below) or pink to deep rose (above) and about 1 in (3 cm) long.

**HABITAT AND RANGE:** Nearly all soil types of all desert habitats. Great Plains and intermountain grasslands and deserts from southern Canada south to Mexico. Occurs in ARCH, BRCA, CANY, CARE, GLCA, GRST, NABR, RABR, and ZION.

**NOTES:** There are several forms of common pricklypear, many of which are sometimes considered distinct species. The forms are separated by characters of the spines; color of the flowers has little bearing on taxonomy. Berry pricklypear (*O. phaecantha*) has yellow petals with red bases and edible, red, fleshy, spineless fruit. Although the fruits of common pricklypear are inedible, young pads can be cooked and eaten if the spines and glochids are removed.

167

# Fremont's indigo-bush
*(Psorothamnus fremontii)*
## Pea Family (Fabaceae)

**DESCRIPTION:** Shrub 1-5 ft (30-150 cm) tall. **Stems** branched, brittle, white. **Leaves** alternate, pinnately compound, 1-2 in (2-6 cm) long with 3 to 7 short-hairy and gland-dotted leaflets. **Inflorescence** from upper leaf axils, narrow, up to 4½ in (11 cm) long with 5 to 30 flowers. **Flowers** deep purple, pea-like, ⅜ in (7-10 mm) long. **Pods** ovoid, gland-dotted, ¼ in (4-6 mm) long.

**HABITAT AND RANGE:** Sandy, gravelly or stony soil of desert shrub, blackbrush or pinyon-juniper communities. Colorado Plateau and Mojave Desert from California east to Utah and Arizona. Occurs in CARE, GLCA, GRST, and ZION.

**NOTES:** Paiute and Shoshoni used a decoction of the roots for stomach ailments. Thompson's indigo-bush (*P. thompsoniae*, below) has gland-dotted twigs.

# Thompson's indigo-bush *(Psorothamnus thompsoniae)*
## Pea Family (Fabaceae)

**DESCRIPTION:** Densely branched, thorny shrub 10-32 in (25-80 cm) tall. **Stems** gland-dotted, short-hairy. **Leaves** are alternate, ½-2 in (1-5 cm) long with 7 to 17 gland-dotted leaflets. **Inflorescence** narrow, on stem tips with 8 to 25 flowers. **Flowers** pinkish to purple, pea-like, ⅜ in (8-11 mm) long. **Pods** are beaked-ovoid, gland-dotted and ¼ in (4-5 mm) long.

**HABITAT AND RANGE:** Sandy or gravelly, sometimes silty soil of

dunes in desert shrub, blackbrush, sand sagebrush and pinyon-juniper habitats. Endemic to the Colorado Plateau of Utah, Arizona and Colorado. Found in CANY, CARE, GLCA, and NABR.

**NOTES:** Thompson's indigo-bush is a species of conservation concern. It has potential as a medicinal plant with anti-bacterial qualities. Dotted indigo-bush (*P. polydenius*) also has gland-dotted stems, but the inflorescence is head-like and the calyx lobes are long-pointed.

# Redbud  (*Cercis canadensis*)
## Pea Family  (Fabaceae)

**DESCRIPTION:** Shrub or small tree to 10 ft (3 m) tall. **Stems** with smooth, gray bark and reddish twigs. **Leaves** alternate, stalked; the blades are glabrous, 1-4 in (3-10 cm) long and orbicular with a broad, basal notch. **Inflorescence** of 3 to 6 stalked flowers from mature twigs. **Flowers** are pea-like (but with a short upper banner petal), pinkish-purple and ½ in (12-15 mm) long. **Pods** oblong, flattened, 2-3 in (4-8 cm) long.

**HABITAT AND RANGE:** Streamsides, hanging gardens or canyon walls at low elevation. Eastern North America and across the southern U.S. Known from GLCA and RABR.

**NOTES:** Our plants are var. *orbiculata* which occurs in the southwest and is sometimes considered a separate species (*C. occidentalis*). Navajo ate the roasted pods, and Havasupai used the wood to make bows. Redbud is a favorite nectar and pollen source for native bumblebees and is now being planted in agricultural settings to enhance pollination of crop plants.

169

# Waxy dogbane (*Cycladenia humilis*)
## Dogbane Family (Apocynaceae)

**DESCRIPTION:** Glabrous perennial 4-14 in (11-35 cm) high with erect stems. **Leaves** opposite and stalked; the blades are oval and 1-2 in (4-7 cm) long. **Inflorescence** is above the leaves, composed of several long-stalked flowers. **Flowers** are pink, funnel-shaped, long-hairy; the tube ½-1 in (18-28 mm) long and nearly as wide at the mouth with 5 wrinkled, spreading lobes. **Fruits** are bean-shaped, 2-3 in (5-7 cm) long, long-hairy at the tip and contain numerous seeds.

**HABITAT AND RANGE:** Sandy or gravelly, gypsum-bearing soil, often on steep slopes, of mixed desert shrub habitats. California, southern Utah and adjacent Arizona. Known from CARE, GLCA, and GRST.

**NOTES:** Our plants are var. *jonesii* which can have two distinctly different-sized flowers in the same population. The species is listed as threatened under the Federal Endangered Species Act.

## Stickseed (*Lappula redowskii*)
### Borage Family (Boraginaceae)

**DESCRIPTION:** Annual. Stems usually branched, 2-14 in (5-35 cm) tall. **Leaves** are basal and alternate, linear, up to 1 in (1-3 cm) long and spreading long-hairy. **Inflorescence** of flower clusters that uncurl with age. **Flowers** are blue, tubular with yellow centers and are about ⅛ in (2-3 mm) across the spreading lobes. **Seeds** 4 per flower have thickened white margins with projecting prickles in 1 row.

**HABITAT AND RANGE:** Often disturbed silty, sandy or gravelly soil throughout the area. Native to Europe and western North America. Found in ARCH, BRCA, CANY, CARE, GLCA, GRST, HOVE, NABR, RABR, and ZION.

**NOTES:** Two forms occur in our area: var. *cupulata* (described above) has conspicuous white-margined seeds, while in var. *redowskii* the prickles are not joined by the white margin.

## Crinklemat
### (*Tiquilia latior*)
### Borage Family
### (Boraginaceae)

**DESCRIPTION:** Mat-forming perennial. **Stems** prostrate, branched, bristly, up to 8 in (20 cm) long. **Leaves** alternate, rigid, stiff-hairy, ⅜ in (5-10 mm) long. **Flowers** are solitary in leaf axils, pinkish, ⅜ in (8 mm) long, tubular with 5 spreading lobes. **Seeds**, 1 or 2, are hard-coated with roughened surfaces.

**HABITAT AND RANGE:** Sandy or gravelly soil of desert shrub and pinyon-juniper habitats. Endemic to the Colorado Plateau of Nevada, Utah and Arizona. Known from ARCH, CANY, CARE, GLCA, GRST, NABR, and RABR.

**NOTES:** Navajo used the plant to treat gastrointestinal problems. The beverage tequila comes from the blue agave (*Agave tequiliana*) which is unrelated despite the similar sounding name.

# Dwarf morning glory
## (*Evolvulus nuttallianus*)
## Morning Glory Family
## (Convolvulaceae)

**DESCRIPTION:** Perennial with long, spreading hairs. **Stems** branched, ascending to nearly prostrate, 2-10 in (5-25 cm) long. **Leaves** are alternate, lanceolate and ¼-1 in (6-20 mm) long. **Flowers** are short-stalked, bell-shaped, lavender with white centers and up to ⅜ in (4-9 mm) long. **Fruit** a few-seeded capsule 3-5 mm long hidden among the leaves.

**HABITAT AND RANGE:** Sandy or gravelly soil of desert shrub, sagebrush and pinyon-juniper habitats. Western Great Plains and warm deserts from Montana south to Arizona and Texas. Found in ARCH, CARE, GLCA, and GRST.

**NOTES:** Navajo inhaled the ground plant to relieve an itchy nose. In flower, this species is easy to see with its morning glory-like flowers. When the flowers are not present, it can be nearly impossible to find. Alkali weed (*Cressa truxillensis*) is vegetatively similar but has white flowers.

# Brittle phacelia
## (*Phacelia demissa*)
## Waterleaf Family
## (Hydrophyllaceae)

**DESCRIPTION:** Low-growing annual up to 6 in (15 cm) high with gland-tipped hairs. **Stems** prostrate to ascending, brittle, branched. **Leaves** alternate, spade-shaped, veiny, up to 1 in (2.5 cm) long. **Inflorescence** compact in leaf axils, several-flowered, curled at first but then unfolding. **Flowers** bell-shaped, 5-lobed, ¼ in (4-7 mm) long, purple; the stamens within the yellow corolla tube.

**HABITAT AND RANGE:** Clay barrens at lower elevations. Colorado Plateau from Arizona and New Mexico north into southwestern Wyoming. Found in ARCH, BRCA, CARE, GLCA, and GRST.

**NOTES:** After a wet winter or spring, clay badlands can become purple from the flowers of this species. Badlands phacelia (*P. cephalotes*) has a similar growth form and habitat, but the leaves are narrowly ovate and the flowers remain in a compact inflorescence.

# Heliotrope phacelia (*Phacelia crenulata*)
## Waterleaf Family (Hydrophyllaceae)

**DESCRIPTION:** Ill-smelling, annual with gland-tipped hairs. **Stems** erect, 4-24 in (10-60 cm) tall, branched above. **Leaves** are basal and alternate, ½-4 in (1-10 cm) long and narrowly oblong with numerous toothed lobes. **Inflorescence** branched with numerous, dense flowers; the branches coiled at first, becoming straight-ascending. **Flowers** bell-shaped, ⅜ in (6-10 mm) long, light purple with stamens extending beyond the 5 corolla lobes.

**HABITAT AND RANGE:** Sandy or gravelly soil of desert shrub and pinyon-juniper habitats. Warm and cold deserts from Nevada to western Colorado and south to Mexico. Occurs in ARCH, BRCA, CANY, CARE, GLCA, GRST, HOVE, and NABR.

**NOTES:** Hopi used the plant to treat injured horses. Contact with the plant may cause a rash. Moenkopi phacelia (*P. constancei*) and Torrey's phacelia (*P. integrifolia*) have less deeply divided corollas and leaves; the former species has hairier leaves than the latter. The seeds of heliotrope phacelia are conspicuously honey-combed; they are well worth putting under a hand lens! The odor of many of the glandular phacelias is described as "mephitic" in technical manuals, which is a fancy word for "skunk-like".

## Dwarf sand-verbena (*Abronia nana*)
### Four-o'clock Family (Nyctaginaceae)

**DIAGNOSTICS CHARACTERS:** Sticky-hairy perennial 2-6 in (5-16 cm) high. **Stems** leafless. **Leaves** are basal and long-stalked, the blades ovate and ¼-1 in (6-30 mm) long. **Inflorescence** umbrella-like at stem tips with 7 to 25 flowers. **Flower**s are light pink, trumpet-shaped; the tube ½-1 in (1-2 cm) long with 5 bilobed, wrinkled, spreading lobes. **Fruits** obovoid, ¼-½ in (5-12 mm) long with 5 longitudinal wings.

**HABITAT AND RANGE:** Clay or sandy soil of desert shrub and pinyon-juniper habitats. Mojave, Great Basin and Colorado Plateau deserts. Found in BRCA, CARE, GLCA, and GRST.

**NOTES:** Fragrant sand-verbena (P. 57) has leafy stems. Chemists have extracted compounds from the roots of dwarf sand-verbena that show promise for treating dementia.

## Winged sandpuff (*Tripterocalyx carneus*)
### Four-o'clock Family (Nyctaginaceae)

**DESCRIPTION:** Fleshy, glabrous or sparsely-hairy annual. **Stems** erect to ascending, 4-16 in (10-40 cm) long. **Leaves** basal and subopposite are short-stalked; the blades broadly ovate and 1-4 in (2-10 cm) long. **Inflorescence** umbrella-like at stem tips with 10 to 25 flowers. **Flowers** are trumpet-shaped; the pink tube is ½-1 in (1-3 cm) long with 5 white, bilobed, wrinkled, spreading lobes; the corolla ¼-¾ in (6-19 mm) wide. **Fruits** ellipsoid, ½-2 in (1-4 cm) long with 3 veiny, translucent wings.

**HABITAT AND RANGE:** Sandy soil of desert shrub, blackbrush and sagebrush habitats. Utah, Colorado, Arizona and New Mexico. Found in CANY, GLCA, GRST, and RABR.

**NOTES:** Small-flowered sandpuff (*T. micranthus*) has smaller flowers, less than ¼ in (6 mm) wide at the top. Fragrant sand verbena (P. 57) is a perennial having fruits with non-translucent wings.

174

# Showy four-o'clock (*Mirabilis multiflora*)
## Four-o'clock Family (Nyctaginaceae)

**DESCRIPTION:** Clump-forming, nearly glabrous perennial. **Stems** are prostrate to ascending, 12-20 in (30-50 cm) long. **Leaves** are opposite, stalked with lanceolate to ovate blades ½-3 in (1-8 cm) long. **Inflorescence** consists of terminal clusters of 6 stalked flower buds subtended by a 5-lobed cup. **Flowers** are magenta, funnel-shaped; the tube 1-3 in (4-8 cm) long with 5 bilobed, spreading lobes. **Fruits** are leathery, ellipsoid, and ⅜ in (6-11 mm) long.

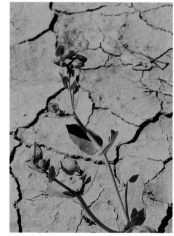

**HABITAT AND RANGE:** Usually sandy or gravelly soil of black-brush and pinyon-juniper communities. California east to Colorado and Texas. Occurs in ARCH, CANY, CARE, GLCA, GRST, HOVE, NABR, RABR, and ZION.

**NOTES:** Navajo used showy four-o'clock to treat rheumatism, and Hopi chewed the root to induce visions. Three varieties are recognized based on differences in fruit characteristics that are rarely available. Winged four-o'clock (*M. alipes*) has smaller flowers, a more deeply divided floral cup and tends to grow on barren clay soils. Hairy-tuft four-o'clock (*M. comata*, right) has smaller flowers and may occur on clay soils.

# Cancerroot
## (*Orobanche ludoviciana*)
### Broomrape Family (Orobanchaceae)

**DESCRIPTION:** Fleshy, purplish, sticky-hairy perennial. **Stems** are erect, leafless, unbranched and 4-12 in (10-30 cm) high. **Inflorescence** terminal and narrow, composed of numerous flowers, each subtended by small bracts. **Flowers** are purple and yellow, about 1 in (2-3 cm) long, bent-tubular with 5 short, unequal lobes at the mouth. **Fruit** an obovoid, many-seeded capsule, ⅜ in (7-10 mm) long.

**HABITAT AND RANGE:** Sandy, silty or gravelly soil of blackbrush, sagebrush and pinyon-juniper communities. Throughout most of western and central North America. Known from ARCH, CANY, CARE, GLCA, GRST, HOVE, NABR, and ZION.

**NOTES:** Cancerroot lacks chlorophyll and parasitizes other plants through underground attachments called haustoria. Species of sagebrush are typical host plants. Clustered broomrape (P. 118) may have either purple or yellow flowers at the end of long stalks.

# Long-flowered gilia
## (*Gilia longiflora*)
### Phlox Family
### (Polemoniaceae)

**DESCRIPTION:** Glabrous annual or biennial. **Stems** erect, branched, 6-24 in (15-60 cm) high. **Leaves** are alternate, ½-2 in (1-5 cm) long, linear sometimes with 1 to 3 pairs of linear lobes. **Inflorescence** diffuse, composed of single flowers on branch tips. **Flowers** are pale lavender to whitish, trumpet-shaped; the tube 1-2 in (3-4 cm) long with 5 spreading lobes ⅜ in (7-12 mm) long. **Fruit** an ellipsoid capsule about ½ in (7-14 mm) long.

**HABITAT AND RANGE:** Sandy soil of desert shrub, sagebrush and pinyon-juniper communities, sometimes on dunes. Great Plains of South Dakota and Wyoming south to the deserts of Arizona to Texas and Mexico. Found in ARCH, CANY, CARE, GLCA, GRST, and ZION.

**NOTES:** Hopi and Navajo used a decoction of long-flowered gilia to treat stomach ache. It is pollinated by long-tongued hawkmoths attracted by sugary nectar. Studies have shown that the concentration of sugar and quantity of nectar decreases with hot and droughty conditions.

# Bristly langloisia (*Langloisia setosissima*)
## Polemoniaceae (Phlox Family)

**DESCRIPTION:** Bristly annual forming small mats. **Stems** prostrate or ascending, ½- 6 in (1-14 cm) long, branched at the base. **Leaves** are basal and alternate and oblong with bristle-tipped triangular lobes, ½-1 in (1-2 cm) long. **Inflorescence** of bristly flower clusters at stem tips. **Flowers** are lavender with a tube ½ in (10-13 mm) long with 5 spreading lobes up to ¼ in (3-6 mm) long. **Fruit** a grooved capsule ¼ in (5-6 mm) long.

**HABITAT AND RANGE:** Gravelly soil of desert shrub, blackbrush and pinyon-juniper communities. Mojave Desert and western Colorado Plateau of California east to Utah and Arizona. Occurs in GLCA, GRST, and ZION.

**NOTES:** Three other species of langloisia, separated by flower and leaf shape, are sometimes united with bristly langloisia into one species. None of these other species occur in our area. With their distinctive, bristle-tipped leaves, *Langloisia* macrofossils have been reliably identified in Mojave Desert packrat middens that are nearly 15,000 years old.

# Longleaf phlox
### (*Phlox longifolia*)
### Phlox Family (Polemoniaceae)

**DESCRIPTION:** Soft-hairy perennial with a woody base. **Stems** prostrate to erect, branched at the base, up to 4-16 in (10-40 cm) high. **Leaves** are opposite, narrow, ½-3 in (1-8 cm) long. **Inflorescence** of few long-stalked flowers at stem tips. **Flowers** are white to pink with a tube ½-1 in (1-3 cm) long and 5 spreading lobes ½ in (7-15 mm) long. **Fruit** an ellipsoid capsule with a style ¼-1 in (6-20 mm) long.

**HABITAT AND RANGE:** Usually sandy or gravelly soil, mainly in sagebrush and pinyon-juniper communities. Throughout most of temperate, mountainous western North America. Found in BRCA, CANY, CARE, GRST, HOVE, NABR, and ZION.

**NOTES:** Plants in our area have a longer flower tube and shorter leaves than those from far north. Havasupai peoples made a decoction of desert phlox roots and used it as a poultice to treat body aches. Other phlox species in the Colorado Plateau have matted or clustered stems, shorter leaves, or notched petal lobes.

# Shooting stars
### (*Dodecatheon pulchellum*)
### Primrose Family (Primulaceae)

**DESCRIPTION:** Glabrous perennial. **Stems** are erect, leafless and 4-8 in (10-20 cm) high. **Leaves** are all basal, stalked; the blades oblanceolate, 1-4 in (2-10 cm) long. **Inflorescence** of nodding, stalked flowers, all arising from the stem tip. **Flowers** have 5 deep pink (sometimes white), upturned petals about ½-¾ in (9-20 mm) long exposing the black and yellow tube of stamens. **Fruit** an ovoid capsule about ½ in (7-17 mm) long.

**HABITAT AND RANGE:** Wet soil of hanging gardens, along streams and around springs. Throughout most of temperate western North America. Occurs in BRCA, GLCA, GRST, and ZION.

**NOTES:** The species is more common at higher elevations. Molecular evidence suggests that shooting stars are directly related to primroses (P. 179). The exserted anthers of shooting stars are "buzz pollinated" by large bees that shake pollen loose and transfer it to the receptive style through vibrations caused by their flight muscles.

# Cave primrose
## (*Primula specuicola*)
### Primrose Family (Primulaceae)

**DESCRIPTION:** Perennial with mealy-white foliage. **Stems** are erect, leafless and 2-12 in (6-30 cm) high. **Leaves** are stalked, oblanceolate with toothed margins and 2-7 in (6-18 cm) long. **Inflorescence** of erect, long-stalked flowers, all arising from the stem tip. **Flowers** are white to pink or light purple with a tube ⅜ in (7-12 mm) long with 5 spreading lobes ¼ in (4-8 mm) long. **Fruit** an ovoid capsule about ¼ in (5-8 mm) long.

**HABITAT AND RANGE:** Hanging gardens and streambanks. Endemic to the Colorado Plateau of Utah and Arizona. Found in ARCH, CANY, CARE, GLCA, and RABR.

**NOTES:** Silvery primrose (*P. incana*) has shorter leaves with mostly smooth margins. Primrose flowers come in two forms that promote cross-pollination: pin flowers have the round stigma elevated near the rim of the corolla tube and well above the short stamens. Thrum flowers are the opposite.

# Dwarf lousewort
## (*Pedicularis centranthera*)
### Figwort Family
### (Scrophulariaceae)

**DESCRIPTION:** Compact, glabrous, perennial. **Stems** 1½-3 in (4-7 cm) high. **Leaves** are stalked, alternate, lanceolate, 2-6 in (6-15 cm) long with numerous, broad, overlapping lobes with toothed margins. **Inflorescence** short, congested, with leaf-like bracts subtending the flowers. **Flowers** are yellowish, tubular and up to 1½ in (3-4 cm) long with a purple mouth and short, curled beak. **Fruit** is an ovoid capsule about ½ in (10-13 mm) long, hidden in the calyx.

**HABITAT AND RANGE:** Stony soil of pinyon-juniper habitats. Oregon and California east to Colorado and New Mexico. Occurs in BRCA, CANY, CARE, GLCA, GRST, NABR, and ZION.

**NOTES:** Louseworts are partially parasitic on the roots of neighboring plants. A decoction of the roots was given to Shoshoni children to treat stomach ache. Dwarf lousewort is one of the earliest flowering plants in pinyon-juniper habitats.

179

# Narrowleaf penstemon
## (*Penstemon angustifolius*)
### Figwort Family  (Scrophulariaceae)

**DESCRIPTION:** Waxy-glabrous perennial. **Stems** erect, unbranched, 8-24 in (20-60 cm) tall. **Leaves** are basal and opposite, fleshy, linear to lanceolate and 1-4 in (2-10 cm) long with long-tapered tips. **Inflorescence** of flower clusters surrounding upper leaf nodes which are spaced more closely above. **Flowers** are blue, ½-1 in (15-22 mm) long and vase-shaped with 5 unequal, spreading lobes and 4 fertile stamens and 1 hairy, sterile stamen within.

**HABITAT AND RANGE:** Usually sandy soil of blackbrush, sagebrush and pinyon-juniper habitats. Deserts and Great Plains from Montana and North Dakota south to Arizona and New Mexico. Found in CARE, GLCA, GRST, and HOVE.

**NOTES:** Leaves of fleshy penstemon (*P. carnosus*, right) and thick-leaf penstemon (*P. pachyphyllus*) are not long-tapered; flower clusters of the former are close together but widely-spaced in the latter. Loa penstemon (*P. ophianthus*) has sticky-hairy stems.

180

# Atwood's penstemon (*Penstemon atwoodii*)
## Figwort Family (Scrophulariaceae)

**DESCRIPTION:** Glabrous perennial with erect or ascending stems 5-20 in (13-50 cm) tall. **Leaves** basal and opposite, are 1-3 in (2-8 cm) long, lower leaves oblanceolate; upper leaves linear. **Inflorescence** sticky-hairy and composed of numerous short-stalked flowers in widely spaced whorls around the axils of upper leaves and bracts. **Flowers** are blue to lavender, up to ½ in (10-12 mm) long, tubular with 5 unequal, spreading lobes and 4 fertile stamens with 1 hairy, sterile stamen within.

**HABITAT AND RANGE:** Sandy, stony or clay soil in pinyon-juniper habitats. Endemic to the Colorado Plateau of south-central Utah. Found in GRST.

**NOTES:** Siler penstemon (*P. linarioides*) also has narrow stem leaves, but basal leaves are lacking. Blue- and purple-flowered penstemons are mostly pollinated by bees, while red-flowered species are pollinated by hummingbirds. The size of the flower dictates the type of bee that can pollinate the plant.

## Thompson's penstemon (*Penstemon thompsoniae*)
### Figwort Family (Scrophulariaceae)

**DESCRIPTION:** White-hairy, ground-hugging perennial. **Stems** mostly prostrate, 2-6 in (4-15 cm) long. **Leaves** are opposite, spoon-shaped to obovate and ¼-¾ in (6-20 mm) long with flake-like hairs. **Inflorescence** of few flowers in upper leaf axils. **Flowers** are lavender, up to ¾ in (1-2 cm) long, broadly tubular with 5 unequal, spreading lobes and 4 fertile stamens and 1 hairy, sterile stamen within.

**HABITAT AND RANGE:** Sandy or clay soil of sagebrush and pinyon-juniper communities. Southeast California and southern Nevada to southern Utah and northern Arizona. Occurs in GRST.

**NOTES:** Matt penstemon (*P. caespitosus*) has a similar growth form but greener foliage.

## Bluestem penstemon
### (*Penstemon cyanocaulis*)
### Figwort Family
### (Scrophulariaceae)

**DESCRIPTION:** Glabrous perennial with erect stems 8-24 in (20-50 cm) tall. **Leaves** opposite and basal, ¾-8 in (2-20 cm) long with wavy margins; basal leaves stalked but stem leaves stalkless. **Inflorescence** has numerous stalked flowers surrounding nodes of upper leaves and leaf-like bracts. **Flowers** are blue, up to ¾ in (14-20 mm) long, conical with 5 unequal, spreading lobes and 4 fertile stamens with 1 glabrous, sterile stamen within.

**HABITAT AND RANGE:** Stony and sandy or silty soil of pinyon-juniper communities. Endemic to the Colorado Plateau of Utah and Colorado. Occurs in ARCH, CANY, and GLCA.

**NOTES:** Bluestem penstemon has short-hairy anthers; Natural Bridges penstemon (*P. strictiformis*) has long-hairy anthers, and those of smooth penstemon (*P. laevis*) are glabrous. Most penstemons have sterile stamens which help prevent the wrong insects from entering the corolla tube to steal nectar.

# Moffat penstemon (*Penstemon moffatii*)
## Figwort Family (Scrophulariaceae)

**DESCRIPTION:** Short-hairy perennial with erect or ascending stems, 3-12 in (8-30 cm) tall. **Leaves** are basal and opposite, ½-2 in (15-60 mm) long; the basal have elliptic blades becoming narrower with wavy margins higher up the stem. **Inflorescence** sticky-hairy, of numerous short-stalked flowers clustered in axils of upper leaves and bracts. **Flowers** are sticky-hairy, blue, ½-1 in (15-25 mm) long and vase-shaped with 5 unequal lobes at the mouth, enclosing 4 fertile stamens and 1 hairy, sterile stamen.

**HABITAT AND RANGE:** Stony, clayey or silty soil in blackbrush, sagebrush and pinyon-juniper habitats. Endemic to the Colorado Plateau and Uinta Basin of Utah and Colorado. Occurs in CARE and GLCA.

**NOTES:** Alice Eastwood named this plant for David Moffat, the president of the railroad that carried her to Colorado where she discovered it. Jones' penstemon (*P. marcusii*) and shortstem penstemon (*P. breviculus*, right) have smaller flowers; corolla lobes of the former are nearly equal.

183

## Silverleaf nightshade *(Solanum elaeagnifolium)*
### Nightshade Family (Solanaceae)

**DESCRIPTION:** Silvery-hairy, rhizomatous perennial. **Stems** ascending or erect, up to 3 ft (1 m) tall, spiny and branched above. **Leaves** alternate, stalked; the blades are linear-lanceolate, up to 6 in (15 cm) long with wavy margins. **Inflorescence** leafy, spiny and branched at stem tips. **Flowers** are blue or purple, dish-shaped, ¾-1 in (2-3 cm) across with 5 triangular lobes that expose a central column of yellow anthers. **Fruit** is a globose, reddish, berry about ½ in (9-15 mm).

**HABITAT AND RANGE:** Disturbed soil of fields and roadsides. Native to California and Mexico east to the southern Great Plains and sporadically introduced elsewhere. Occurs in CARE, GLCA, GRST, and ZION.

**NOTES:** Navajo used silverleaf nightshade to treat sore eyes. Like the shooting stars (P. 178), silverleaf nightshade is buzz-pollinated by large bees that vibrate pollen loose from the anthers. Buffalo bur (*S. rostratum*, right) is also native and has lobed leaves and spiny fruit.

184

# Desert snowberry (*Symphoricarpos longiflorus*)
## Honeysuckle Family (Caprifoliaceae)

**DESCRIPTION:** Highly-branched shrub up to 3 ft (100 cm ) tall. **Twigs** finely hairy, becoming glabrous. **Leaves** are opposite, elliptic and up to 1 in (5-20 mm) long. **Flowers** few together on branch tips or paired in leaf axils, are pink, tubular and up to ¾ in (10-18 mm) long with 5 whitish, spreading lobes. **Fruits** are ellipsoid, white berries ⅜ in (8-10 mm) long.

**HABITAT AND RANGE:** Often stony soil of sagebrush or pinyon-juniper habitats. Southern Oregon and Idaho south through California to Texas and Mexico. Occurs in ARCH, CANY, CARE, GLCA, GRST, NABR, and ZION.

**NOTES:** Mountain snowberry (*S. oreophilus*, left) occurs in sagebrush habitats or higher and has shorter flowers without spreading lobes. The inside of the flower of mountain snowberry is woolly-hairy, and the style is glabrous, while desert snowberry has the inside of the corolla glabrous, but the style is hairy. Paiute used a decoction of the plant to treat stomach pain.

185

# Prostrate vervain
## (*Verbena bracteata*)
## Vervain Family (Verbenaceae)

DESCRIPTION: Long-hairy annual or short-lived perennial. **Stems** prostrate, branched, 4-20 in (10-50 cm) long. **Leaves** are ovate in outline, ½-2 in (1-5 cm) long with deeply lobed and toothed margins. **Inflorescence** is narrow, with sessile flowers in axils of linear bracts at branch tips. **Flowers** light blue or pink, about ⅛ in (4 mm) long, tubular with 5 spreading lobes. **Fruit** is 4 hard, linear-ellipsoid sculpted seeds less than ⅛ in (2 mm) long, enclosed in the stiff-hairy calyx.

HABITAT AND RANGE: A native weed in disturbed soil of fields and roadsides. Found throughout temperate North America but perhaps only native in the west. Found in ARCH, BRCA, CANY, CARE, GLCA, GRST, NABR, and ZION.

NOTES: Goodding's vervain (*V. gooddingii*) has erect stems and more densely-flowered inflorescences with bilobed corollas.

# Frosted mint
## (*Poliomintha incana*)
## Mint Family (Lamiaceae)

DESCRIPTION: Aromatic, densely short-hairy shrub. **Stems** silvery-green, hairy, erect, to 3 ft (1 m) high, branched below. **Leaves** are opposite, narrowly oblong and ½-1 in (1-3 cm) long. **Inflorescence** elongate, composed of open whorls of flowers in upper leaf axils. **Flowers** are lavender to pale pink or blue, ½ in (10-14 mm) long, hairy, and tubular with 4 short, flaring lobes. **Fruit** consists of 4 smooth, hard seeds.

HABITAT AND RANGE: Sandy soil of dunes and desert shrub, blackbrush and pinyon-juniper habitats. Colorado Plateau and Chihuahuan Desert of Texas and Mexico. Known from ARCH, CANY, CARE, GLCA, and GRST.

NOTES: Navajo used the plant to treat sores, and Hopi employed it to treat rheumatism. Purple sage (P. 187) differs in having conspicuous, broad, purple flower bracts, stamens that extend well past the corolla, and a more compact inflorescence.

# Purple sage *(Salvia dorrii)*
## Mint Family (Lamiaceae)

**DESCRIPTION:** Aromatic, silvery-hairy shrub to 32 in (80 cm) high. **Stems** rigid, whitish, sometimes thorny. **Leaves** are opposite, gland-dotted, spoon-shaped and ½-1½ in (1-4 cm) long. **Inflorescence** of terminal flower clusters subtended by conspicuous purple bracts. **Flowers** light purple, blue, or rarely white, ½ in (10-12 mm) long with 4 spreading lobes and strongly exserted stamens. **Fruit** consists of 4 smooth, hard seeds.

**HABITAT AND RANGE:** Silty or gravelly soil of blackbrush, sagebrush and pinyon-juniper habitats. Sagebrush steppe and deserts from Washington south to California and Arizona. Found in GLCA, GRST, and ZION.

**NOTES:** A decoction of the leaves was used to treat convulsions by the Hopi. Frosted mint (P. 186) is another shrub in the mint family, but the flowers do not have exserted stamens or purple bracts and are arranged in a more elongated inflorescence. Purple sage is a mint and not related to sagebrush.

# Arizona thistle
## *(Cirsium arizonicum)*
## Sunflower Family (Asteraceae)

**DESCRIPTION:** Spiny perennial. Stems branched, 1-3 ft (30-90 cm) tall. **Leaves** are dark green above, whitish underneath, 3-16 in (7-40 cm) long with toothed margins bearing sharp, yellow spines. **Heads** solitary on stem and branch tips, 1-2 in (20-40 mm) high, distinctly longer than wide. Involucral bracts are lance-shaped and spine-tipped. **Disk flowers** usually bright red to pink or purple. **Ray flowers** absent. **Seeds** with feathery bristles at the tip.

**HABITAT AND RANGE:** Brushy slopes and pinyon-juniper woodlands, occasionally in shrubby deserts. Colorado Plateau and Great Basin, Mojave and Sonoran deserts. Known from BRCA, GLCA, GRST, and ZION.

**NOTES:** Caineville thistle (P. 188) is similar but has lighter-colored flowers and broader flowering heads. Arizona thistle is easy to recognize with its elongate heads and often carmine-colored flowers that are regularly pollinated by hummingbirds. This and many other species of thistle may live for several seasons but flower only once before they die.

## **Caineville thistle** (*Cirsium calcareum*)
### Sunflower Family (Asteraceae)

**DESCRIPTION:** Spiny perennial. **Stems** branched, 1-3 ft (20-90 cm) tall. **Leaves** are toothed with spiny margins, sparsely to densely long-hairy and 2-16 in (3-40 cm) long without petioles. **Heads** are solitary on stem and branch tips, about 1 in (2-3 cm) high and about as long as wide. Involucral bracts lance-shaped with long hairs and long-spined on the tip. **Disk flowers** pink to light purple, rarely white. **Ray flowers** absent. **Seeds** have feathery bristles at the tip.

**HABITAT AND RANGE:** Mostly sandy soil of canyon bottoms and slopes. Nearly endemic to the Colorado Plateau of Utah and Colorado. Found in ARCH, BRCA, CANY, CARE, GLCA, GRST, NABR, and ZION.

**NOTES:** Thistles are often difficult to confidently identify to species. The lines separating some species are often not as clear as the botanist might wish because most characters vary within as well as among species. It is common for plants to be intermediate between the descriptions of two or more species. Caineville thistle tends to replace Arizona thistle (P. 187) in the northern part of the Colorado Plateau, but can be difficult to distinguish where their ranges overlap in southern Utah. Rydberg's thistle (*C. rydbergii*) has reflexed involucral bracts, basal leaves over 1 foot long, and is almost always in hanging gardens.

188

# Pretty daisy
## (*Erigeron bellidiastrum*)
## Sunflower Family (Asteraceae)

**DESCRIPTION:** Branched annual covered with short, curved hairs. **Stems** erect or ascending, 4-16 in (10-40 cm) long. **Leaves** are alternate, slender and up to 2 in (5 cm) long. **Heads** occur on branch tips and are less than ¼ in (3-5 mm) high. Involucral bracts linear, barely overlapping. **Disk flowers** yellow. **Ray flowers** 30 to 40, white to light purple. **Seeds** have long bristles at the tip.

**HABITAT AND RANGE:** Sandy soil of blackbrush and pinyon-juniper habitats. Wyoming and South Dakota south to Arizona, New Mexico and Texas. Found in ARCH, CANY, CARE, GLCA, GRST, HOVE, and RABR,

**NOTES:** Spreading daisy (P. 75) is similar but has somewhat longer rays, straight hairs on the stems, and both long and short bristles at the tip of the seed.

# Utah daisy
## (*Erigeron utahensis*)
## Sunflower Family
## (Asteraceae)

**DESCRIPTION:** Perennial usually covered with dense, short hair. **Stems** numerous, 4-24 in (10-60 cm) tall, usually with felt-like white hairs at the very base. **Leaves** are linear, mostly alternate on the stem and up to 4 in (10 cm) long. **Heads** up to ¼ in (3-6 mm) high, solitary on stems or branch tips. Involucral bracts are narrowly lance-shaped, brownish, overlapping and covered with appressed hairs. **Disk flowers** yellow. **Ray flowers** 10 to 40, white to bluish-white. **Seeds** have a mixture of bristles and short, narrow scales at the tip.

**HABITAT AND RANGE:** Sandstone ledges or sandy or stony soil of desert shrub, blackbrush and pinyon-juniper habitats. Colorado Plateau and southern Mojave Desert of Utah, Colorado, Arizona and New Mexico. Found in ARCH, CANY, CARE, GLCA, GRST, HOVE, NABR, RABR, and ZION,

**NOTES:** Two forms are recognized in Utah; var. *utahensis* is pictured here. Silver daisy (*E. argentatus*) has similar flowers but a persistent basal rosette.

# Rush pink (*Lygodesmia grandiflora*)
## Sunflower Family (Asteraceae)

**DESCRIPTION:** Perennial. **Stems** are often branched, 2- 20 in (6-50 cm) tall and exude milky sap. **Leaves** narrow, mostly glabrous and up to 5 in (13 cm) long. **Heads** slender, nearly 1 in (17-24 mm) high. Involucral bracts are linear and of 2 distinct lengths, the outer much shorter. **Disk flowers** absent. **Ray flowers** 5 to 12, pink to blue, 5-lobed at the tip. **Seeds** have numerous long, unbranched bristles on the tip.

**HABITAT AND RANGE:** Sparsely-vegetated, usually sandy soil of blackbrush, sagebrush and pinyon-juniper habitats. Colorado Plateau north to Wyoming. Found in ARCH, BRCA, CANY, CARE, GLCA, GRST, HOVE, and ZION.

**NOTES:** Up to 5 different forms of this species have been described for the Colorado Plateau based on differences in number of rays, plant size and leaf width. Navajo ate the leaves and used the sap to treat sunburn sores. Brightwhite (*L. exigua*) has much smaller flower heads. Species of wirelettuce (P. 191) usually bloom later and have feather-like bristles on the seed tips. The ray flowers of rush pink and its close relatives are easily confused for petals, especially when there are just 5 rays per head. It is easy to confuse such plants with species in the Pink Family (Caryophyllaceae); these latter species do not bleed white latex when broken.

# Annual wirelettuce (*Stephanomeria exigua*)
## Sunflower Family (Asteraceae)

DESCRIPTION: Annual. **Stems** branched, 4-24 in (10-60 cm) tall, glabrous with milky sap. **Leaves** are lobed or toothed, ½-2 in (1-6 cm) long, mainly basal and withered at flowering. **Heads** numerous, ⅜ in (5-10 mm) high. Involucral bracts are few and of two lengths: short on the outside and long on the inside. **Disk flowers** absent. **Ray flowers** 4 to 8, pink or light lavender, 5-toothed at the tip. **Seeds** have several feather-like bristles on top.

HABITAT AND RANGE: Desert shrub, salt desert shrub and pinyon-juniper communities. Southeast Oregon and Idaho south to California through Texas. Occurs in ARCH, BRCA, CANY, CARE, GLCA, GRST, and ZION.

NOTES: Stems of robust plants may be hollow. Hopi used this plant as a diuretic for venereal disease. Individuals of annual wirelettuce can differ significantly in overall size within the same population, but this pattern has been found to be environmentally dictated, rather than based on genetic differences. Few-flowered wirelettuce (*S. pauciflora*) and slender wirelettuce (*S. tenuifolia*) are similar but both are perennial; the stems of the latter are more slender. See rush pink (P. 190).

191

# Common tansy-aster (*Machaeranthera tanacetifolia*)
## Sunflower Family (Asteraceae)

**Description:** Annual. **Stems** branched, 2-16 in (5-40 cm) tall. **Leaves** are 1-4 in (2-10 cm) long, fern-like, and 1 to 3 times divided into spine-tipped lobes with sparse, long hair and crystal-like glands. **Heads** ⅜ in (6-10 mm) high. Involucral bracts overlap and are spreading and glandular. **Disk flowers** yellow. **Ray flowers** 11 to 23 are blue and sharp-pointed. **Seeds** hairy with numerous long bristles on the tip.

**HABITAT AND RANGE:** Sandy or silty, disturbed or sparsely-vegetated soil in desert shrub, salt desert shrub, sagebrush, and pinyon-juniper habitats. Western Great Plains and intermountain deserts from Canada south to Mexico. Occurs in ARCH, CANY, CARE, GLCA, GRST, and ZION.

**NOTES:** Navajo used a decoction of this plant for stomach ache. Common tansy-aster blooms from spring to fall. Small-flowered tansy-aster (*M. parviflora*) has less deeply lobed leaves and smaller heads.

# Brownfoot (*Acourtia wrightii*)
## Sunflower Family (Asteraceae)

**DESCRIPTION:** Perennial from a brown-wooly root crown. **Stems** branched, up to 3 ft (100 cm) tall. **Leaves** are alternate, 2-5 in (5-13 cm) long with toothed margins and covered with stalked glands. **Heads** numerous, few-flowered, ⅜ in (6-9 mm) high. Involucral bracts overlap. **Flowers** pink with 2 unequal strap-like lobes; the smaller one 2-lobed, the other with 3 teeth at the tip. **Seeds** are sticky with numerous long bristles on the tip.

**HABITAT AND RANGE:** Desert shrub and pinyon-juniper communities. Deserts from Mexico north to southern Utah and Nevada. Found in GLCA, GRST, and RABR.

**NOTES:** Brownfoot flowers seem intermediate between typical disk and ray flowers. Hualapai used the brown hair of the root crown as a poultice for open wounds.

192

# Mojave woody-aster (*Machaeranthera tortifolia*)
## Sunflower Family (Asteraceae)

**DESCRIPTION:** Perennial subshrub. **Stems** sometimes branched, 6-20 in (15-50 cm) tall. **Leaves** are alternate, 1-3 in (2-9 cm) long, sticky and sparsely long-hairy with sharp-toothed margins. **Heads** solitary, up to ¾ in (12-20 mm) high. Involucral bracts overlap and are long-pointed and sticky. **Disk flowers** yellow. **Ray flowers** numerous, blue (sometimes white) with rounded tips. **Seeds** are hairy with bristles on top.

**HABITAT AND RANGE:** Sparsely-vegetated, sandy or gravelly soil in the sagebrush, blackbrush and pinyon-juniper habitats. Deserts of Utah, Nevada, California and Arizona. Found in ARCH, CANY, CARE, GLCA, GRST, and RABR.

**NOTES:** Our plants are var. *imberbis* which is endemic to the Colorado Plateau. Havasupai carried ground leaves in their clothes to act as a deodorant.

## Cisco woody-aster (*Machaeranthera venusta*)
### Sunflower Family (Asteraceae)

**DESCRIPTION:** Perennial, shrubby below. **Stems** sometimes branched, 4-16 in (10-40 cm) tall. **Leaves** are alternate, 1-3 in (2-9 cm) long, narrowly oblong and sparsely long-hairy with smooth margins. **Heads** solitary, up to 1 in (12-20 mm) high. Involucral bracts are long-pointed and barely overlapped. **Disk flowers** yellow. **Ray flowers** numerous, blue or white with rounded tips. **Seeds** are hairy with bristles on top.

**HABITAT AND RANGE:** Clayey or silty, sparsely-vegetated soil in salt desert shrub habitats. Colorado Plateau and Uinta Basin of Utah and adjacent Colorado. Known from ARCH, CANY, CARE, GLCA, and NABR.

**NOTES:** Mojave woody-aster (P. 193) has toothed leaves and usually blue rays. Many species of *Machaeranthera* are selenium accumulators and in the past have been blamed for livestock deaths, though this conclusion has recently been questioned based on the low palatability of these plants and aversion to them by stock.

194

## Spiderwort (*Tradescantia occidentalis*)
### Spiderwort Family (Commelinaceae)

**Description:** Glabrous perennial 4-20 in (10-50 cm) tall. **Stems** unbranched. **Leaves** are alternate, grass-like, up to 1 in (2-20 mm) wide, widest at the base. **Inflorescence** terminal, composed of several stalked flowers subtended by 2 or 3 leaf-like bracts. **Flowers** have 3 blue petals about ½ in (7-16 mm) long. **Fruits** are pendulous, few-seeded capsules, ¼ in (4-7 mm) long.

**Habitat and Range:** Usually sandy soil of sagebrush and pinyon-juniper communities. Great Plains and warm deserts from Canada south to Arizona through Louisiana. Known from CARE, GLCA, GRST, RABR, and ZION.

**Notes:** Navajo used an infusion of the plant as an aphrodisiac for both people and livestock. The filaments of the anthers of spiderwort are deep purple and densely hairy, like the hairs of a spider. Spiderwort foliage is rich in gooey mucilage which helps conserve moisture and reduce herbivory.

195

## Sinuous mariposa *(Calochortus flexuosus)*
### Lily Family (Liliaceae)

**DESCRIPTION:** Glabrous perennial. **Stems** are prostrate to erect, often sinuous and 3-20 in (8-50 cm) long. **Leaves** few, narrow, 4-10 in (10-25 cm) long, grass-like, V-shaped in cross-section. **Flowers** few to several, each subtended by a leaf-like bract. Petals are 1-2 in (20-45 mm) long, pale purple with a reddish semicircle on the inner base surrounded by yellow. **Fruit** is an ovoid, 3-angled capsule 1-1½ in (25-35 mm) long.

**HABITAT AND RANGE:** Silty or stony soil of desert shrub and pinyon-juniper habitats. California east to Colorado and New Mexico. Found in CANY, GLCA, GRST, HOVE, NABR, RABR, and ZION.

**NOTES:** Sinuous mariposa often grows within the canopy of low shrubs and the stems are protected and supported by the shrub's branches. Gunnison's mariposa (*C. gunnisonii*) also has purplish petals but with a transverse, dark purple band on the inside. Cisco mariposa (*C. ciscoensis*, right) of eastern Utah has solid pink or white petals and straight stems.

196

# Tapertip onion
## (*Allium acuminatum*)
### Lily Family  (Liliaceae)

**DESCRIPTION:** Glabrous perennial. **Bulbs** with a membranous, mesh-like coat. **Stems** erect, unbranched, 4-12 in (10-30 cm) tall. **Leaves** 2 to 4, mainly basal, linear with a U-shaped cross-section. **Inflorescence** of several equal-stalked flowers arising from the stem tip subtended by 2 membranous bracts. **Flowers** with 2 unequal sets of 3 light purple petals up to ½ in (15 mm) long.

**HABITAT AND RANGE:** Silty or gravelly soil of sagebrush and pinyon-juniper communities. Grasslands and steppe from British Columbia south to California, Arizona and New Mexico. Found in BRCA, CARE, GRST, and ZION.

**NOTES:** Geyer's onion (*A. geyeri*) has pink or white flowers and a fibrous bulb coat. Palmer's onion (*A. bisceptrum*) also has a membranous bulb coat, but the veins are sinuous rather than strictly rectangular.

# Pretty wild buckwheat
## (*Eriogonum bicolor*)
### Knotweed Family
### (Polygonaceae)

**DESCRIPTION:** Cushion-forming perennial 1-3 in (2-8 cm) high with white-wooly foliage. **Leaves** basal, broadly linear and up to 1 in (5-20 mm) long. **Inflorescence** a terminal cluster of stalked flowers arising from a cup-shaped involucre ⅛ in (2-4 mm) high. **Flowers** are cup-shaped with 6 white to rose-colored, glabrous petals ⅛ in (2-4 mm) long. **Seeds** are short-hairy.

**Habitat and Range:** Silty, clayey or gravelly, often salty soil of desert shrub, salt desert shrub and pinyon-juniper habitats. Endemic to the Colorado Plateau of Utah and adjacent Colorado. Occurs in ARCH, CANY, CARE, and GLCA.

**Notes:** Shockley's wild buckwheat (*E. shockleyi*) and woodside wild buckwheat (*E. tumulosum*) have white-wooly flowers as well as leaves; the former has stems greater than 1 cm high, while those of the latter are shorter. Shortstem wild buckwheat (*E. brevicaule*) is usually taller and does not usually form cushions.

# Currant-leaf globemallow (*Sphaeralcea grossulariifolia*)
## Mallow Family (Malvaceae)

**DESCRIPTION:** Perennial. **Stems** several, 4-40 in (10-100 cm) tall. **Leaves** are alternate and stalked; the blades ½-2 in (1-5 cm) long, ovate in outline, deeply 3- to 5-lobed and covered with star-shaped hairs, giving the foliage a grayish look. **Inflorescence** slender with clusters of short-stalked flowers. **Flowers** are orange with 5 petals ca. ½ - ¾ in (8-20 mm) long and the

style and stamens united into a column. **Fruits** are disk-shaped, ¼ in (5-7 mm) across and divided into several radial segments like pie slices.

**HABITAT AND RANGE:** Usually sandy or gravelly soil throughout the desert and pinyon-juniper habitats. Intermountain deserts from Washington south through Arizona and New Mexico. Occurs in BEAR, CANY, CARE, GLCA, GRST, and ZION.

**NOTES:** Plants with bright green foliage (due to the sparsity of hairs) have been segregated as var. *moorei*. Roots of this plant were used by the Hopi as a diuretic. Common globemallow (*S. coccinea*, left) is often a smaller plant with solitary flowers at each branch in the inflorescence. Small-leaf globemallow (P. 199) has greenish leaves that are only shallowly toothed.

198

# Small-leaf globemallow (*Sphaeralcea parvifolia*)
## Mallow Family (Malvaceae)

**DESCRIPTION:** Perennial. **Stems** several, 6-22 in (15-55 cm) tall. **Leaves** are alternate and stalked; the blades ½-2 in (15-50 mm) long, broadly ovate with 3 to 5 shallow, toothed lobes and star-shaped hairs. **Inflorescence** slender with several solitary, widely-spaced stalked flowers. **Flowers** are orange with 5 petals less than ½ in (8-12 mm) long and the style and stamens united into a column. **Fruits** are disk-shaped, ¼ in (4-6 mm) across and divided into several radial pie-like segments.

**HABITAT AND RANGE:** Common in most habitats and soils throughout our area including roadsides. Great Basin and Colorado Plateau deserts of California east to Colorado and New Mexico. Occurs in ARCH, BEAR, BRCA, CANY, CARE, GLCA, GRST, HOVE, NABR, and ZION.

**NOTES:** Many plants in the Colorado Plateau are intermediate between small-leaf and currant-leaf (P. 198) globemallows and can only be distinguished by examining the net-like vein patterns on ripe fruit wedges. Hopi employed the root of small-leaf globemallow to relieve constipation. Mojave globemallow (*S. ambigua*) has similar leaves but larger petals and fruits.

# Slender-leaf globemallow
## (*Sphaeralcea leptophylla*)
## Mallow Family (Malvaceae)

**DESCRIPTION:** Perennial. **Stems** several, wand-like, 6-22 in (15-55 cm) tall. **Leaves** are alternate and stalked; the blades ½-1 in (1-3 cm) long, divided into 3 linear leaflets and grayish with star-shaped hairs. **Inflorescence** slender with clusters of short-stalked flowers. **Flowers** are red-orange with 5 petals less than ½ in (8-12 mm) long and the style and stamens united into a column. **Fruits** are disk-shaped, ¼ in (4-6 mm) across and divided into several 1-seeded, radial pie-like segments.

**HABITAT AND RANGE:** Sandy or gravelly soil of desert shrub, blackbrush and pinyon-juniper habitats, often on stream terraces. Colorado Plateau south to west Texas. Occurs in ARCH, BEAR, CANY, GLCA, and HOVE.

**NOTES:** Slender-leaf globemallow is mostly restricted to the vicinity of Canyonlands National Park. Jane's globemallow (*S. janeae*) has similar leaves but they are not gray with dense hair.

# Red triangles
## (*Centrostegia thurberi*)
## Knotweed Family
## (Polygonaceae)

**DESCRIPTION:** Diffusely-branched annual 2-6 in (4-16 cm) high. **Inflorescence** reddish, sticky-hairy, branched at nodes of 3-lobed bracts. **Leaves** are basal, oblong and up to 1 in (¼-3 cm) long. **Flowers** are tiny; small clusters are enclosed in reddish, vase-shaped involucres, ca. ¼ in (3-7 mm) long, that bear 3 conspicuous, spine-tipped wings at the base. **Seeds** are glabrous, 3-sided and ⅛ in (2-3 mm) long.

**HABITAT AND RANGE:** Sparsely-vegetated, sandy or gravelly soil of blackbrush, saltbush, and pinyon-juniper habitats. Deserts from California west to Arizona and southern Utah. Found in GRST and ZION.

**NOTES:** Short spineflower (*Chorizanthe brevicornu*) has a similar growth form but has linear basal leaves and the involucres lack wings.

# **Claret-cup** (*Echinocereus coccineus*)
## Cactus Family (Cactaceae)

**DESCRIPTION: Stems** few to usually many in a clump, 3-6 in (8-15 cm) high and short-cylindrical with 9 to 10 ribs. **Central spines** 1 to 3 per cluster, ½-2 in (1-4 cm) long, straight, round in cross-section. **Flowers** are borne below the apex on side branches. Petals deep red, ca. 1 in (2.5 cm) long and rounded at the tip.

**HABITAT AND RANGE:** Silty or gravelly soil of blackbrush, sagebrush or pinyon-juniper habitats. Nevada to Colorado and Texas and south to Mexico. Occurs in ARCH, BEAR, BRCA, CANY, CARE, GLCA, GRST, HOVE, NABR, RABR, and ZION.

**NOTES:** Spineless plants occur occasionally throughout our area. The common phase in the Colorado Plateau is var. *mojavensis* (treated as *E. mojavensis*, in most recent floras) which differs in having separate male and female flowers on the same plant and minutely rough-bumpy spines (only visible under magnification).

201

## Scarlet gilia (*Gilia aggregata*)
### Phlox Family (Polemoniaceae)

**DESCRIPTION:** Ill-smelling biennial or short-lived perennial with long, sometimes sticky hairs. **Stems** erect, usually unbranched, 8-40 in (20-100 cm) tall. **Leaves** are basal and alternate and 1-3 in (2-8 cm) long, with several pairs of linear, pinnately divided lobes. **Inflorescence** of several short side branches bearing clusters of short-stalked flowers. **Flowers** are red, pink, or whitish and trumpet-shaped; the tube ½-2 in (15-50 mm) long with 5 spreading lobes ⅜ in (6-13 mm) long. **Fruit** a capsule ¼ in (4-8 mm) long.

**HABITAT AND RANGE:** Often gravelly soil in sagebrush and pinyon-juniper communities. Throughout most of intermontane western North America from British Columbia to Mexico. Known from ARCH, BEAR, BRCA, CANY, CARE, GLCA, GRST, NABR, RABR, and ZION.

**NOTES:** Two forms occur in our area; var. *aggregata* is pictured here. Flower color can change within popultions during the growing season. Red flowers are produced when hummingbirds are present, and pink flowers are produced to attract moths when hummingbirds migrate. Coral gilia (*Gilia subnuda* below) has red flowers and entire or toothed leaves.

## Coral gilia (*Gilia subnuda*)
### Phlox Family (Polemoniaceae)

**DESCRIPTION:** Sticky-hairy, short-lived perennial. **Stems** erect, sometimes branched, 5-20 in (13-50 cm) high. **Leaves** are basal and alternate, oblanceolate and 1-3 in (2-9 cm) long with finely toothed margins. **Inflorescence** of erect branches with clusters of short-stalked flowers. **Flowers** are red; the tube about ½ in (11-17 mm) long with 5 spreading lobes up to ¼ in (5-8 mm) long. **Fruit** an ovoid capsule about ⅛ in (3-4 mm) long.

**HABITAT AND RANGE:** Sparsely-vegetated, sandy soil, sometimes on slickrock, dunes or roadsides in sagebrush and pinyon-juniper habitats. Endemic to the Colorado Plateau. Found in ARCH, BEAR, CANY, CARE, GLCA, GRST, and NABR.

**NOTES:** Scarlet gilia (above) has red flowers but the leaves are deeply pinnately lobed. Sticky gilia (*G. pinnatifida*) and Uinta gilia (*G. stenothyrsa*) are both biennials with deeply lobed leaves and bluish flowers. Navajo employed the ground flowers of coral gilia to ease labor pains. Several species of gilia are now placed in the genus *Ipomopsis*.

# Firecracker penstemon *(Penstemon eatonii)*
## Figwort Family  (Scrophulariaceae)

**DESCRIPTION:** Short-hairy or glabrous, short-lived perennial. **Stems** erect, unbranched, 1-3 ft (30-100 cm) tall. **Leaves** are basal and opposite and 2-4 in (5-10 cm) long; the blades elliptic to ovate below, becoming narrower above. **Inflorescence** of several stalked, nodding flowers in axils of upper leaves and bracts. **Flowers** are red, about 1 in (2-3 cm) long, tubular with 5 short lobes at the mouth, enclosing 4 fertile stamens and 1 glabrous, sterile stamen.

**HABITAT AND RANGE:** Dry grasslands and woodlands to moist meadows throughout our area. Idaho south to California through New Mexico and Mexico. Found in ARCH, BEAR, BRCA, CANY, CARE, GLCA, GRST, NABR, RABR, and ZION.

**NOTES:** Both var. *eatonii*, with glabrous foliage, and var. *undosus*, with short-hairy herbage, occur in our area. Navajo used firecracker penstemon to treat spider bites and stomach troubles. The red flowers attract hummingbirds. The anthers of firecracker penstemon open only at the tips, like a salt shaker, and carefully control the amount of pollen released at any time. The pollen lands on the face of a hummingbird, which then deposits it on the long stigma of the next flower it visits.

203

# Utah penstemon (*Penstemon utahensis*)
## Figwort Family (Scrophulariaceae)

**DESCRIPTION:** Waxy-glabrous perennial with erect stems 6-24 in (15-60 cm) tall. **Leaves** are opposite and basal, oblanceolate to oblong and ½-4 in (1-10 cm) long. **Inflorescence** of several short-stalked flowers in widely-spaced clusters above leaf-like bracts. **Flowers** are carmine, up to ¾ in (14-20 mm) long, tubular with 5 unequal, spreading lobes, 4 fertile stamens and 1 glabrous, sterile stamen.

**HABITAT AND RANGE:** Often sandy or stony soil in all habitats, especially pinyon-juniper. Mojave Desert of California and Nevada to the Colorado Plateau. Found in ARCH, BEAR, BRCA, CANY, CARE, GLCA, GRST, HOVE, NABR, RABR, and ZION.

**NOTES:** Utah penstemon has the red coloration of hummingbird-pollination, but the broad landing platform on the corolla tube of bee-pollinated species. It may be recently evolved from blue-flowered ancestors. Mistaken penstemon (*P. confusus*, right) has somewhat smaller flowers that are pink to purplish.

204

## Slickrock paintbrush  (*Castilleja scabrida*)
### Figwort Family  (Scrophulariaceae)

**Description:** Short-hairy perennial. **Stems** ascending, unbranched, 2-10 in (5-25 cm) tall with reduced tan leaves at the base. **Leaves** are alternate, narrowly lanceolate, ½-1½ in (1-4 cm) long, upper leaves usually with 1-5 linear lobes. **Inflorescence** of short-stalked flowers, each subtended by a red, lobed, leaf-like bract. **Flowers** are ½-1½ in (2-4 cm) long; the greenish, tubular corolla has a snout-like beak which protrudes from the red, 4-lobed calyx. **Fruit** is an ovoid capsule, ca. ½ in (9-12 mm) long, enclosed in the calyx.

**Habitat and range:** Stony or shallow soil or crevices of slopes and sandstone outcrops in the sagebrush and pinyon-juniper communities. Deserts of Nevada east to Colorado and New Mexico. Occurs in ARCH, BEAR, CANY, CARE, GLCA, GRST, HOVE, NABR, and ZION.

**Notes:** Paintbrush species are partial parasites that obtain water and nutrients by attaching their roots to those of their neighbors. Slickrock paintbrush is the common paintbrush on the red Navajo Sandstone walls on the east side of Zion NP. Desert paintbrush (*C. chromosa*, right) is usually a taller plant with unreduced leaves at the stem base. Wyoming paintbrush (P. 206) has narrower leaves with a more elongate inflorescence.

# Wyoming paintbrush
## (*Castilleja linariifolia*)
## Figwort Family
## (Scrophulariaceae)

**DESCRIPTION:** Glabrous or short-hairy perennial. **Stems** erect, unbranched, 8-32 in (20-80 cm) tall. **Leaves** are alternate, linear, ½-4 in (1-10 cm) long; the uppermost often with a pair of linear lobes. **Inflorescence** narrow with short-stalked flowers, each subtended by a leaf-like bract. **Flowers** are 1-2 in (3-5 cm) long; the greenish, tubular corolla has a snout-like beak which protrudes from the red 4-lobed calyx. **Fruit** is an ovoid capsule, ca. ½ in (9-13 mm) long, enclosed in the calyx.

**HABITAT AND RANGE:** Grasslands and meadows in sagebrush and pinyon-juniper habitats. Southern Washington to Montana south to Mexico. Found in ARCH, BEAR, BRCA, CANY, CARE, GLCA, GRST, NABR, RABR, and ZION.

**NOTES:** Hopi used a decoction of Wyoming paintbrush for birth control. Annual paintbrush (*C. exilis*) has red flowers and linear leaves but is an annual of wet habitats.

# Giant helleborine
## (*Epipactis gigantea*)
## Orchid Family  (Orchidaceae)

**DESCRIPTION:** Rhizomatous, mostly glabrous perennial. **Stems** erect, 9-12 in  (30-100 cm) tall with bladeless sheaths at the base. **Leaves** are alternate, oblanceolate below, lanceolate above, 2-8 in (5-20 cm) long with parallel veins. **Flowers** solitary in axils of upper leaves have 3 yellowish-green sepals ½ in (12-15 mm) long, 2 pinkish petals pointing up and a larger, sac-shaped, blood-red, lower petal longer than the upper. **Fruit** an ellipsoid capsule about 1 in (20-25 mm) long with abundant minute seeds.

**HABITAT AND RANGE:** Hanging gardens and wet sandy soil along small streams. Across temperate western North America, but rare throughout much of this range. Found in ARCH, BEAR, BRCA, CANY, CARE, GLCA, GRST, NABR, RABR, and ZION.

**NOTES:** In the northern portion of its range giant helleborine is restricted to spring-fed habitats that do not freeze hard in the winter.

# Veiny dock (*Rumex venosus*)
## Knotweed Family (Polygonaceae)

**DESCRIPTION:** Glabrous, rhizomatous perennial. **Stems** ascending, branched, 4-16 in (10-40 cm) high. **Leaves** are alternate, stalked with membranous sheaths where they meet the stem; the blades are lanceolate to ovate and 1-6 in (2-14 cm) long. **Inflorescence** a short-branched cluster of flowers. **Flowers** have 6 red petals less than ¼ in (4-5 mm) long. **Fruits** have 3 reddish semicircular, veiny wings up to 1½ in (15-35 mm) long with a tiny seed near the base.

**HABITAT AND RANGE:** Sparsely-vegetated dunes or other sandy habitats in pinyon-juniper communities. Columbia Plateau and Great Plains south through the Great Basin and Colorado Plateau. Known from ARCH, CANY, GLCA, and GRST.

**NOTES:** Paiute Indians used a decoction made from the roots to treat stomachache. Sand dock (P. 208) has clustered tuber-like roots and a basal rosette.

## Sand dock (*Rumex hymenosepalus*)
### Knotweed Family (Polygonaceae)

**DESCRIPTION:** Mostly glabrous perennial with tuberous roots. **Stems** erect, 8-40 in (20-100 cm) tall, unbranched below. **Leaves** are basal and alternate and stalked with membranous sheaths where they meet the stem; the blades are oblanceolate with wavy-toothed margins and 3-10 in (8-25 cm) long. **Inflorescence** about half the height of the plant, with flowers in a branched panicle. **Flowers** have 6 reddish petals ⅛ in (2-4 mm) long. **Fruits** are heart-shaped and have 3 pink, ovate, veiny wings about ½ in (8-18 mm) long with a tiny seed near the base.

**HABITAT AND RANGE:** Sandy soil of desert shrub and blackbrush communities, often on stream terraces. Montana south to California through Texas and Mexico. Found in ARCH, BEAR, CANY, CARE, GLCA, GRST, HOVE, NABR, RABR, and ZION.

**NOTES:** Willow dock (*R. salicifolius*) has smaller brownish fruits and narrower leaves and is usually found in moister environments. Veiny dock (P. 207) has an elongate below-ground rhizome and lacks a basal rosette of leaves.

208

# Southern maidenhair fern (*Adiantum capillus-veneris*)
## Fern Family (Polypodiaceae)

**DESCRIPTION:** Fern with drooping thin fronds scattered along a rhizome. **Fronds** 4-16 in (10-40 cm) long, lanceolate in outline, twice pinnately branched; the hand-shaped leaflets (pinnae) ovate, ⅜-1 in (8-25 mm) long with round lobes. **Spores** borne on the inrolled undersurface of the leaflet tips.

**HABITAT AND RANGE:** Wet soil of seeps and hanging gardens in sandstone or limestone cliffs. Southern United States from California and Mexico east to Virginia and Florida. Known from ARCH, BEAR, CANY, CARE, GLCA, GRST, NABR, RABR, and ZION.

**NOTES:** Green fronds usually occur among copious brown leaves from previous years. Navajo used an infusion of the fronds to treat bee and centipede stings.

# Poverty weed
## (*Monolepis nuttalliana*)
## Goosefoot Family (Chenopodiaceae)

**DESCRIPTION:** Nearly glabrous annual. **Stems** to 12 in (30 cm) tall, usually branched. **Leaves** alternate, stalked; the blades are thick, ½-1 in (1-3 cm) long, lanceolate to triangular, and often with a pair of lobes at the base. **Inflorescence** of clusters of succulent bracts and small flowers in leaf axils. **Fruits** are lens-shaped, and about ⅛ in (1-2 mm) long with a honeycomb exterior.

**HABITAT AND RANGE:** Sparsely-vegetated, silty or clayey, sometimes saline soils of salt desert shrub, blackbrush, sagebrush and pinyon-juniper habitats. Throughout most of western North America. Found in ARCH, CANY, CARE, GLCA, GRST, RABR, and ZION.

**NOTES:** Both Navajo and Hopi used the seeds for food.

## Spider milkweed (*Asclepias asperula*)
### Milkweed Family (Asclepiadaceae)

**DESCRIPTION:** Perennial with milky sap. **Stems** clustered, erect and 8-24 in (20-60 cm) tall. **Leaves** are narrowly lanceolate, minutely hairy, alternate and 3-8 in (8-20 cm) long with a short petiole. **Inflorescence** globose with long-stalked flowers. **Flowers** are fragrant and ca. ¼ in (6-8 mm) across with 5 greenish, curved petals surrounding 5 purple, blunt hoods radiating from a greenish central axis. **Fruits** are oblong and ribbed, 2-5 in (4-13 cm) long, and borne erect on S-shaped stalks. **Seeds** have tufts of long hair at the tip.

**HABITAT AND RANGE:** Gravelly or stony soil in desert shrub, sagebrush and pinyon-juniper habitats. Deserts of California and Nevada east to Kansas and Texas. Found in ARCH, BEAR, BRCA, CANY, CARE, GLCA, GRST, HOVE, NABR, RABR, and ZION.

**NOTES:** All other milkweeds in southern Utah differ in having recurved or spreading white, pink, red, or purplish petals that do not curve up to partly hide the flower horns. Cutler's milkweed (*A. cutleri*) and Rusby's milkweed (*A. rusbyi*) have very narrow, alternate leaves; the former has stems to 8 in (20 cm) tall and pendulous pods, while the latter is usually more than 8 in tall with erect fruits.

## Russian thistle
### (*Salsola tragus*)
### Goosefoot Family
### (Chenopodiaceae)

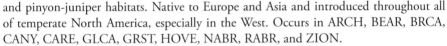

**DESCRIPTION:** Nearly glabrous annual, 4-32 in (10-80 cm) high. **Stems** red- and white-striped, branched; branches opposite near the base. **Leaves** alternate, linear, succulent, spine-tipped and ½-2 in (1-5 cm) long. **Inflorescence** of 1 to few flowers in leaf axils. **Fruits** consist of a small seed surrounded by 3 whitish, membranous, petal-like wings that form a disk less than ¼ in (ca. 5 mm) across.

**HABITAT AND RANGE:** Disturbed soil of fields, roadsides and overgrazed rangeland, especially in sagebrush and pinyon-juniper habitats. Native to Europe and Asia and introduced throughout all of temperate North America, especially in the West. Occurs in ARCH, BEAR, BRCA, CANY, CARE, GLCA, GRST, HOVE, NABR, RABR, and ZION.

**NOTES:** Larger plants form rounded, shrub-like plants that break off at the base. These tumbleweeds disperse seed as they are blown before the wind. Barbwire Russian thistle (*S. paulsenii*) has shorter, more rigid leaves.

## Alkali seepweed (*Suaeda nigra*)
### Goosefoot Family
### (Chenopodiaceae)

**DESCRIPTION:** Mostly glabrous shrubs 8-40 in (20-100 cm) tall. **Stems** branched, woody near the base. **Leaves** are alternate, cylindrical, linear, succulent and ½-1 in (1-3 cm) long. **Inflorescence** linear with clusters of few, small, green flowers in axils of leaf-like bracts. **Fruits** are small, black seeds enclosed in the fleshy, green flowers, ⅛ in (1-2 mm) across.

**HABITAT AND RANGE:** Saline, silty or clayey soil of flats and terraces in salt desert shrub communities. Alberta and Saskatchewan south to California through Texas and Mexico. Found in ARCH, BEAR, BRCA, CANY, CARE, GLCA, GRST, and HOVE.

**NOTE:** Navajo boiled the seeds to make a porridge. Broom seepweed (*S. calceoliformis*) is an annual with unequal calyx lobes. Hairy forms of alkali seepweed are sometimes recognized as a distinct species.

# Pinyon dwarf mistletoe
## (*Arceuthobium divaricatum*)
## Mistletoe Family
## (Viscaceae)

**DESCRIPTION:** Yellowish, tree-branch parasite. **Stems** 2-4 in (5-10 cm) long. **Leaves** reduced to tiny scale pairs surrounding the stem at nodes. **Inflorescence** of few flowers of separate sex on short branches from the nodes. **Male flowers** are about ⅛ in (2-3 mm) across with 3 lobes and 3 stamens. **Female flowers** have a short conical cap on top of the ovoid ovary. **Fruit** an ellipsoid, 1-seeded berry about ⅛ in (3-4 mm) long.

**HABITAT AND RANGE:** Parasitic on pinyon pine. California east to Colorado and Texas. Found in ARCH, BEAR, BRCA, CANY, CARE, GLCA, GRST, NABR, and ZION.

**NOTES:** Dwarf mistletoe berries "explode," expelling the seed to other parts of the tree or even nearby trees. Many species of mistletoe cause their host tree to produce a "witches' broom," an area of abnormally dense branching; however, pinyon dwarf mistletoe rarely does this.

# Juniper mistletoe
## (*Phoradendron juniperinum*)
## Mistletoe Family  (Viscaceae)

**DESCRIPTION:** Yellow-green, branch parasite. **Stems** branched, 4-10 in (10-25 cm) long. **Leaves** reduced to tiny pairs of scales surrounding the stem at nodes. **Inflorescence** of 2 (female) or several (male) flowers on short branches from the nodes. **Male flowers** are less than ⅛ in (ca. 2 mm) across with 3 lobes and 3 stamens. **Female flowers** are reduced to 3 tiny lobes on top of the ovoid ovary. **Fruit** a pink to white, globose, 1-seeded berry less than ¼ in (3-5 mm) long.

**HABITAT AND RANGE:** Parasitic on junipers. Oregon south to California and east to Colorado through Texas and Mexico. Known from ARCH, BEAR, BRCA, CANY, CARE, GLCA, GRST, NABR, and ZION.

**NOTES:** Birds eat the berries and defecate the seeds onto other branches of the same or neighboring trees. The seeds are inedible and covered in thick mucous, which allows it to adhere to a branch long enough for the seed to germinate and send its stem into a cut or break in the host's stem. Navajo used the plant to treat warts.

# Bud sage
## (*Artemisia spinescens*)
## Sunflower Family
## (Asteraceae)

**DESCRIPTION:** Low, aromatic shrub. **Stems** 2-12 in (5-30 cm) long, often spreading and somewhat thorny. **Leaves** alternate, long-hairy, wedge-shaped, up to 1 in (2 cm) long with 3 to 5 toe-like lobes at the tip. **Heads** about ⅛ in (2-4 mm) high and long-hairy are ball-like in leaf axils or on on stem tips. Involucral bracts green and leaf-like. **Disk flowers** inconspicuous, cream-colored, long-hairy. **Ray flowers** absent. **Seeds** long-hairy but without pappus.

**HABITAT AND RANGE:** Clay, sometimes saline soils of salt desert shrub, blackbrush, sagebrush and pinyon-juniper communities. Intermontane valleys and deserts from Montana south to California, Arizona and New Mexico. Known from ARCH, BEAR, CANY, CARE, GLCA, GRST, HOVE, and NABR.

**NOTES:** Thorns are short, dead, side branches. There are many species of sagebrush (*Artemisia* spp.) on the Colorado Plateau, but only this one flowers in spring. Paiute used the plant to treat stomach cramps, cough and rheumatism.

# Four-wing saltbush
## (*Atriplex canescens*)
## Goosefoot Family
## (Chenopodiaceae)

**DESCRIPTION:** Intricately branched, evergreen shrub 2-5 ft (60-200 cm) tall. **Stems** rigid with glabrous, gray bark. **Leaves** are alternate, narrow, 1-2 in (2-5 cm) long and covered with whitish, flake-like hairs. **Inflorescence** of clusters of small yellowish-green flowers in axils of upper leaves. **Fruits** are ca. ½ in (10-17 mm) long and consist of a central seed with four ruffled semi-circular wings.

**HABITAT AND RANGE:** Often sandy soil of desert shrub, blackbrush, sagebrush and pinyon-juniper habitats. Western Great Plains and intermountain region from Alberta south to northern Mexico. Occurs in ARCH, BEAR, BRCA, CANY, CARE, GLCA, GRST, HOVE, NABR, RABR, and ZION.

**NOTES:** Male and female flowers are on separate plants. Plants can change sex from one year to the next, and female plants will often shift to "male" the year after making a large fruit crop. Hopi used a lather of the leaves to wash hair.

## **Shadscale** (*Atriplex confertifolia*)
## Goosefoot Family (Chenopodiaceae)

**DESCRIPTION:** Hemispheric, evergreen shrub 1-3 ft (30-80 cm) tall. **Stems** rigid with short, thorn-like branches and smooth, gray bark. **Leaves** are ovate, alternate, closely-spaced, up to 1 in (1-3 cm) long and covered with whitish, flake-like hairs. **Inflorescence** of stalkless, globose to short-stalked, linear clusters of tiny, green to yellowish flowers in leaf axils. **Fruits** are rhomboid to ovoid, whitish-green and up to ½ in (5-13 mm) long without distinct wings.

**HABITAT AND RANGE:** Silty or clayey, often saline soil of salt desert shrub, blackbrush or sagebrush habitats. Western Great Plains and intermountain region from Oregon to North Dakota south to northern Mexico. Found in ARCH, BEAR, BRCA, CANY, CARE, GLCA, GRST, HOVE, NABR, and ZION.

**NOTES:** Male and female flowers are on separate plants, so some bushes will not have fruit. Shadscale will hybridize with other species in the genus *Atriplex*. Hopi smoked the plant to treat epileptic fits and used the salty leaves to spice foods. Shadscale is an important browse speces for livestock and wildlife.

## Gardner's saltbush *(Atriplex gardneri)*
### Goosefoot Family (Chenopodiaceae)

**DESCRIPTION:** Low, spreading shrub, 4-32 in (10-80 cm) tall, woody only toward the base. **Stems** spreading with erect branches. **Leaves** are ovate, alternate, ½-2 in (1-6 cm) long and covered with whitish, flake-like hairs. **Inflorescence**, sometimes branched, is composed of clusters of tiny green or brownish flowers in axils of upper leaves or leaf-like bracts. **Fruits** are about ¼ in (3-9 mm) long, gray-green, obovoid to nearly circular, with or without bumpy projections on the faces.

**HABITAT AND RANGE:** Usually saline, silty or clayey soils of salt desert shrub and sagebrush habitats. Western Great Plains and intermountain region from southern Canada south to Arizona and New Mexico. Found in ARCH, BRCA, CANY, CARE, GLCA, HOVE, and NABR.

**NOTES:** Most of our plants are var. *cuneata* (pictured) with ovate leaf blades; var. *welshii* has strap-shaped leaves and is found only in a small area north of Arches National Park. Male and female flowers are on separate plants, so some bushes will not have fruit. Gardner's saltbush was named in honor of Alexander Gordon, a Scotish nobleman and botanist who explored western North America in the 1840s. Unfortunately the scienstist who named the species could not decipher Gordon's sloppy handwriting and misspelled his name (a lesson for us all).

215

# Mat saltbush
## (*Atriplex corrugata*)
## Goosefoot Family
## (Chenopodiaceae)

**Description:** Low, shrub 2-8 in (5-20 cm) tall. **Stems** spreading to ascending with pale gray bark. **Leaves** are narrow, mainly basal, less than 1 in (3-20 mm) long and covered with whitish, flake-like hairs. **Inflorescence** cylindrical on erect branches with clusters of small, green or yellow flowers, subtended by leaf-like bracts on female plants. **Fruits** are ¼ in (4-6 mm) long, gray-green, obovate and flattened with wrinkled faces.

**Habitat and Range:** Gravelly or clay, shale-derived, often saline soil in salt desert shrub communities. Endemic to the Colorado Plateau of Utah, Colorado and New Mexico. Known from ARCH, CARE, GLCA, and GRST.

**Notes:** Mat saltbush helps prevent erosion in otherwise barren soil and has been used for landscaping highway rights-of-way and mine reclamation. Male and female flowers are on separate plants, so some bushes will not have fruit.

# Winterfat
## (*Krascheninnikovia lanata*)
## Goosefoot Family
## (Chenopodiaceae)

**Description:** Shrub 8-32 in (20-80 cm) tall, woody toward the base. **Stems** erect, branched below. **Leaves** are alternate, linear, ½-2 in (1-5 cm) long, U-shaped in cross-section and covered with small star-shaped hairs and longer straight hairs. **Inflorescence** of 1 to few small flowers in upper leaf axils. **Fruits** are ca. ¼ in (4-8 mm) long, 4-lobed and densely white long-hairy.

**Habitat and Range:** Silty or gravelly soil in all habitats. Great Plains and Intermountain Region from southern Canada to Mexico. Found in ARCH, BEAR, BRCA, CANY, CARE, GLCA, GRST, NABR, and ZION.

**Notes:** Some plants in extreme southeast Utah are up to 4 ft tall and woody for more than half their height and are referred to as var. *ruinina*. As the common name implies, winterfat is important wildlife forage, especially during winter. Male and female flowers are on separate plants, so some bushes will not have fruit.

# Spiny hopsage *(Grayia spinosa)*
## Goosefoot Family (Chenopodiaceae)

**DESCRIPTION:** Densely-branched shrub 1-4 ft (30-120 cm) tall. **Stems** with gray bark, rigid, often becoming thorn-like. **Leaves** are alternate, obovate, ½-1 in (1-3 cm) long with scurfy, branched hairs on the surface. **Inflorescence** of clusters of tiny flowers in upper leaf axils. **Fruits** are green, yellow or red-tinged, glabrous, disk-like and up to ½ in (7-14 mm) long.

**HABITAT AND RANGE:** Silty or clay, often saline soils of mainly salt desert shrub and sagebrush habitats. Washington to southern Montana, south to California, Arizona and northern New Mexico. Occurs in ARCH, BEAR, CANY, CARE, GLCA, GRST, HOVE, RABR, and ZION

**NOTES:** Male and female flowers are on separate plants, so some bushes will not have fruit. This is an important browse plant for wildlife and livestock during spring months.

217

# Siltbush (*Zuckia brandegeei*)
## Goosefoot Family
## (Chenopodiaceae)

**DESCRIPTION:** Shrubs 4-20 in (10-50 cm) tall. **Stems** branched, woody near the base. **Leaves** are alternate, ½-3 in (1-8 cm) long and grayish with branched hairs. **Inflorescence** of clusters of small green to yellow flowers arranged linearly in upper leaf axils. **Fruits** are flattened disks with wing-like margins, about ½ in (7-14 mm) long.

**HABITAT AND RANGE:** Silty, usually saline soil in salt desert shrub, sagebrush and pinyon-juniper communities. Intermountain region from Wyoming south to Arizona and New Mexico. Found in ARCH, BEAR, BRCA, CANY, CARE, GLCA, GRST, and NABR.

**NOTES:** Two forms of siltbush occur in our area; var. *brandegeei* (pictured here) is a Colorado Plateau endemic with narrow leaves, while var. *plummeri* has a more northern distribution and spoon-shaped leaves. Arizona siltbush (*Z. arizonica*) has leaves similar to var. *plummeri* but fruits that are much wider than high.

# Greasewood
## (*Sarcobatus vermiculatus*)
## Greasewood Family
## (Sarcobataceae)

**DESCRIPTION:** Nearly glabrous shrubs to 6 ft (2 m) tall. **Stems** rigid with thorny side branches and white-barked twigs. **Leaves** are alternate or opposite, linear, succulent and ½-2 in (1-5 cm) long. **Inflorescence** of a terminal, cone-like, green to purple spike of male flowers with small, green, solitary female flowers in leaf axils below. **Fruits** have an ellipsoid seed surrounded by a whitish, membranous, skirt-like disk ½ in (8-14 mm) across.

**HABITAT AND RANGE:** Often forming solid stands in silty or clay, saline soil of flats and terraces in salt desert shrub habitats with a high water table. Throughout most of temperate western North America. Found in ARCH, BEAR, BRCA, CANY, CARE, GLCA, GRST, HOVE, NABR, and ZION.

**NOTES:** This and a second species of the Mojave Desert are the only members of this family. Fossil pollen data indicate that the range of greasewood has not changed much since before the Pleistocene, despite significant environmental changes.

## Mormon tea (*Ephedra viridis*)
### Ephedra Family (Ephedraceae)

**DESCRIPTION:** Shrub to 4 ft (120 cm) tall. **Stems** mostly glabrous and highly branched; twigs are green, opposite and nearly erect. **Leaves** are about ⅛ in (2-4 mm) long, brownish, scale-like and quickly falling from the stem joints. **Male cones** are short-stalked, yellow, ¼ in (5-7 mm) long and paired or several at stem joints. **Female cones** are brownish and mostly paired at the joints.

**HABITAT AND RANGE:** Gravelly, sandy or stony soil of desert shrub, blackbrush and pinyon-juniper habitats. Intermountain region and Sonoran Desert from southern Oregon and Wyoming south to Mexico. Known from ARCH, BEAR, BRCA, CANY, GLCA, GRST, HOVE, NABR, RABR, and ZION.

**NOTES:** Two forms are recognized in our area; var. *viridis* (pictured here) has glabrous stems, but var. *viscida* (= *E. cutleri*) has somewhat sticky stems and a grass-like growth form when found in shifting sand dunes. An infusion was used by many Native American tribes and white settlers to cure a number of ailments. "Mormon tea," a beverage created by pioneers from stems of this plant, contains the stimulant ephedrine. Torrey's ephedra (*E. torreyana*) has cones and leaves in groups of 3 at the nodes.

219

# Coyote willow (*Salix exigua*)
## Willow Family (Salicaceae)

**DESCRIPTION:** Colonial shrub with stems up to 10 ft (3 m) tall and brown to gray twigs. **Leaves** alternate, short-stalked; the blades linear, loosely white-hairy, 1-4 in (2-10 cm) long with minutely toothed margins. **Inflorescence** many-flowered, cylindrical, ascending catkins 1-4 in (2-10 cm) long; male and female on different plants. **Fruits** numerous, green, glabrous, pear-shaped capsules ca. ¼ in (3-7 mm) long containing minute cottony seeds.

**HABITAT AND RANGE:** Stream margins. Throughout temperate western North America. Occurs in ARCH, BEAR, BRCA, CANY, CARE, GLCA, GRST, HOVE, NABR, RABR, and ZION.

**NOTES:** Our plants are var. *exigua*. This is our most common willow; clones can form dense streamside thickets. Havasupai used young vigorous twigs to make baskets. The inner bark of willows is the source of salicylic acid, an ingredient in aspirin and acne creams.

# Yellow willow
## (*Salix eriocephala*)
## Willow Family
## (Salicaceae)

**DESCRIPTION:** Large shrub to 16 ft (5 m) high with multiple stems and yellow to gray twigs. **Leaves** alternate, stalked; the blades are lanceolate, whitish-waxy beneath and 1-3 in (2-8 cm) long with minutely toothed margins. **Inflorescence** many-flowered, cylindrical, ascending catkins 1-3 in (2-7 cm) long; male and female flowers on different plants. **Fruits** numerous, green, glabrous, narrowly-

ovoid capsules ca. ¼ in (3-6 mm) long containing minute cottony seeds.

**HABITAT AND RANGE:** Stream margins. Throughout temperate North America. Found in ARCH, BEAR, BRCA, CANY, CARE, GLCA, GRST, NABR, and ZION.

**NOTES:** Our plants are var. *watsonii* which occurs throughout most of the West. Several other willow species occur in similar habitats in our area. Peach-leaf willow (*S. amygdaloides*) and black willow (*S. goodingii*) usually attain tree stature; Scouler's willow (*S. scouleriana*) has leaves that are broader toward the tip and can occur in more upland habitats.

**Appendix A.** Scientific names in the left column are used by either *A Utah Flora* (Welsh et al. 2003) or the *Flora of North America* (FNA Editorial Committee 1993-2016). Names in the right column are those used by the *Intermountain Flora* (Cronquist et al. 1972-2012) and in this book.

| Synonym | Names in this book |
|---|---|
| Achnatherum aridum | Stipa arida |
| Achnatherum hymenoides | Oryzopsis hymenoides |
| Agropyron triticeum | Eremopyrum triticeum |
| Aliciella latifolia | Gilia latifolia |
| Aliciella leptomeria | Gilia leptomeria |
| Allium biceptrum | Allium bisceptrum |
| Aquilegia caerulea | Aquilegia coerulea |
| Arabis demissa | Boechera demissa |
| Arabis perennans | Boechera perennans |
| Arabis pulchra | Boechera pulchra |
| Arenaria fendleri | Eremogone fendleri |
| Arenaria macradenia | Eremogone macradenia |
| Arida parviflora | Machaeranthera parviflora |
| Berberis fremontii | Mahonia fremontii |
| Boechera formosa | Boechera pulchra |
| Castilleja minor | Castilleja exilis |
| Ceanothus pauciflorus | Ceanothus greggii |
| Ceratoides lanata | Krascheninnikovia lanata |
| Chorizanthe thurberi | Centrostegia thurberi |
| Cycladenia jonesii | Cycladenia humilis |
| Dalea oligophylla | Dalea candida |
| Delphinium andersonii | Delphinium scaposum |
| Dichelostemma capitatum | Dichelostemma pulchellum |
| Dieteria canescens | Machaeranthera canescens |
| Dithyrea wislizenii | Dimorphocarpa wislizenii |
| Dyssodia acerosa | Thymophylla acerosa |
| Dyssodia pentachaeta | Thymophylla pentachaeta |
| Echinocereus triglochidiatus | Echinocereus coccineus |
| Elymus elymoides | Sitanion hystrix |
| Elymus smithii | Agropyron smithii |
| Elymus spicatus | Agropyron spicatum |
| Elymus trachycaulus | Agropyron trachycaulum |
| Encelia nutans | Enceliopsis nutans |
| Erigeron concinnus | Erigeron pumilus |
| Eriogonum flexum | Stenogonum flexum |
| Eriogonum salsuginosum | Stenogonum salsuginosum |
| Erythranthe floribunda | Mimulus floribundus |

| Synonym | Names in this book |
| --- | --- |
| Erythranthe rubella | Mimulus rubellus |
| Erythranthe suksdorfii | Mimulus suksdorfii |
| Euphorbia fendleri | Chamaesyce fendleri |
| Euphorbia virgata | Euphorbia esula |
| Festuca octoflora | Vulpia octoflora |
| Forsellesia meionandra | Glossopetalon spinescens |
| Forsellesia nevadensis | Glossopetalon spinescens |
| Frangula betulifolia | Rhamnus betulifolius |
| Grindelia hirsutula | Grindelia fastigiata |
| Heliomeris longifolia | Viguiera annua |
| Heliomeris soliceps | Viguiera soliceps |
| Hesperostipa comata | Stipa comata |
| Hesperostipa neomexicana | Stipa neomexicana |
| Heterotheca villosa | Chrysopsis villosa |
| Hoffmanseggia repens | Caesalpinia repens |
| Ipomopsis aggregata | Gilia aggregata |
| Ipomopsis congesta | Gilia congesta |
| Ipomopsis gunnisonii | Gilia gunnisonii |
| Ipomopsis longiflora | Gilia longiflora |
| Ipomopsis polycladon | Gilia polycladon |
| Ipomopsis pumila | Gilia pumila |
| Lappula occidentalis | Lappula redowskii |
| Leptosiphon nuttallii | Linanthastrum nuttallii |
| Lesquerella fendleri | Physaria fendleri |
| Lesquerella intermedia | Physaria intermedia |
| Lesquerella kingii | Physaria kingii |
| Lesquerella ludoviciana | Physaria ludoviciana |
| Lesquerella rectipes | Physaria rectipes |
| Linanthus caespitosus | Leptodactylon caespitosum |
| Linanthus pungens | Leptodactylon pungens |
| Linanthus watsonii | Leptodactylon watsonii |
| Linum perenne | Linum lewisii |
| Opuntia erinacea | Opuntia aurea |
| Packera cana | Senecio canus |
| Packera multilobata | Senecio multilobatus |
| Pascopyrum smithii | Agropyron smithii |
| Perezia wrightii | Acourtia wrightii |
| Peritoma lutea | Cleome lutea |
| Peritoma serrulata | Cleome serrulata |
| Picrothamnus desertorum | Artemisia spinescens |
| Platyschkuhria integrifolia | Bahia nudicaulis |
| Populus fremontii | Populus deltoides |

| Synonym | Names in this book |
|---|---|
| Prenanthella exigua | Lygodesmia exigua |
| Pseudoroegneria spicata | Agropyron spicatum |
| Psorothamnus polyadenius | Psorothamnus polydenius |
| Purshia mexicana | Purshia stansburiana |
| Rhus trilobata | Rhus aromatica |
| Salix lutea | Salix eriocephala |
| Salsola pestifer | Salsola tragus |
| Scabrethia scabra | Wyethia scabra |
| Sclerocactus whipplei | Sclerocactus parviflorus |
| Senecio longilobus | Senecio flaccidus |
| Sisymbrium linifolium | Schoenocrambe linifolia |
| Stenotus acaulis | Haplopappus acaulis |
| Stenotus armerioides | Haplopappus armerioides |
| Stipa hymenoides | Oryzopsis hymenoides |
| Strigosella africana | Malcolmia africana |
| Swertia albomarginata | Frasera albomarginata |
| Swertia utahensis | Frasera paniculata |
| Talinum brevifolium | Phemeranthus brevifolius |
| Talinum parviflorum | Phemeranthus confertiflorus |
| Tetraneuris acaulis | Hymenoxys acaulis |
| Tetraneuris ivesiana | Hymenoxys argentea |
| Viguiera longifolia | Viguiera annua |
| Xanthisma grindelioides | Machaeranthera grindelioides |
| Xylorhiza confertifolia | Machaeranthera confertifolia |
| Xylorhiza glabriuscula | Machaeranthera glabriuscula |
| Xylorhiza tortifolia | Machaeranthera tortifolia |
| Xylorhiza venusta | Machaeranthera venusta |
| Zuckia brandegeei | Zuckia arizonica |

# Index

225

226

227

228

229

232

233